RELIGION AND THE DEVELOPMENT OF THE AMERICAN PENAL SYSTEM

Andrew Skotnicki

University Press of America
Lanham • New York • Oxford

Copyright © 2000 by
University Press of America,® Inc.
4720 Boston Way
Lanham, Maryland 20706

12 Hid's Copse Rd.
Cumnor Hill, Oxford OX2 9JJ

Library of Congress Cataloging-in-Publication Data

Skotnicki, Andrew.
Religion and the development of the American penal system /
Andrew Skotnicki.
p.   cm.
Includes bibliographical references and index.
1.   Prisons—United States—History. 2. Imprisonment—United
States—History. 3. Imprisonment—Religious aspects—Protestantism.
4.   Religion and social problems—United States—History.
5. Religion and justice. I. Title.
HV9471.S59   2000   365'.973—dc21   00-060712 CIP

ISBN 0-7618-1810-3 (cloth: alk. ppr.)

♾™ The paper used in this publication meets the minimum
requirements of American National Standard for Information
Sciences—Permanence of Paper for Printed Library Materials,
ANSI Z39.48—1984

Contents

CHAPTER 1

RELIGION AND THE PENAL SYSTEM

Few of the many thousands of cars that traverse the San Rafael Bridge each day take the first exit on reaching the west bank of the San Francisco Bay. Tourists may instinctively pull off the expressway after having captured glimpses of the majestic panorama, but they quickly find their way back to the safety and anonymity of the road. Those who are drawn to this exit are not sightseers. They are principally correctional staff and officers, as well as the relatives and friends of the inhabitants of the California State Prison at San Quentin.

On past occasions, and again more recently, groups of religious adherents have also felt compelled to gather at the prison gate. The members usually bear candles and placards that give witness to rival theological and ethical positions with regard to capital punishment. One group decries violence of any sort and silently prays in protest. The other supports the state in its enforcement of a sentence which, they argue, safeguards the well-being of the community, and reveals the will of God secured through legitimate authority.

The scene just described is as metaphorical as it is descriptive. What is common to the two groups outside the walls is that they *are* outside the walls, peripheral to the event. Their denunciation or sanction is largely irrelevant to the life and death drama being carried out within the ominous structure before them.

Within the walls, what is arguably the one unimpeded function of religion is vividly captured in a comment by a former Warden of San Quentin, James Johnston.

> As soon as I stepped into the cage, the man could tell it was all over. Generally he said 'Good-bye' and thanked me for whatever I had done for him. The guards slipped a leather belt around his waist and strapped his wrists to his sides. We began our march, the priest praying as we moved along (Johnston 1937, 322).

I suggest that these images reveal common assumptions, and indeed misperceptions, concerning the impact of religion on the American penal system, namely, that it is not integral to the social structures that have arisen in response to criminal misbehavior. As with the priest on execution day, its duty is commonly understood as the performance of rituals that anticipate the world to come, not to involve itself in the one in which we live.

One could easily assume that the roots of the practice of using confinement as a form of punishment were religious in nature. A simple linguistic analysis suggests as much. Many of the terms common to the lexicon of penal life—cell, penitentiary, reformatory—have a religious, even monastic, quality. What the author did not know, and sought to investigate, were the processes by which this influence had been severed, or perhaps transformed.

A fruitful, analytical starting point was an examination of the richly prosaic reports of the inspectors of the first penitentiaries in the United States. Through textual analysis, perhaps a hypothesis could be generated concerning the development of penal theory and practice, concentrating on the location and subsequent attenuation of religious inspiration. This research, however, revealed a more thorough impact than had been suspected.[1]

It became clear that the religious community itself had substantially affected the developments that saw the post-revolutionary evangelical emphasis on conversion translate into the first penitentiaries.

In the early nineteenth century, a confident and committed evangelical Protestantism dominated the American religious economy. It was schooled in the first Great Awakening of the 1740s, and was undergoing a renewed period of revival that would culminate in another Great Awakening in the 1820s. The roots of this revival mentality were deeply significant both theologically and socially. They traced to significant permutations within Calvinism, spearheaded by groups seeking to replace the arbitrariness of divine judgment, and God's "secret will," with a more rational and public theology centered in the covenant.[2]

The shift to progressive thinking later in the century likewise represented a further transformation of the religious ethos. This occurred as key church leaders began to employ scientific methods to provide causal explanations for increased criminal behavior in the years following the Civil War. The movement led to the widely-held assumption that the institutions of modern industrial society could be revitalized, and made the stable foundation of God's reign, by employing the methods and assumptions of positivist science.

The oversight I had committed in my preliminary analysis, and it is a common one among interpreters of religion, was to theorize about the role and social value of religion by focusing attention on its institutional presence, and not on the dynamic movements that preceded the institutions and that eventually must subject them to judgment. H. Richard Niebuhr spoke of this very tendency when arguing that a religious analysis that focuses only on institutions is "very partial," for it "cannot do full justice to the institution since this developed out of the movement" (1937, 12).

The bulk of historical scholarship in the area of corrections has fallen prey to this tendency to equate the impact of religion with its empirically visible or pragmatic function. And from an empirical standpoint, it was apparent that religion, despite any early influence it might have had on the penal system, was virtually eliminated as a significant visible force shortly after the Civil War, if not before in the eyes of not a few.[3] All that has remained, in the opinion of most who comment on the subject, is a superficial and ceremonial presence, as in the woeful and ornamental chaplain at the execution.

The irony, and there are many in this story, is that religious movements, in effect, had not retreated or been forced from the debate over the penal system. They had become intimately united with the penal project. Religion was not an external force outside the walls, simply reacting to events, but an integral part of the internal logic by which the prisons were governed.

In the pages that follow I hope to convince the reader of the vibrant nature of the American religious ethos as it pertains to institutional life. It certainly lies at the roots of the penal system. Theological understandings of person and society may require attention once more if the expanding correctional complex is to be resurrected from the aimlessness and cynicism that seem its only sure attributes.

This study will conflict with those scholars who maintain that religion has had a function in penal development: as a mask and justification for economic and political subjugation of the lower classes by the social elite.[4] The role of religion in penal development is complex and involves layers of meaning across several academic disciplines. Notwithstanding the noteworthy critique of some of these writers, there is evidence to substantiate the claim that religious inspired systems, particularly in Pennsylvania, provided an effective and humane system of corrections motivated by specifically theological concerns.

In a theoretical sense, the initial empirical analysis of primary source material triggered a rereading of social scientific theory, concentrating on those writers who would help provide a theoretical model and conceptual categories for the data being recorded. Figures such as Emile Durkheim and Talcott Parsons examined the development of society and its institutions by giving primary emphasis to cultural and linguistic factors. There was substantial accord between their belief that religious imagery and ethics provide the basis of social organization, and the penal documents under consideration. Their ideas help locate religion in a role of providing moral meaning and motivation to a social system. They also highlight the inclusive character of religious dynamism—one that lays claim to social movements that might not on first look appear to be religious. This will be of particular importance in understanding how religion seemingly was supplanted by the advent of Positivism and social scientific methodology when, in principle, it provided the incentive and background for these very movements.

The text also owes a theoretical debt, at least in part, to the Weberian concept of rationalization. Partial, in that it explains various internal developments in penal evolution but not the overall evolution itself.

Weber's noted thesis concerning Protestantism and the development of Capitalism argues that economic rationalization in the West was immeasurably aided by its affinity to the type of asceticism necessary to Protestantism, especially Calvinism. Calvinist Christians, facing a "disenchanted" world through denial of the means of spiritual comfort provided by the "otherworldly" ethic of Catholicism, must prove themselves "solely through the ethical quality of [their] conduct in this world" (Weber 1946, 291).

Following Weber's scholarship, one can connect the development and increasing complexity of capitalist society to the religious anxiety of the believer, who must seek salvation ethically, and yet within the context of economic success. This will prove to be a significant insight with regard to the development of the penal system, particularly its dominant expression initiated at the Auburn penitentiary in New York, as rehabilitation could not be envisioned without concrete evidence of economic vitality within the institutions.

Another conceptual element in the text focuses on the integration of scientific thinking and methodology into the social system by way of the same controlling Protestant ethos. This rationalization was affected substantially by the methodical approach of the natural sciences, especially as they are expressed in Positivism. This latter phenomenon dominated American thought in the latter part of the nineteenth century, and came to subsume penal methodology under its rubric by the instigation of the religious community, particularly the chaplains. Robert Bellah maintains that the favorable attitude of Ascetic Protestantism to modernization "contributed to the relatively smooth course of development in areas where it predominated and to the absence of social movements evidencing a high degree of emotional rejection of modernity" (1970, 68). He notes that it is not surprising that "it was on Protestant soil that the modern ideology of science first took root" (1970, 67).

The process of penal evolution, like the process of modernization itself, "is always a moral and religious problem" (1970, 64). The challenge to each society is the integration of increasingly complex areas of social and personal life within a unified symbolic framework.

These basic sociological principles support my contention that the penitentiary did not fall into disfavor due to its inability to fulfill its original purpose—to institutionalize the means of calling both the inmate and the wider society to a conversion of heart.[5] Rather, it disappeared as a result of pressures within Protestantism itself, developments triggered by the union of Calvinist and social scientific analysis, with the attendant pressure for economic solvency. These led to a gradual and increasingly profound division within the Protestant community. The threads of this separation are witnessed in the evolution of the Social Gospel movement within the liberal wing of American Protestantism. It featured a growing insistence on institutional reform as the catalyst for the continued unfolding of the reign of God. This dominant trend led to calls for new institutional configurations that precipitated the inauguration of the reformatory and the modern prison. The conservative, evangelical wing of Protestantism continued to place its emphasis on the traditional program of personal conversion. Although it continued, as it does today, to have periodic bursts of revivalism, it was diminishing as the governing logic of the American religious community and, indeed, of the American social ethos.

I believe that this thesis can be substantiated by an analysis of the data provided by the reports of prison directors, legislators, religious leaders, and voluntary associations in the states of New York, Massachusetts, and Pennsylvania from 1824 to 1913.

New York and Pennsylvania developed the two prototypical American penitentiaries (Auburn and the Eastern State Penitentiary) in the 1820s, reflecting the religious beliefs of the two states. New York was home to numerous religious bodies, but the great immigration of Yankee settlers with their literate clergy, skilled in the areas of organization and publishing, made it dominantly Presbyterian and Calvinist. This influence was felt in the penal philosophy of the silent system, which was instituted first at Auburn, and shortly thereafter at Sing Sing. Quaker theology was the principal force behind the formation and implementation of the separate system at the Eastern State Penitentiary in Philadelphia, and at the Western State Penitentiary near Pittsburgh.

Massachusetts is very important in the history of American penology because of its important Auburn-style penitentiary at Charlestown, and due to the influence of the Reverend Louis Dwight and the Boston Prison Discipline Society. Dwight was the first national figure in the area of corrections, and through the society circulated the first national publication on prisons. He was the spokesperson for the Auburn system and was singularly instrumental in spreading its influence throughout the United States.

The New York and Pennsylvania systems were the focus of considerable national and world attention. The debate on the merits and demerits of the two institutions raged for decades, most notably in Dwight's writings. The predominance of these two models mirrors the influence of the three states chosen for this inquiry. As David Rothman argues, Boston, New York, and Philadelphia "set the pace of change" in the period under study (1971, xiii-xiv).

The era to be investigated begins with the opening of the Auburn penitentiary in 1824. The facility had been in operation since 1821, but the silent system originated at that point. The penitentiaries at Philadelphia and Pittsburgh began the separate in system in 1829, the same year that the silent system was inaugurated at Charlestown.

The analysis ends in 1913 when the Eastern Penitentiary in Philadelphia ended the separate system. This action officially terminated the penitentiary era. The focus of American corrections was then fully directed to the progressive programs instituted in the reformatories. The rudiments of the progressive treatment program, reflecting the positivist approach, remained in vogue until the major prison riots of the late sixties and early seventies. Indeed, many of its innovations—probation, parole, the indeterminate sentence, the primacy of psychological and environmental factors in explaining criminal behavior—remain to this day.

The fact that the analysis is of two expressions of penal philosophy assumes a comparative format. This is indeed true but it is not my primary interest. I am less concerned with comparing the merits and demerits of the silent and separate systems than in defining the religious movements that fashioned them, and how they slowly came to merge under the ideological edifice of Progressivism.

The historical and sociological research undertaken in this endeavor has led to several assumptions which guide the approach taken in the pages that follow. The first is that the current marginal involvement of the churches in the criminal justice enterprise is a result of developments in the social system which they themselves initiated. Modernism, with its new epistemology and psychology centered on the autonomous individual, may be officially secular. However, it owes its existence and philosophical underpinnings to religious movements. As Weber states, the modern, capitalist world built on the foundations of Ascetic Protestantism now "rests on mechanical foundations" and "needs its support no longer" (1958, 181-82).

I argue throughout that the chaplains and religious leaders of the mid-nineteenth century inaugurated the positivist shift in penal thinking that created the conditions for the Social Gospel phenomenon in Protestant Christianity. This development transferred the evangelical emphasis on personal conversion to a need to create new institutions responsible for generating the reign of God on earth. The fact that the result was a diminished religious voice does not negate the theological foundation of the newly secular institutions.

A second assumption in this presentation is that the penitentiary is a microcosm of the society in which it functions. It is "an indicator of the social organization and moral values of the larger society" (Jacobs 1977, x) as well as its mode of production (Rusche and Kirchheimer 1968, 5). Penal practice reflects "a particular conceptualization of the human person," as well as "implicit assumptions about the purpose of law and society" (McHugh 1978, 3). These ideas will generally be coherent with those of the dominant class in society. I maintain, however, that religion has an autonomy, indeed a priority of influence, in the social milieu. Rationalization, bureaucratization, and other values associated with capitalism will affect and limit decisions made in the institutional sphere, but the movements that precede social change cannot be reduced to extensions of the mode and relations of production.

A third assumption is that there is a recurring tension between prison administrators and reformers, and therefore within society itself, concerning the particular punitive logic that operates in the penal context. There is an obvious difference between the deterrence or obedience model favored in the Auburn-style penitentiaries, and the individual treatment model that was the mark of the Pennsylvania system and of the progressives. A vocal and unified religious presence mitigates the symbolic incoherence and structural "anomie" that occur when competing punishment theories offset one another, as they did in New York, and as they continue to do today.

For purposes of clarity I will define some of the terms that will be used throughout the study. Positivism refers to the belief that the methods of the natural sciences constitute the person's "sole possible significant cognitive relation to external (non ego) reality" (Parsons 1968, 61). This framework complements the rationalism of Utilitarianism and conceives the explanation of human action in biological terms, concentrating on the factors of heredity and environment (Parsons 1968, 67).

Evangelicalism in a strict sense means the preaching of the gospel. It is generally applied to the beliefs held by Christians that stress the sinfulness of human nature, the personal relationship of the human person to God, divine salvation through faith, and the need for conversion through preaching and other means (Cole 1977, 4-5). These means of evangelical conversion are usually expressed in an emotionally charged manner. All evangelicals stress Martin Luther's "sola scriptura," that the bible is the medium through which saving grace is channeled to the person of faith.

Ascetic Protestantism, or Culture Protestantism, represents the blending of Calvinism with the Baptist doctrine of freedom and with Pietistic rigorism. It retains the Calvinist democratic political emphasis within the context of the free church or congregational system. There is less emphasis on predestination, and a greater accent on ethical conduct in the world as the expression of one's sanctification. It is associated with liberalism, democracy, a strong self-controlled individualism, and utilitarianism in secular affairs (Troeltsch 1931, 688-91).

A prison refers to an edifice built for the purpose of deprivation of liberty through the imposition of a time sentence. Although present in limited ways throughout history, the prison as the dominant means of societal punishment does not emerge until the eighteenth century. Before that, deviants were detained mainly to await corporal punishment, while itinerants and those lacking habits of industry were confined in workhouses.

The term "penitentiary" is first mentioned in the seventeenth century in connection with the writings of the Benedictine monk, Jean Mabillon. Its purpose was to use the time sentence as a pretext to reform the inmate through silence, work, and spiritual counsel. It came into international prominence in the New York and Pennsylvania systems, both echoing Mabillon's ideas (Sellin 1927, 581-602).[6]

Historians of the development of punishment and penal institutions probably resonate with the statement in the book of Ecclesiastes that there is "nothing new under the sun" (Eccl. 1:9). Virtually all of the debates currently raging over the nature and effects of punishment, alternatives to prison, prison factories, inmate skill training, and a host of other remedies to the problem of deviancy have been in the correctional milieu for at least a century. Indeed, it seems that the only new phenomenon in the current situation is an abiding cynicism and an abandonment of constructive dialogue in favor of "technologies of power." Foucault comes closest to baring the logic behind the contemporary practice of making everyone a suspect. What he and other analysts of the phenomenon of crime have done, however, is surrender to the modernist ideological critique of religion. Such a frame of reference leads one to conclude that it is at best a noble attempt that failed, at worst a perverse superstition that suppresses human freedom and dignity.[7]

This historical study in religious sociology confers on the religious community a primary place in constructing permeable institutions that owe their existence to an understanding of society based on theological assumptions. It is a vision founded on the belief that the quality of human life and human community are divine concerns, safeguarded in the molding of social structures to be constantly evaluated in terms of their congruence with theological and moral principles. The fact that conflicts exist within this community, that its members are deeply affected by social, economic, and psychological factors, that they often became prisoners of their own prejudices, does not negate the ongoing dynamism of the religious voice and the movements for social reform that it inevitably creates.

Chapter 2 will present the social and intellectual movements that paved the way for the penitentiary era, the most significant of which was the Great Awakening of the early eighteenth century. The religious revolution that ensued maintained the Calvinist heritage of political involvement, but was driven by the twin forces of emotional conversion and a millennial mission to transform the institutions and mores of American life.

In Chapter 3 the development of the two competing systems of penitentiary discipline in New York and Pennsylvania will be outlined. The role of the religious community will be illuminated as it mediated the developments during the post-revolutionary era when the penitentiaries rose to national prominence and, especially in New York, became a national scandal.

Chapter 4 argues that the seeds of the Progressive Era in the penal system, and the nation at large, were sown by religious figures, chiefly prison chaplains, who splintered the then remarkable cohesiveness of evangelical Protestantism by their development of basic sociological investigative techniques. Frustrated by the explanatory inadequacy of a social hermeneutic based on personal conversion, and through the medium of the interview and the subsequent employment of statistical data, the chaplains opened the religious community to the ideology and methodology of Positivism. This procedural and theological shift provided the basis for the Social Gospel phenomenon in American Protestantism, and for the development of the Progressive Era in penology.

Chapter 5 will briefly present how the ideology of Progressivism, born in religious movements and embodied in the reformatory, erased both the practical significance and the actual existence not only of the penitentiaries, but of religion as a dynamic and creative force in the correctional arena. The conclusion that follows argues that American penology has lost and desperately needs to recover a moral organizational principle that can give meaning and coherence to the whole system. This is a role that is the historical and functional province of the religious community. It cannot be carried out solely by the state.

Put another way, this study contends that the groups demonstrating at the prison gate, and the chaplain walking the condemned to the electric chair, are the descendants of the principal architects of the American penal system. Their voices are not only echoes of what has been done in American penology to this point; they are voices that cannot remain outside the prison walls if society is to develop a just and more effective solution to the problem of crime.

Chapter 2

THE EVANGELICAL MILLENNIUM AND THE RISE OF THE PENITENTIARY

In 1831 Gustave de Beaumont and Alexis de Tocqueville were sent by the government of France to examine the penitentiaries in the United States. Only two years earlier Pennsylvania had begun what was known as the separate system in its state penitentiaries. Less than a decade had elapsed since the inauguration of the silent system in Auburn, New York. In this brief time the attention of the nation and the world had been drawn to the contentious debate that had arisen between the two plans of penal discipline.

The French visitors were not alone. England, Prussia and many other European countries had sent delegations. There were observers from Canada, Latin America and Japan as well. All were hoping to derive a workable solution from these experiments to the enduring problem of the social deviant.

What made the French delegation so important were neither its purpose nor its recommendations; it was the observant mind of de

Tocqueville himself. He was convinced that the penitentiary was not an isolated phenomenon but a significant symbolic expression of the foundational American vision.

> If we carefully examine the social and political state of America, after having studied its history, we shall remain perfectly convinced that not an opinion, not a custom, not a law, I may even say not an event is upon record which the origin of that people will not explain (1945, 29).

Institutions, he might have said, cannot be superimposed upon a people but proceed from the original social and moral imagination of the society. The circumstances that accompanied nations and "contributed to their development affected the whole term of their being" (1945, 28). The American penitentiary, therefore, like American democracy itself, had to be interpreted in light of the original Puritan vision of society, a vision drawing much of its inspiration from the theology of John Calvin.

The Calvinist Worldview

The descendants of Calvin were in many ways apprehensive individuals.[1] The reformation had left them free of both the domination and the security of the vast symbolic world of Catholicism. Predestination removed the redemptive significance of action in the world, but had not diminished the responsibility to fashion the earthly realm into a "theater of God's glory."

A central focus of Calvin's theology was the permanent estrangement of human beings from their God. Like Luther, he held out no hope that a life of virtuous action could assuage one's anxiety concerning salvation. Unlike Luther, however, who had prescribed faith as the solution to this dilemma, Calvin upheld an uncompromised notion of obedience.

> As I have said, God's right remains unviolated only when we adhere unquestioningly to his service and are convinced that no consideration is important enough to permit us to make it lawful for us to deviate in the slightest degree from that course of action which he commands by his word and which he requires of us (Calvin 1958, 242).

Calvin demanded that his followers participate in transforming both church and state into disciplinary associations conformed to the revelation of Scripture. The task of the church was to bring men and women into the "obedience of the Gospel." As one Presbyterian pastor expressed it, neither the "lion's den" nor the "furnaces of hell" could dissuade the Christian from this duty: "We will dare do it in the face of all interdicts, of all opposition, even, as Luther said when on his way to Worms, if there were as many devils in our path, as tiles upon the houses" (Adams 1851, 32-33).

The state, in recognition of its divine purpose, and given the sinful inclinations of its citizens, was to be no less than an established order of repression. For the number of the elect is small and "therefore it is necessary that the rest of the crowd be restrained by a forcible curb. For the sons of God are intermingled with great, savage beasts, or with wolves and false men" (Calvin 1958, 188). A properly ordered church and state would lead to the creation of a holy commonwealth, one that would assure not only the provision of basic necessities to each citizen, but also one whose organization would fulfill the higher command to magnify the greatness of God.

> [I]ts objects are that idolatry, sacrileges against the name of God, blasphemies against his truth, and other offenses against God may not openly appear and be disseminated among the people; that the public tranquility may not be disturbed; that every person may enjoy his property without molestation; that men may transact their business together without fraud or injustice; that integrity and modesty may be cultivated among them; in short, that there may be a public form of religion among Christians, and that humanity may be maintained among men (Calvin 1950, 46-47).

This great hallmark of Calvinism, that the government is solemnly pledged to obey God, was deeply established in the Puritan mind set and continued to influence the discourse and social vision of its descendants. The Congregational pastor, Samuel Wolcott, echoed this theme in an election sermon to the Massachusetts legislature.

> It is a most pleasing and impressive religious usage, which provides that your entrance to the halls of legislation shall be through the sanctuary of God. This service is a devout recognition of the truth, that the kingdom is the Lord's, and he is the governor among the nations. The special design of these exercises is secured, when you carry hence to your respective posts of public service a solemn sense of your accountability to the Supreme Ruler, of your obligation to promote, to the fullest practicable extent, the best interests of your fellow-men (MA Senate 1853, 32-33).

De Tocqueville showed foresight in tracking the development of American institutions from the ethos of the first settlers. Indeed the impact of Calvinism, extended and modified by the Puritans, on the shape of Anglo-American social and political structure is most profound. Calvinist theology, as Michael Walzer summarizes it, transformed previously passive individuals by providing them with the methods of political activity by which they could give shape to and successfully participate in "that ongoing system of political action that is the modern state" (1965, 18). Virtually all the expressions of contemporary democratic life can trace their origin to Calvin's political theology and the Puritan saints who carried it into English and subsequently American political life. Representative councils, a national constitution, the public presentation of demands and the formation of voluntary associations to implement those demands, the appearance of political journalism, and the insistence on the continuing reform of public life were all elements of seventeenth century revolutionary politics that the Puritans brought with them to America (Walzer 1965, 10).

The other form of activity that provided a degree of solace to the descendants of Calvin was economic endeavor. Weber remarks that the mendicant religious orders of the Middle Ages had made begging an accepted state that not only raised the level of the poorest members of society, but also gave the well-to-do an opportunity to assuage guilt by means of charitable action (1958, 177). Lacking this form of religious assurance, the affluent Calvinist found a degree of spiritual comfort by expanded achievement in the economic arena. As the bourgeois came to justify their life not by good works but by everyday conduct, divine benediction became equated with diligent attention to their specific calling and by the level of success they attained in the world. Wealth lost its mark of sinfulness and, as Rusche and Kirchheimer suggest, "the idea of voluntary generosity toward the poor as absolution for the sin involved in wealth became meaningless" (1968, 35-36). Calvinism may have been only a contributing factor in the development of capitalism in the West, but there can be no doubt that it offered a welcome intellectual foundation for the social and economic philosophy of the Protestant states (Weber 1968, 36-37).[2]

A significant issue that surfaces repeatedly in the history that follows is the connection between punishment and economics. Early penal reformers in America insisted on enforced labor, vocational training, and repeatedly placed institutional value on a par with economic solvency. In so doing, they not only revealed a pragmatic ethic; they bore witness to a primary tenet of the Calvinist theology that informed their past and did so much to shape their social vision for the future.

The Enlightenment

There is a necessary debt that the process of modernization owes to the theological and ethical attitudes of Calvinism. According to Talcott Parsons, among others, one must understand social and psychological development as a result of a shift in ethical norms. In the case of the Enlightenment, it must be viewed as the culmination of movements begun in the Protestant Reformation.

The Reformation led to the introduction of radical political and economic ideas. In the wake of William of Ockham and Nominalism, it emphasized the idea of freedom, preeminently the religious freedom of the individual. The impact of freedom on the idea of faith is unquestioned, but of similar importance is its impact on epistemology. In embracing the normative starting point that social conduct proceeds from the faith of the individual, the early Protestants at the same time came to exalt the idea of freedom of conscience. The Catholic metaphysical assumptions that constructed limits on intellectual investigation were pushed back. The social system took on decidedly rational and scientific overtones within the normative context provided by individual freedom (Parsons 1968, 87).

Parsons argues that the immediacy of the individual to God was accompanied by a parallel devaluation of attachment to one's fellows. The human actor was encouraged to reduce relationships to "impersonal, unsentimental terms and to consider others not so much from the point of view of their value in themselves as of their usefulness, ultimately to the purposes of God, more immediately to his own ends" (1968, 54-55). This evolution in social thought away from the more organic approach of Thomist Catholicism produced the conditions for the rational means-end analysis of utilitarianism (Parsons 1968, 55).

The characteristic aims of the Enlightenment: natural rights, personal liberty, democracy, rationality, and scientific procedure were derived in large part from the ideas of the Reformation in general and Calvin in particular. When Locke wrote his political philosophy, with the concepts of contract, accountability, and power centered in the governed, he revealed the influence of Richard Hooker who, in turn, was schooled in the ideas of Calvin. In Locke's concern for individual felicity and personal liberty he similarly extended and developed basic themes of the Swiss Reformation.[3]

When the Enlightenment reformers turned their attention to the question of crime and punishment, they necessarily brought a new framework to an old problem. What was formerly a brutal art that sought to exact societal vengeance on the body of the convicted was now reinterpreted in terms of the new ethical and epistemological considerations.[4] The Encyclopedists, especially Montesquieu, held that punishments must be made to fit the crime, that moderation in their employment reflected the level of advancement of equality within society: "The severity of punishments is fitter for despotic governments, whose principle is terror, than for a monarchy or republic, whose spring is honor and virtue" (Montesquieu 1762, 88).

Utilitarians, such as Bentham and Beccaria,[5] evaluated the treatment of the criminal in cost/benefit terms, with deprivation of liberty replacing capital punishment as a primary vehicle of punishment. Beccaria wrote: "such punishments and such method of inflicting them ought to be chosen, therefore, which will make the strongest and most lasting impression on the minds of men, and inflict the least torment on the body of the criminal" (1963, 42). The fact that Beccaria was trained as an economist also lent further credibility to the assertion that quantitative approaches were better suited to a rational understanding of social problems such as crime. Evidence of this argument can be seen in his belief in expanded economic productivity as the best criminal deterrent, an argument not lost on the evolving religious economy of America:[6]

> The surest way to keep citizens in their country is to increase the relative well-being of each of them. Just as every effort ought to be made to turn the balance of trade in our favor, so it is in the greatest interest of the sovereign and of the nation that the sum of happiness, compared with that of surrounding nations, be greater than elsewhere (Beccaria 1963, 82).

The evolution of Reformation thought in the Enlightenment was to make its way across the Atlantic. In such diverse and important thinkers as Benjamin Rush and especially Jonathan Edwards it would have an impact on the development of the American penal system.

The New England Experience

The Puritans who arrived in New England in the seventeenth century represented the radical wing of the English Reformation. Their strict demeanor bore testimony to their Calvinist-inspired interpretation of the Holy Scripture. They sought to create in America that "city on the hill" of which John Winthrop spoke that would be a light to the nations and a vivid representation of God's reign on earth. Even before the influential writing of Hobbes and Locke, of Montesquieu, Beccaria and the great penal reformer, John Howard, they were intent on reforming the brutality of English criminal law. The number of executions in England had increased dramatically during the turbulent seventeenth century, the processions to the gallows tree being a common occurrence. From the end of the reign of Charles II to the beginning of the nineteenth century, 187 new capital offenses were added to the criminal law (Newman 1978, 134).

The Puritans formulated a strict biblical basis for punishment, corresponding to their belief that crime was tantamount to sin. As the theologian Thomas Hooker expressed it:

> Learn therefore to see how far your rebellions reach. It is not arguments you gainsay, not the counsel of a minister you reject, the command of a magistrate ye oppose, evidence of rule or reason ye resist, but be it known to you, you fly in the very face of the Almighty (Miller 1956, 158).

Although the corporal nature of correction was upheld, their adherence to biblical evidence as the sole justification for punishment led them to reduce the number of capital crimes to twelve (Preyer 1982, 332-33).

The New England colonists exhibited the Calvinist belief of adherence to divine sovereignty in social and political affairs by way of three basic principles: a Christian constitutionalism based on the idea of covenant, a commitment to church independence via the organizational principle of Congregationalism (the free church), and a sense of limits on the authority of secular rulers.[7] As H. Richard Niebuhr maintains, "the pilgrims of Plymouth were a church before they were a commonwealth and became a commonwealth only in order that they might maintain themselves as a church" (1937, 58, 68).

The Puritan experiment was rooted in the premise that the state and the church could be one. The basis of this unity was not in organization or immediate purpose, but in their common recognition of the sovereignty of God. This conviction, when joined with the freedom and optimism of the Enlightenment, would usher in the providential belief that an abundant land and a favoring deity were guiding the creation of God's reign in America.

Changes in Penal Philosophy

In order to develop a theory that explains the development of the American penal system one must weave together several threads of social history and ethical methodology. Already we have noted the presence of Enlightenment thinkers within this fabric, as well as the obedience-centered Scriptural ethic of the Puritan settlers in New England. One must also take note of developments in England prior to and during the period of Continental Rationalism and British Empiricism. These were the movements to establish first the workhouse and subsequently the penitentiary.

There can be no doubt that the Puritans brought English criminal theory and practice with them to the colonial settlements. Their emphasis on hard work and thrift led them to adopt the idea of the workhouse.

The workhouse was a form of sanction aimed at vagabonds and disorderly locals. Its origin can be traced to Tudor England where an experimental facility was established in the revitalized royal palace at Bridewell in 1557 (Hirsch 1992, 13-14). The supporters of the idea, on both sides of the Atlantic, hoped that enforced labor and loss of liberty would act as a deterrent to communal deviants while expressing a fitting form of enlightened punishment (Rothman 1971, 25). The first workhouse was opened in Massachusetts in 1629. Its success led the Massachusetts General Court to order each county in the Bay State to open similar establishments (Hirsch 1992, 27).

These early attempts at correction expressed the social and theological understanding of the community. They bore witness to the evolution of Calvinist thought away from the rigid dictum of predestination to one more centered on accountability and amendment of the will to perform works of righteousness.[8] *The Cambridge Platform* states:

> In dealing with an offender, great care is to be taken that we be neither over strict or rigorous, not too indulgent or remiss; our proceeding herein ought to be with a spirit of meekness, considering ourselves, lest we also be tempted (Gal.6:1), and that the best of us have need of much forgiveness from the Lord (Matth. 18: 34, 35) (Vaughan 1972, 110).

This shift in theology led to the belief in England, and subsequently in America, that the function of the workhouse could be expanded to provide the vagrant with the environment necessary for a reformed spirit. These new houses of correction were proposed by religious figures and philanthropists who sought to emulate the cellular plan featuring silence, prayer, and, in some cases, work, that had been attempted in the prisons on the European continent.[9]

The combination of Enlightenment rationalism and a more optimistic theology led to dramatic changes in the social response to crime and deviancy in New England. By the late eighteenth century all the forms of public punishment characteristic of the earliest Puritan communities–the pillory, stocks, and, in large part, the gallows–were either radically reduced or fully eliminated. This report of the New York Assembly captures the tenor of the new approach to crime and punishment showing the particular influence of John Locke and the Enlightenment.

> In the state of nature, then, man did not possess the right to take the life of his fellow, except in self-defense. Since nature, says a writer on the law of nations, has given to man the right of using force only when it becomes necessary for their defence and the preservation of their rights; and since society is founded upon the delegation of certain natural rights, it necessarily follows, that society is not authorized to use force in any case where it would not have been right for an individual to have exercised it (Assembly Doc. 187 1832, 9).

If one accepts the premise that Enlightenment values influenced the new outlook on crime, one must ask at what juncture and through what process these now secularized values merged with the largely orthodox Calvinism of the Puritan colonies. It is this question that illuminates the most significant of the eighteenth century developments that affected the course of the penal system and, indeed, that of the nation itself: the Great Awakening and the figure of Jonathan Edwards.

The Great Awakening

It was certain that if Enlightenment thinking could spread in New World communities it would further modify the strict Calvinism of the early Puritans. Edwards (1703-1758) is a key figure in pioneering that development. Although philosophical logic and rational analysis were held in high regard by the Puritans, Edwards was a guiding figure in blending these forces within an experiential framework suited to the particular spiritual hunger of the age. As William Frankenna notes, he marks the beginning of a tradition of teleological and utilitarian thinking strongly opposed to the deontological intuitionism prevalent in American ethics (Edwards 1960, viii).

Although he was a Calvinist, he sought to ground his ethics on empirical and rational grounds. He based his system on the concept of the "beautiful," an apprehension of the divine presence within others and a corresponding sense of benevolence toward them (Edwards 1960, 3). This mystical union with being, in Calvinist fashion, was only the province of the elect (Edwards 1960, 100), but its effect on American religion was considerable. By incorporating the ideas of Locke and Newton into his thought, as well as those of the moral sense theorists, Hutcheson and Butler, Edwards was able to infuse the spirit of the Age of Reason into his ancestral faith. As Sydney Ahlstrom states, he helped inaugurate "the great spiritual transition that marks the end of a period when American culture was still recognizably medieval in its outlook and inner spirit, and the emergence of distinctly 'modern' religious ideas" (1972, 351).

The Great Awakening of the 1740s injected a spirit of emotionalism into religious experience, a tangible "feeling" of saving grace. As it gained momentum, it would go far beyond the rather conservative theology of Edwards. The experience of conversion was destined to become not only *the* central religious issue, but arguably the dominant social force in American life well into the nineteenth century. Edwards, and preachers such as Whitefield, Frelinghuysen, and the Wesley's, brought an impassioned sense of election to the soul of the American people that could elevate them above the torment that had so troubled them in regard to their salvation.

Emanating from a wing of Lutheranism, Pietism also easily accommodated itself to the religious excitement and ferment of the era. The Pietists protested against intellectualism and formalism in religious matters. This revivalist movement aimed at making the relation to God more experientially meaningful as well as socially relevant. While it stressed a religious subjectivism, its moral emphasis led directly to active charitable concerns and to a great flourishing of Christian philanthropy.[10]

Faith, democracy, and a spirit of optimism about the human prospect were to generate a commission to benevolence and direct social action. After a revival in 1744, Samuel Blair noted that one could distinguish the truly regenerated from those who were simply trying to imitate the demeanor of the sanctified. In the converted, he noted, "Their Walk is habitually Tender and Conscientious; their Carriage toward their Neighbor Just and Kind; and they appear to have an agreeable and peculiar Love one for another, and for all in whom appears the Image of God" (Bushman 1970, 77).

The Great Awakening served to break the unified spirit of Congregationalism, exemplified in creedal statements such as *The Cambridge Platform*, within the religious economy of New England. It created an often acrimonious split within Calvinist communities between what were called the "old lights" and the "new lights," orthodox and revisionist believers respectively. Among the more ecclesiastically centralized Presbyterians the controversy was particularly bitter. A synod of the church in Philadelphia in 1741 expelled the "new light" members "to preserve this swooning church from a total expiration" (Bushman 1970, 97).

In fine, a continued union, in our judgment, is most absurd and inconsistent, when it is so notorious, that our doctrine and principles of church government, in many points, are not only diverse, but directly opposite. For how can two walk together, except they be agreed? (Bushman 1970, 100)

The controversy continued well into the nineteenth century prefiguring the current split within Protestantism between "high church" formalists and "low church" evangelicals. *The Presbyterian Review* remarked, "there must be, if piety and good conscience is preserved, a living protest in the body, and a perpetual controversy" (June 1852, 21-22).

The theology of Jacob Arminius (1560-1609) found a receptive audience during the period of the Awakening.[11] He was a Dutch Calvinist who rebelled against the arbitrary character of predestination. His acclamation of free will and the universal quality of grace, while welcome news to those on the fringes of orthodoxy, had remained a bold yet dubious assertion to the average believer. With Edwards and the first great wave of Evangelists, however, theological barriers that formerly seemed unassailable were beginning to erode. The Arminians, although skeptical of the emotionalism of the revivals, found a far more hospitable climate for their ideas. Their theology was more rationally based and emphasized an expansive optimism concerning the scope and merit of ethical conduct; a position vilified by its accusers for approaching the dreaded justification by works. There would be a slow but steady transition within a wing of New England Calvinism as Arminian ideas came to dominate the religious imagination of Boston's educated and cosmopolitan citizenry, preparing New England soil for the seeds of Unitarianism. Arminian ideas removed the grim determinism of predestination. Together with the social activism of Calvinism and the optimism of the Enlightenment, they produced a marriage of forces that would culminate in the social reform movements that gave birth to the penitentiaries.

Another less dramatic offshoot of the theology of Edwards is important to this study. As differentiation occurred within the religious and cultural environment there were, as we have seen, strict, "old light" Calvinists, "new light" or "Consistent Calvinists," and Arminians. There was also substantial growth among Unitarians, Universalists, and Methodists as well as among the Calvinist revival sects, the Baptists and Quakers. One of the disciples of Edwards was Samuel Hopkins who encouraged the believer to disinterested benevolence as the proper expression of humble obedience. His followers were often engaged in crusades for moral reform. Among those influenced by Hopkins was the Reverend Louis Dwight who exerted an unparalleled influence on the development of the American penal system.

Revivalism, Conversion, and Social Reconstruction

The nineteenth century opened with another wave of revivalism. As Weber stated, charismatic movements have the tendency to become routinized as the emotional fires of conversion are cooled with the passage of time and daily organizational demands, eventually settling into more methodical forms of behavior (1978, 246-48). If the religious system grounded in a visceral spiritual experience was to maintain its influence, it would need periodic renewal. Inasmuch as historians concede that evangelical religion dominated national life throughout much of the nineteenth century, one can trace a consistent pattern of revivalism throughout the period.[12]

The most important religious event of the first half century was the Second Great Awakening which began in the mid 1820s and, by most accounts, ended with the economic recession of 1837. It was preceded by several noteworthy developments: a turn of many intellectuals to Deism with a corresponding depletion of religious fervor in favor of more secular, republican themes, and the expansion of the nation westward without a preestablished religious presence.

Deism was an eighteenth century notion entirely inimical to the Protestant belief that human beings were fallen creatures unable to escape damnation save through the action of divine grace. Evangelical leaders were greatly disturbed as they observed the undisciplined frontier settlements. Reverend Timothy Dwight, president of Yale and the grandson of Edwards, described the Maine frontier in 1797 as the haunt of "vicious men" who had fled society to give more liberal reign to their "idle and licentious dispositions" (Weisberger 1958, 11). At the same time, the liberal Unitarians were making deep inroads at Harvard, which they would come to dominate, and could claim by 1812 that they held within their communion most of Boston's clergy as well as the majority of the city's "respectable" laity (Weisberger 1958, 15).

The Second Awakening tapped the boundless enthusiasm of the expanding nation and the spirit of voluntarism that de Tocqueville had recognized, as well as the native tendency for "ultraism" that had been identified in the revivals of the previous century. Thousands of "new light" Congregationalists and Presbyterians joined the Methodist and Baptist Churches, where the revival mentality was less inhibited by the stubborn values of community inclusiveness and strict authority residing in the older denominations.

Evangelical publications blossomed and throughout the land there was a persistent cry to save the lost through the revival of religion. *The Evangelical Repository* was one of many channels through which the trumpet of revivalism was sounded:

> Look around us in our own immediate neighborhood. How many families can we count, who, although not heathen, are living equally "without God, and without hope in the world?" Among these can we not see some of our friends-companions? In our very midst, around our doors, in our families, thousands of our fellow creatures are sinking down into the flames of hell (July 1842, 50).

In tandem with such soteriological concerns was the belief of religious leaders that the growth of Protestantism was synonymous with social progress. They were insistent that America's political and economic advance was the direct result of the Protestant stamp upon the nation. The Baptist leader, Francis Wayland, stated that "the doctrines of Protestant Christianity are the sure, nay, the only bulwark of civil freedom" (Cole 1977, 154). Only a turn away from sinful behavior, individually and collectively, could assure God's continued blessings on the land: "anyone who has not seen the vials of wrath, pouring on the head of our guilty nation, standing as she does with her feet on the Sabbath, and stained with the blood of millions, must have been sleeping, when God was abroad in the earth" (Evangelical Repository July 1842, 58).

Despite the tensions that existed between the churches and civil society during the Jacksonian era, the natural affinity between evangelical Christianity and republicanism mollified these differences and helped usher in new institutional forms to express the optimistic tenor of the times. Whitney Cross captures well the unique alliance between religious ideas and the tenor of the age, one that was itself the product of deep religious roots.

> The wedding of humanitarian movements and revivalism followed upon a lengthy betrothal . . . Tendencies deeply rooted in the age contributed to their growing congeniality. Jacksonian democracy, whose marked worldliness and hints of outright infidelity pointed out the necessity for spiritual and moral progress, drove them into each other's arms (1981, 168).

This is not, of course, to argue that there were not reform movements apart from those generated by the revivalists. Radicalism was deeply rooted in the American tradition to which the likes of Thomas Paine and Robert Owen give witness. Indeed, much of this reform tradition was anticlerical in its outlook as that attitude was very much a companion of the Enlightenment. Yet however one argues for an independent tradition of secular radicalism, it never achieved substantial popularity with the American public. Rather, it was those movements firmly planted in the soil of evangelical piety that produced the major changes in American society.

The Second Great Awakening and the prevailing social optimism combined to initiate a great wave of millenialism. The belief was dominantly post-millenarian, that America was witnessing the second coming of Christ and the inauguration of a thousand-year reign of peace and progress. A new dispensation of grace was available to the sinner, and just as the American political system would lead the world to the equality that de Tocqueville admired, so the revivals would establish the governance of Christ before the end of the world. As one editorial expressed it, "[W]e are standing on the *verge of the millennium*. The present and the coming age will be crowded with strange events; the cleansing of the sanctuary, the rising of the witnesses—the ushering in of the glorious millennium. It is already the Saturday evening of the world" (Evangelical Repository July 1842, 58). The greatest preacher of the day, Charles Finney claimed: "As the millennium advances, it is probable that these periodical excitements will be unknown. Then the church will be enlightened, and the counteracting causes removed, and the entire church will be in a state of habitual and steady obedience to God" (Finney 1960, 11).

Progressivism was born in these religious movements. The optimistic belief in God's providential guidance of America, however, was still accompanied by the old Calvinist sobriety. While the grace of conversion was available to all, there remained the conviction that the natural human tendency, barring conversion, was toward degeneracy. Charles Sutton, who served for many years as warden of the "Tombs" in New York City, spoke of how the "substratum of society is seamed with sin" and that beneath the "sun-lit surface is a dark, surging sea, tempest tossed by the winds of brutality, ignorance and license." He spoke of the "wall" which guards the social system: "That wall is the law, its battlements and turrets are the jails" (Sutton 1874, 17). Another example of the continued belief in human sinfulness is found in this cautionary reminder:

> [People] cannot choose holiness of heart, speech, or behaviour. They cannot choose the image of God, conformity to his divine law, or

communion with him. It is never until the infinite power of the Holy
Spirit . . . that they can choose the good, and refuse the evil. Thus the
very nature of the Holy Spirit, shows that man is incapacitated either
to choose salvation, or work it out. Because before he can either
possess or desire it, he must be born again (Evangelical Repository
August 1842, 106).

Also common to the period was the wider unfolding of a concept
prefigured in the Puritan covenental theology, that human corruption was
provoked by external as well as by internal factors. Whereas many "old
light" religionists did not feel that personal sinfulness could be mitigated
by the control of social structures, the idealism of the new era began to
portray deviancy and crime as symptomatic of an unredeemed social
order.[13]

The evangelicals, with millenarian enthusiasm, thought it possible
"to ferret out corruption and eliminate crime" (Rothman 1971, 68-69).
Social structures could act as a catalyst for inner conversion. Human
reason and will, liberated from sin by grace, were sufficiently wise and
selfless to make an ideal society possible.

Although there were numerous denominations in the country, the
remarkable achievement of the Jacksonian era revivals was to create a
united evangelical outlook that controlled the pace of virtually all religious
groups within the land. There were repeated calls to sublimate doctrinal
differences for the greater good of spreading the gospel with one clear and
powerful voice. The evangelist Albert Barnes remarked that the revivals
"have done more than any other single cause to form the public mind in
this country" (Cole 1977, 7). *The Evangelical Repository* called on the
churches to "present one undivided front, one unbroken phalanx to the
enemy" (July 1842, 56-57). A writer in the *Sunday School Journal*
declared that if all Christians could be heard, a great majority would favor
relaxing denominational bonds and strengthening "those which unite them
as followers of Christ. The sentiment of the church at this time is for
union" (Smith 1957, 42).

The calls for union were so pervasive and the pressure so unrelenting
that many Unitarians were likewise affected. A Unitarian periodical, *The
Christian Examiner*, after reviewing Comte's philosophy of Positivism,
that would later make deep inroads into the liberal religious psyche, called
him an "infidel" (March 1851, 196). In another issue we find this
declaration:

We may as well say, however, in advance, that to our apprehension
there is, but one Saviour in the New Testament,—one Christ, one

Christology . . . there it is, simple, unique, defying opposition, and
calmly advancing to universal dominion. It describes itself in terms
of marvelous grandeur:"The power of God and the wisdom of God
unto salvation" (March 1852, 273-74).

The evangelical movement was channeled by means of a four-tiered
program of religious conversion and social reform that would be
duplicated by the chaplains in the penitentiaries. First, the revivals would
kindle a zeal for the missionary enterprise. With the millennium at hand
and many souls in the balance there was little time to waste: "How many
families in this Christian land are without the Bible? How many
professing Christians in our 17,000,000? Scarcely 2,000,000; among
these how many are there, who, not laying hold of Christ, must sink
forever?" (Evangelical Repository July 1842, 51) The second and third
stages of the strategy were the formation of local and national missionary
societies, including many bible and tract societies, and the establishment
of Sunday schools and educational programs. An 1825 address of the
Executive Committee of the American Tract Society commented: "Next
to the Bible and the living Ministry, one of these means of light and
salvation will be found to be, short, plain, striking, entertaining, and
instructive Tracts, exhibiting in writing some of the great and glorious
truths of the Gospel" (The American Tract Society 1972, 4). Finally, out
of this organizational base, crusades for moral reform were initiated. The
New York State Society for the Abolition of Capital Punishment noted:

> During this week Societies for the distribution of Bibles, for the
> establishment of missions, for the suppression of American and
> foreign slave dealing, for the support of Sunday schools, for the
> promotion of African colonization, for the distribution of Tracts, for
> the Education of the Blind and the Deaf and Dumb, for the
> amelioration of the condition of the Jews, for the promotion of
> Temperance, for the encouragement of the sacred observance of the
> Sabbath, and many other humane and religious societies . . . will
> deservedly excite great interest among our citizens (1848, 2).

Here was a rich and varied expression of what de Tocqueville saw
as the hope of American democracy, the voluntary association: "[The
people] must go forward and accelerate the union of private with public
interests . . . At the present time civic zeal seems to me to be inseparable
from the exercise of political rights" (1945, 252).[14]
Just as there was a clearly defined method for bringing the sinner to
conversion, so also was there a set of strict behavioral principles that were
to be its fruit. Finney claimed: "Let Christians in a revival BEWARE,

when they first find an inclination creeping upon them, to shrink from self-denial, and to give into one self-indulgence after another. It is the device of Satan, to bait them off from the work of God" (Finney 1960, 285). Profanity, dueling, labor on Sunday and gambling were vices to be avoided. A turn from sexual immorality was also a common theme. Adultery, fornication, masturbation and all biblically proscribed forms of sexual expression were frequently upbraided. It was a common assumption of the time that not only was masturbation a spiritual malady, it was also a cause of death to those who frequently practiced it.[15] As late as 1883 a warning card was hung in each cell of the Eastern State Penitentiary in Philadelphia. It stated that besides debilitating and deadly physical, emotional and mental effects: "It debases the moral faculties, because it is a sin against nature and a sin against God." One who practices it cannot "appreciate the doctrines and precepts of Revealed Religion. He destroys himself" (Teeters and Shearer 1957, 176-77).

Of all the moral cognates of the act of conversion, none was more insistently promoted than temperance. The revivals not only raised the use of intoxicants to the level of sin, instead of a mere departure from decency; they also considered the existence of intemperance the major hindrance to the renewal of spirituality that was to mark the millennium. A sermon by the Reverend Austin Dickinson stated:

> Happy! thrice happy ye! who may thus have the honor of dashing away for ever the cup of drunkenness and washing this foul stain from our country's glory. Happy the generation! who may rise up instead of the fathers, and, like the rainbow above the retiring cloud, reflect from one end of the earth to the other, the glories of the millennial sun (The National Preacher 1830, 320).

Our current fascination with the connection between criminal behavior and intoxication can hardly match the national frenzy of evangelicals directed at eliminating this practice. It was, said a report of the Secretary of State of New York, "a fruitful source of pauperism and misery" (NY Assembly Doc. 85 1824, 2). Finney compared intemperance with the descent into hell and the pledge with the rise to new life (Cross 1981, 168). Chaplain Dickerson of Sing Sing State Prison, in a report revealing the tendency of chaplains to compile factual data in order to ascertain the cause of crime, had this to say concerning the temperance issue:

> By the request of the agent I have spent considerable time in ascertaining the cause of crime, with special reference to

intemperance, and have pursued a course which would be most likely to lead to a true result; it is truly melancholy to find the frequent recurrence of *intemperance - intemperance - under the influence of liquor, &c.* and that too, in many instances, for the express purpose of perpetrating some horrid deed, without hesitation or fear. May this avenue to crime and death speedily be closed up (NY Senate Document [Sen. Doc.] 14 1832, 10).

One of the key features of revivalism was its individuality. Although it established the tradition of the "camp meeting" and other forms of emotional mass participation, it shaped a kind of religious thinking that was intensely individual, making the apex of Christian experience for each separate man or woman a personal change of heart which came about suddenly and publicly under "excruciating emotional pressure" (Weisberger 1958, 21). Calls for national reform hinged on saving one soul at a time. Chaplain Jared Curtis, writing a former prisoner, mirrored the dominant theological preoccupation of the day: "pray to God, and put your trust in him, and you shall find rest for your soul . . . If we expect to be saved, we must be saved through the blood and righteousness of Jesus Christ" (The Boston Prison Discipline Society [PDS] 1842, 10-11).

Thus one could argue that despite the impressive calls for social improvement that were to emanate from this phenomenon, the method was essentially conservative. Martin Marty takes a sober view of the moral reform of the revivalists:

> As for reform, the Protestants readily faced up to those personal vices that were not costly to reformers because self-improvement inconvenienced no one except the individuals involved. The voluntary associations and churches moved with passion to eradicate what one might call breaches of the simple virtues: dueling, profanity, drunkenness, whoring. But these same agencies seemed powerless to affect the controversial issues of freedom, equality, and justice, which are complex because their pursuit does inconvenience others (1984, 227-28).[16]

Expressed in another way, the era of reform was limited by the inability of the Protestant churches to envision the reign of God in terms other than those provided by the particular socioeconomic parameters of American society. Proceeding from a millennial identification of American values with divine approbation, and lacking the transnational character of Catholicism, the evangelicals could not imagine a horizon beyond America and the institutions developed to bring about the divine rule within its national boundaries. Therefore, institutions could be critiqued but the critique was self-limiting.[17] Niebuhr says the localist character of the Protestant evangelical vision was unable to deal with "social crisis, with national disease and the misery of human groups" (1937, 162). It was as if the modernist assumptions of capitalism, individualism, and democracy were largely metaphysical realities that were protected under the umbrella of revealed truth.

Despite these inherent limitations one must use caution in trying to summarize the meaning of complex social movements, with multiple layers of meaning, in a reductionist manner. The sociological tradition amply demonstrates that there are often unintended consequences to social movements; what Ernst Troeltsch terms "accidents," what Weber refers to under the rubric of "elective affinity," or what Robert K. Merton calls "latent functions." The penitentiaries, for example, may have been constructed as vehicles to individual renewal, but these institutions had a profound social and political influence far beyond the intentions of their founders. The philosophy behind them raised anthropological questions, issues of group identity and cohesion, the limits of communal interference in individual life, the extent to which economic solvency can be factored into socially beneficial programs, and a host of other social and moral issues that were addressed, at least in part, in an original and compelling way.

However critically one views the merits of the evangelical program to renew society, one cannot deny that a passionate social agenda was at the heart of the revivalist campaigns. With Charles Finney, one of the final vestiges of Calvinist determinism disappeared. His claim "that the sinner's cannot is a 'will not'" flowed easily into his demand that some kind of relevant social action follow the act of conversion. He reformulated a traditional Calvinist belief in his insistence that the turn to "God and the interests of his kingdom" was to be expressed in terms of moral government: "the cause of peace, the cause of antislavery, and that of the overthrow of licentiousness must lie near the heart of every truly benevolent mind" (Niebuhr 1937, 155-56).

Thus did the faith of the nineteenth century approach a measure of integration that was tolerant of minor denominational differences, ethically motivated, and democratically Arminian. The formation of the "Evangelical United Front" during these years seemed to stoke the fires of millenialism and its unity of belief (Cross 1981, 200).

As long as the revivals flourished and individual sinners could be called to public repentance and spiritual renewal, the movement was immensely powerful. It hinged, one might say precariously, on the receptivity of the faithful and the social and economic forces that predisposed them to embrace the revivals. This fact would be significant in institutions such as the penitentiary which, like any institution, developed its own internal logic. Penal facilities will respond to the play of external pressure but, in the absence of such public interest, will proceed according to other determinants necessary for survival—internal order, administrative appointments, and financial concerns.

These observations will be verified as we continue to assess the evolution of penology in America.

The Prison Becomes the Penitentiary

We have seen that the significant development that occurred in the Puritan colonies during the initial Great Awakening was the introduction of Enlightenment ideas of optimism and individual liberty into orthodox Calvinist theology and social theory. The concept of confinement as simply a prelude to physical punishment was challenged by reformers in Europe and produced noteworthy penal experiments throughout the continent and in the colonies.[18] One traditional idea that remained was the Puritan belief that crime was a free act of the will. Matthew Gordon, chaplain at Sing Sing, spoke for generations of criminal thinkers when he said that what has befallen criminals is directly connected with "their own voluntary misconduct" (NY Sen. Doc. 5 1847, 92). As has been noted, this does not suggest that evangelicals were unaware of the importance of social factors in leading the sinner astray. They were, however, insistent that the conversion of the individual heart was the prelude to social action, and without a heart renewed in Christ, no amount of reform could restrain the dissolute from falling into error.

As the Christian reformers surveyed the national landscape and saw the prevalence of vices driving the unrepentant to a perdition that could be avoided, and mocking the abundant graces available at the advent of the millennial kingdom, the idea developed that the rootless and degenerate members of society needed to be placed in institutions that offered a curative environment. It was believed that a methodical regimen regulating every aspect of the inmate's life could produce the conditions where revival preaching might find an open heart. As Rothman states: "The institution would become a laboratory for social improvement. By demonstrating how regularity and discipline transformed the most corrupt persons, it would reawaken the public to these virtues" (1971, 107).

During the post-revolutionary era experiments were inaugurated in New York and Pennsylvania that evolved into the first penitentiaries whose philosophies were orchestrated into a national debate in Massachusetts. These developments will best be understood by summarizing the religious sociology and penal philosophy of these three states.

The Different States Examined

Pennsylvania

In 1681, William Penn was given a tract of land by Charles II with permission to establish a "Holy Experiment" in an area west of the Delaware river. Pennsylvania, as it came to be called, was to be in Penn's words a model community whose aim was to magnify "the Glory of Almighty God and the Good of Mankind" (Peckman 1976, 128).

Penn was a friend and associate of the founder of the Quakers, George Fox (1624-1691). The movement had developed in England out of left-wing Puritanism. Ahlstrom says, "it exhibits the relentless movement of the Puritan-Reformed impulse away from the hierarchical, sacramental, and objective Christianity of the Middle Ages towards various radical extremes in which intensely individualistic and spiritual motifs become predominant" (1972, 76). The Quakers did not differ from other Calvinists in their confession of the need to establish the dominion of God on earth, but their theological emphasis was on God as the Lord of conscience and the inner life (Niebuhr 1937, 53). Politics and economics were important but secondary to the belief that God's reign could come to men and women in their own lives. Penn stated that each one was endowed with "Native Goodness" which was equally "his Honour and his Happiness" (Peckman 1976, 117). If individuals could turn from their own will and submit themselves to God they could be wholly free. This tendency toward perfectionism was more optimistic than the Puritan belief that a community of discipline was necessary to insure obedience and maintain the integrity of individual commitment. These different systems of social ethics clearly demonstrate the natural disparity of outlook that would occur when the two religious bodies began to contemplate the shape of correctional institutions.

Penn's penal philosophy was more humane than any that had been enacted in either England or its colonies, retaining the death penalty only in the case of homicide done with "Malice or premeditation" (Peckman 1976, 129). In lieu of courts, the Quaker settlers believed that persons could reconcile their differences by reasoning together, with the occasional aid of arbitrators, and abide by the accords they reached. "Peacemakers" were appointed by the judges to settle disputes and the "peace bond" was developed as an alternative to prosecution. The effects were such that not only were minor offenses freed of court action, but also harmonious community correction was exhibited: "in every precinct 3 persons shall be yearly chosen, as common peacemakers in that precinct, and that Arbitrations may be as Valid as the Judgments of the Courts of Justice" (Peckman 1976, 145). Finally, the Quakers began to experiment in the late seventeenth century with the use of "Imprisonment in the house of Correction at hard labor":

> [E)very County . . . at their own Cost and Charge [must] erect, build, or cause to be built . . . a sufficient house at least 20 foot square for Restraint, Correction, Labour & punishment of all such persons as shall be there unto Committed by Law (Peckman 1976, 187).

A number of factors contributed to the erosion of this novel and cooperative approach to criminal justice. The population of Pennsylvania increased by 500 percent between 1700 and 1750. Immigration was bringing to this most tolerant of all the colonies settlers schooled in different social practices. Oftentimes the newcomers were the drifters, beggars, and social deviants expelled from other less accommodating communities. Crime rates rose accordingly and, in 1718, England imposed its harsh criminal code on the colony (Preyer 1982, 343-45).

The vision of William Penn endured, however, in the Quaker communities. As the revolution came to an end, a number of articulate voices uniting the principles of Quaker religion with Locke's empirically based psychology and the penal ideas of Beccaria and John Howard came to be heard. In 1787, William Bradford, Caleb Lownes, and other influential Quakers met in the home of Benjamin Franklin to discuss a paper by Dr. Benjamin Rush entitled, "An Enquiry into the Effects of Public Punishments Upon Criminals and Upon Society."[19] The gathering motivated the group to seek to abrogate the English criminal code. They decided to reassemble a committee, initially founded in 1776, that had been banned by the British during the revolution—The Philadelphia Society for Alleviating the Miseries of Public Prisons. Although dominated by Quakers, the reorganized society elected William White, the presiding bishop of the Protestant Episcopal Church in the United States, as its first president, a post he would hold for more than four decades (Barnes 1927, 84). The society used its social and political leverage to sway the legislature to adopt new criminal statutes in 1787 with, once again, the death penalty only permissible in cases of first-degree murder.

The Philadelphia Society was to have a lasting effect on the development of the penitentiary system. Its list of accomplishments in steering Pennsylvania's correctional approach was unparalleled and it provided the original vision of silence, labor, and spiritual supervision that led to the initial penitentiary experiment in New York. The religious foundation of the society was clear and consistent throughout its long history. The preamble to its constitution was a commentary on the last judgment in the gospel of Matthew.

> When we consider that the obligations of benevolence, which are founded on the precepts and example of the Author of Christianity, are not canceled by the follies or crimes of our fellow creatures; and when we reflect upon the miseries which penury, hunger, cold, unnecessary severity, unwholesome apartments, and guilt . . . involve with them; it becomes us to extend our compassion to that part of mankind, who are subjects of these miseries (Barnes 1927, 81-82).

One of the first projects of the society was to reorganize the Walnut Street Jail in Philadelphia. The facility, constructed in 1774 and reflecting the British model, was a house of detention and correction where the shiftless were given work and the indicted awaited trial. No attempt was made to isolate the residents and there was no systematic program of reform. It is significant that the first recorded activity of the prison society was the introduction of religious services at the jail, "the first religious service ever conducted in an American penal institution" (Barnes 1927, 85).

Religious worship, however, was only the beginning. In 1788, the society appealed to the state legislature for a bold new program aimed at the more recalcitrant inmates. They had been in frequent communication with John Howard, and blending their own religious philosophy with ideas he had adopted while studying the European prisons, especially St. Michael's in Rome and the 'Maison de Force' in Ghent, they petitioned for the following:

> . . . SOLITARY LABOUR, would more successfully tend to reclaim the unhappy objects, as it might be conducted more steadily and uniformly and the kind and proportion of labour be better adopted to the different abilities of the criminals, and evils of familiarizing young minds with vicious characters be removed (The Pennsylvania Journal Jan. 1845, 3-4).

The legislators agreed to the proposal and the seeds of the penitentiary were first sown on the grounds of the Walnut Street Jail. The administration was directed to "cause a suitable number of cells to be constructed in the yard of the gaol . . . for the purpose of confining therein the more hardened and atrocious offenders" (Richard Vaux 1872, 15).

The problems of Walnut Street were far from over, however. While a small group was isolated in the new building, the great and ever increasing body of residents were crowded together with little to do save "contaminate" one another.

Edward Livingston, who directed the reform of penal facilities in Louisiana and was a strong proponent of the Pennsylvania approach of "individual seclusion," stated in a letter that even when the number of inmates confined together "was reduced to two, one of them would generally be found qualified to corrupt the other" (Livingston 1828, 6).

Similarly, when de Beaumont and de Tocqueville spoke of the jail in Philadelphia they isolated two principal faults: "it corrupted by contamination those who worked together. It corrupted by indolence the individuals who were plunged into solitude" (1833, 3).

The members of the prison society were of a similar mind and began to insist that all incarcerated persons should experience solitary confinement combined with labor as "the most efficient element of discipline" (The Pennsylvania Journal Jan. 1845, 5-6). They were thwarted in their efforts, however, because the facility at Walnut Street was simply too overcrowded to allow for such an arrangement. Disorder and violence became the order of the day in the communal sections of the jail. Serious riots erupted in 1817, 1819, 1820 and 1821. The state inspectors concluded in their 1821 report: "It was intended to be a school of reform; but it is now a school of vice" (Report on Punishments and Prison Discipline 1828, 12).

The Philadelphia Society, in that same year, urged the legislature "to pass a law for the erection of a penitentiary for the Eastern District of the State, in which the benefits of solitude and hard labour may be fairly and effectually approved" (Richard Vaux 1872, 17-18). A member, C.C. Cleveland wrote:

> At the quarterly meetings of our Society, the subject had often been introduced, and every member, I believe, felt how utterly inconsistent it was for a Christian community to imprison their fellow beings convicted of crime, ostensibly for reformation, without promoting any adequate means for reaching the seat of all reformation—THE HEART (The Pennsylvania Journal Jan. 1845, 79).

Meanwhile, penal reformers in the Western part of the state were promoting a different type of facility, based on the ideas of Jeremy Bentham and his Panopticon.[20] William Strickland designed a prison based on strict solitary confinement without labor that was approved by the legislature in 1818. The act called on the inspectors to "secure and accomplish a full completion of the outward towers, main building, panopticon cells and culvert, with all other necessary conveniences, so as to be suitable for the reception and solitary confinement of convicts" (Barnes 1927, 139). The new edifice was named the Western State Penitentiary and was opened in July 1826.

The Philadelphia advocates for penal reform were not in disagreement with the belief that solitude and conversion were necessary components of penal discipline. They were convinced, however, that labor was an essential link in the chain of reformation.

Their concerted opinion was summarized in a statement by a legislative committee: "without labor the unfortunate convict would be driven, in solitary confinement, to madness or death" (Report of Joint Committee 1835, 23). Led by Roberts Vaux and Samuel Wood, the first warden at the Philadelphia site, they continued to lobby for a penitentiary based on their philosophy. They could point to the failure of the early experiment of solitude without labor at Auburn to substantiate their position.

In 1819 the legislature of New York had authorized the inspectors at Auburn "to alter or change the interior plan" of a section of the prison "so as to render the same more suitable for confining each prisoner in a separate cell" (Powers 1826, 30). By 1821, this solitary wing, in emulation of the experiment at Walnut Street, had been constructed. The results were disastrous. Five of the prisoners died in the first year, several by suicide, and the physician stated that "sedentary life, no matter in what form, disposes to debility, and consequently to local disease." Gershom Powers, an influential voice in the development of the New York system and later an agent (warden) at Auburn, added that such confinement "operates upon the existing germ of diseases, and hastens the progress of all those that must have otherwise terminated in death" (de Beaumont and de Tocqueville 1833, 151-52). De Beaumont and de Tocqueville stated: "this absolute solitude, if nothing interrupt it, is beyond the strength of man; it destroys the criminal without intermission and without pity; it does not reform, it kills" (1833, 5). Statistics concerning recidivism were equally discouraging. Fourteen of the twenty-six prisoners pardoned after the experiment were rearrested within a short time (1833, 5-6). This data was augmented by the sobering fact that the construction of the Western Penitentiary was, as the French delegation remarked, "so defective, that it is very easy to hear in one cell what is going in another; so that each prisoner found in the communication with his neighbor a daily recreation" (1833, 8).

Roberts Vaux, who with his successor and son, Richard, would combine to lead the progress of the Pennsylvania method for seventy-five years, was the key figure in the fight to abandon the system of solitary confinement without labor. He was a devout Quaker who felt that "the moral and religious treatment of convicts, with a view to their reformation" was the main regard of imprisonment (Roberts Vaux 1827, 5-6). On the occasion of his sister's death he "solemnly entered into covenant with his Maker to devote the residue of his days to the benefit of his fellow creatures" (The Pennsylvania Journal April 1846, 111). At the time of his death his obituary stated: "He remained steadfast to the religious principles in which he was educated, and never ceased to exhibit, by his dress, speech, and demeanor, his connexion with that excellent body of Christians" (Ibid.).

In 1821, Vaux and his associates at the Philadelphia society were able to convince the legislature to begin construction of the Eastern State Penitentiary outside Philadelphia (Richard Vaux 1872, 33). When the cornerstone of the new prison was laid on May 23, 1823, it was Vaux himself who presided over the ceremonies. By the time the new penitentiary opened in 1829, the group had also secured the passage of an act that made the system of solitary confinement with labor, silence, and religious instruction the norm for both the Eastern and Western penitentiaries: "every person who shall be convicted in any court in the western district . . . shall instead of Penitentiary punishments heretofore prescribed, be sentenced by the proper court to suffer punishment *by separate or solitary confinement at labour*" (Richard Vaux 1872 36).

On the occasion of the victory, Vaux wrote William White, Zachariah Poulson, and Thomas Wistar, the only surviving members of the Philadelphia Society's reorganization in 1787:

> Of the thirty-seven individuals who associated almost half a century ago, for the beneficent and wise purposes of softening the needless rigours of imprisonment, of endeavoring to restore the tenants of the jails to virtue and to happiness, and promoting reform in the penal code of Pennsylvania, *you are the only survivors.*
>
> Through the numerous difficulties and anxieties which have arisen in the progress of this work of mercy, and of justice, you have continued its devoted friends and it is your privilege and reward now to witness, a near approach to the completion of your labours, in this department of your civil and Christian duties (The Journal of Law October 1830, 120-21).

New York

It is the contention of this study that the three states under investigation derived their modes of punishing and reforming the offender from their particular religious structures. The shape of Pennsylvania's penal system was decisively Quaker. The overall developments in New York were attributable to the fact that it was primarily a Calvinist settlement and the state most amenable to the revival crusades. This was particularly true in Western New York where the first penitentiary was to develop.

Frequent revivalism concentrated in Western New York as in no other portion of the country during its pioneering era. Emotional religion was thus a congenital characteristic, present at birth and developed throughout the youth of the section (Cross 1981, 4).

New York had been settled by numerous groups: Dutch Reformed, Episcopalians, Quakers coming up the Susquehanna from Pennsylvania, and many others, but no group was more prevalent or influential than the waves of New Englanders who began to move beyond the Appalachian mountains after 1790. The term "Genesee Fever" became popular as not only individuals but entire neighborhoods moved westward (Cross 1981, 5).[21]

Accompanying migration and eventually fueling the revivals was an agreement forged between the two main Calvinist-inspired bodies of the nation, the Congregationalists and the Presbyterians. The Plan of Union was precipitated by the accelerated growth of Deism and Unitarianism in areas that had been Calvinist strongholds. The two denominations agreed to a systematic development aimed at maintaining local unity and minimizing infighting. All church settlements in New England would join the Congregational fold and those west of New England would become Presbyterian (Cross 1981, 18-19). The two religious bodies widely proclaimed the benign character of the plan and the nondenominational tone of their benevolent organizations such as the American Home Missionary Society and the American Tract Society. In point of fact, however, their animus against rival groups—Catholics, Masons, Unitarians, and Universalists—and their belief that their intellectual training made them superior in the evangelizing mission, prompted them to use the societies to steer members into their structure of belief. This was especially true of the Presbyterians in New York who controlled not only the major religious periodicals, but also the seminaries: Union Theological in New York City, and Auburn (Cross 1981, 46-48). Thus "new light" concerns such as antimasonry, antislavery, temperance, revivalism, perfectionism, and millenialism flourished in the "Yankee belt." This helps explain the strong ideological link that existed between New York and Massachusetts when the debate over penology flared throughout the nation.

The evangelical strategy for converting America was put to full and extensive practice throughout the region, animated by the traditional attack on infidelity and apostasy made more immediate by the waves of immigrants and seasonal workers who flooded the state to build the Erie Canal. Revivals, benevolent societies, bible distribution, Sunday schools, Sabbath promotion, and temperance crusades were so fervently utilized that Western New York came to be called the "burned-over district." Ashbell Wells of Auburn seminary founded fourteen new Sabbath schools in six weeks in 1827. The next year, Auburn students helped local benevolent societies cover twenty-six counties, visiting every Presbyterian Church and going from house to house to enroll every child in religious schools (Cross 1981, 129).

The high crime rates in the canal area stimulated the reform minded Christians. They were anxious to implement the evangelical program of conversion at the recently completed facility at Auburn.

The First Penal Experiments

The first prison in New York, Newgate in Greenwich Village, had been constructed through the efforts of a Quaker merchant, Thomas Eddy, in 1796. Eddy, like his Quaker counterparts, was influenced by the European reformers but also had an evangelical bent.[22] He was deeply impressed by William Penn, a person "actuated by the pure principles of a Christian and a philosopher," and the efforts of his coreligionists at Philadelphia's Walnut Street Jail (Eddy 1801, 8). Motivated by the enthusiasm of William Bradford, a judge of the Pennsylvania Supreme Court, and aided by General Philip Schuyler, he successfully petitioned the legislature to enact laws abolishing the death penalty for all but three crimes and prescribing lengthy prison sentences in lieu of corporal or capital punishment (Eddy 1801, 14). The law authorizing the construction of the new prison was passed on March 3, 1796 with only one dissenting voice (Eddy 1801, 12-13).

Eddy became the first agent of the prison and set out to prove that reformation of the inmate was possible under the proper conditions. He made one of the principal duties of the inspectors, "to admonish the bad, applaud the good, and encourage all to amendment and reformation; and to give them such advice as may awaken virtuous sensibility, and promote their moral and religious improvement" (1801, 20). All prisoners were to attend Sunday services and Eddy issued an open invitation to all "Ministers of the Gospel" to "visit and examine the prison at their pleasure" (1801, 21).

The experiment, however, was doomed from the start. With eight prisoners confined together in each room, Eddy had overlooked one of the key principles of the penal reformers he so admired: that frequent social interchange among inmates defeats the reformative ideal (1801, 38). Acts of violence became commonplace and several riots erupted. At the same time, Eddy, a Federalist, encountered difficulties with the prison inspectors who were Jeffersonians. Political infighting, a frequent theme in penal history, was compounded by a legislature reluctant to provide appropriations for an unproven experiment. Exasperated, Eddy resigned his post in 1804 (W. D. Lewis 1965, 33-34).

Violence and inadequate funding were certainly detrimental to Newgate's fortunes, but ultimate blame, in Eddy's mind, rested on the link between overcrowding and the early pardoning of offenders. Pardons undermined both the Enlightenment dictum of swift, certain punishment and the contention of religious leaders that reformation could only be accomplished over a period of time. Eddy had clearly expressed his feelings on the subject:

> No man who enters the prison with vicious habits, can be reasonably expected to be divested of them in less than 4 or 5 years; and it would greatly injure the penitentiary system, to pardon any prisoner before the expiration of that time, unless in extraordinary cases, which may possibly, but very rarely, happen (Eddy 1801, 69). ·

The failure of Newgate convinced the legislature that the construction of a new prison was mandatory. They chose Auburn as the site. The bitter lessons Eddy had learned led him to argue against the continuance of crowding inmates together in their cells. He said it was "the best possible mode of increasing the number of thieves, robbers and vagabonds" (Roscoe 1827, 16). He wanted Auburn built on the cellular plan and expressed as much in a letter to Governor Dewitt Clinton: "No benefit, as it regards reformation, ever has been, nor ever will be produced, unless our prisons are calculated to have separate rooms . . . so that every man can be lodged by himself" (W. D. Lewis 1965, 51). His petition, however, went unheeded. Auburn was opened in 1817 still patterned on the Newgate model.

Perhaps Eddy's greatest problem was that he sought to influence an area with much closer ties to Calvinist New England than Quaker Philadelphia. The new institution did not reflect the Quaker doctrine of the inner light as much as the Calvinist belief in the natural depravity of men and women. Consequently, normative guidelines were established in accord with Calvinist values of order and financial stability.[23]

Thus did the contract system find its way into penal history. It was a practice whereby outside business interests would employ inmates within a given facility and pay a fixed rate to the state. Introduced at Auburn in 1817, it would have a long and controversial history in American corrections, its roots in the Puritan ethos providing the sustenance to nourish it. As in later incarnations, its first appearance in New York failed to match expectations. Monetary losses and escalating violence influenced the legislature to place greater emphasis on the other durable value of the Calvinist heritage, obedience. An act was passed in 1819 legalizing flogging at both Newgate and Auburn (W. D. Lewis 1965, 46).

The discouraging results of these early developments revealed a prison possessing the destructive traits of Eddy's first experiment, without exhibiting as yet either reform of the inmates or the desired financial viability. By 1821, the legislature was disposed to seek another innovation. At Governor Clinton's, and, by extension, Eddy's behest, they approved the Quaker practice developed at Walnut Street of separating the criminals into classes (W. D. Lewis 1965, 79). The main body of residents would continue to reflect the original congregate plan,[24] but the most recalcitrant individuals were to be placed in a new wing of solitary cells where it was believed that enforced solitude, without labor, would purge their souls and lead to reform. The inspectors stated: "no radical change can be expected until their stubborn spirits are subdued, and their depraved hearts softened by mental suffering" (W. D. Lewis 1965, 68). The results, as mentioned earlier, were disastrous, suicide and insanity being more commonplace than reform.

This shift in penal philosophy, however, began an irreversible process of innovation that would eventually fuse the Calvinist concerns of obedience and economic productivity with the revivalist desire to reform the hearts of the wayward. As the French delegation was to point out:

> [The] idea was not given up, that the solitude, which causes the criminal to reflect, exercises a beneficial influence; and the problem was, to find the means by which the evil effect of total solitude could be avoided without giving up its advantages. It was believed that this end could be attained, by leaving the convicts in their cells during night, and by making them work during the day, in the common work-shops, obliging them at the same time to observe absolute silence (de Beaumont and de Tocqueville 1833, 6).

The new approach was to come largely from a cadre of conservative individuals associated with the facility: a New England native and former army captain, Elam Lynds, another former military officer, John D. Cray, a local Federalist magistrate, Gershom Powers, and the first agent of the prison, William Britten. It would be praised before the nation and the world from the spiritual and physical birthplace of many of the New Yorkers, New England. The charismatic figure who would lead the crusade was the Reverend Louis Dwight.

Massachusetts

Massachusetts was undergoing a divisive and acrimonious battle in the early decades of the nineteenth century, principally between Unitarians and "new light" evangelicals. There were lingering tensions between these groups and "old light" Calvinists as well. John Adams symbolized the degree to which the Boston establishment, animated with the new ideas of republicanism and freedom, now embraced a faith in which reason furnished the only acknowledged revelation. For the Unitarians, morality and not mystery was the proper companion of religion. They stood firm against the claim of their opponents that humans wallow in depravity and that men and women "love darkness rather than light" (Presbyterian Magazine 1821, 157-58). Their greatest orator was William Ellery Channing (1780-1842) who stressed not human sinfulness and repentance, but human perfectibility and the enclosure of religion within Enlightenment rationality and humanitarianism. Many Unitarians included a "humanized" Jesus within their secular spirituality. One writer said he "was a brave, a good man, superendowed by nature with spiritual gifts" but not divine:

> If he be the Deity . . . then the beloved and tender hero disappears
> . . . The theory of an atoning Saviour filled the world with brutality,
> bloodshed, hate, inquisitions, and as far as it is accepted to-day it
> keeps men apart and uncharitable (Kirby 1971, 139-40).

Unitarianism was not only a regional phenomenon. It was becoming the preferred religious philosophy of the Boston upper class (Ahlstrom 1972, 400-02).

From such "new light" Congregational strongholds as the churches at Park Street and Hanover Street in Boston, the evangelicals fought for revivalism and the evangelical program of social reform. Timothy Dwight saw an identical relationship between liberal religion and infidelity. He lamented as he saw influences whereby "our sons become the disciples of Voltaire" and insisted on the need for revivals to reawaken sinners (Weisberger 1958, 63). Lyman Beecher carried out a spirited campaign for decades against the Unitarians from his Connecticut congregation, eventually moving to Boston itself in 1826 to be the champion "of the faith once delivered to the saints" (Beecher and Scoville 1888, 82).

> As to the importance of the stand in Boston . . . It is here that New England is to be regenerated, the enemy driven out of the temple they have usurped and polluted, the college to be rescued, the public sentiment to be revolutionized and restored to evangelical tone. And all this with reference to the resurrection of New England to an undivided and renovated effort for the extension of religious and moral influence throughout the land and through the world (Lyman Beecher 1961, 48).

Timothy Dwight and Beecher broadened the more exclusive theology of Edwards and promoted the belief that repentance and religious fidelity would produce a universal outpouring of social benevolence. They, however, were not the only ones who traced their social commitment to Edwards. Another community of Christians was no less repelled by the Unitarians and liberals. They were the disciples of Samuel Hopkins. Hopkins stressed a compromise approach in his two volume work, *System of Doctrines* (1793). "Regeneration" was entirely the imperceptible work of the Holy Spirit but provided a foundation in the mind "for holy exercises, for hungering and thirsting after righteousness" (Ahlstrom 1972, 407-09). This combination of revivalism and intellectualism combined covenanted church membership with rational criteria of regenerated behavior, chief among them being "disinterested benevolence," even if it led to being damned for the glory of God. A Universalist publication in New York derided the somber philosophy: "Admitants to Hopkinsian churches are asked '*Are you willing to be damned* and made miserable forever, for the glory of God?' And all who prefer *hell* to heaven are considered as '*born again*'" (The Gospel Herald 1821, 191-92).

The importance of this doctrine is that it provided an important link between strict Calvinists and evangelicals. The followers of Hopkins could appreciate the role of individual desire and a voluntary commitment to virtuous behavior, while at the same time hallowing the importance of discipline and strict obedience to the commands of God channeled through civil and ecclesiastical institutions. The most noteworthy disciple of Hopkins, Louis Dwight, would use this theological stance to reconcile the strict, unremitting discipline of Elam Lynds and his co-workers at the Auburn and Sing Sing penitentiaries, with the revivalist concerns of the evangelicals. So successful was he that he attracted conservative Calvinists in Boston and Auburn (an anti-republican stronghold), as well as Unitarians and evangelicals, even Lyman Beecher himself, to membership in his Boston Prison Discipline Society.

Louis Dwight

Louis Dwight was born in 1793 to a family "of the old Puritan stock of New England" and from an early age was attracted to a life of religious dedication and the ministry. His biographer relates that a constant preoccupation was "[his] individual responsibility to God, and his own wretched failure to love the Lord with 'his whole heart'" (Jenks 1856, 9-10). He attended Yale toward the end of the long presidency of his relative, Timothy Dwight, and was a witness to the regular revivals at that institution. His dream of becoming a preacher ended in 1813, when an accident during a chemistry experiment caused his lungs to hemorrhage, precipitating a lifelong series of physical ailments.

Upon graduation, he entered the seminary at Andover, a Hopkinsian stronghold, from which he was ordained. His sickly constitution, which he viewed as an opportunity to share "with my Saviour's sufferings," restricted his ministerial options (Jenks 1856, 15). He chose employment with the American Tract Society and, subsequently, with the American Education Society. At the latter post, a noteworthy aspect of his personality was revealed. His father-in-law noticed in him "a peculiar aptitude and ability in arranging statistical information, and condensing accounts of facts" (Jenks 1856, 17-18). His health, however, once again betrayed him and he was forced to resign his position.

It was during this time that he discovered that riding long distances on horseback was physically beneficial. He therefore decided to embark on a missionary venture, delivering bibles to penal institutions, eventually convincing the newly-formed American Bible Society to sustain him in the effort (Jenks 1856, 19-20). Calvinist asceticism and sobriety were deeply inbred and soon would impress themselves on the philosophy of American penology.

> I accept no invitation to dine or take tea. I make no visits of ceremony or pleasure. I see few persons, except my own appropriate business. All this is almost literally true. I cannot accomplish much without adhering to this general rule. In my business I am happy and successful (Jenks 1856, 20).

Dwight was horrified by the conditions of the jails, workhouses, and prisons that he visited, among them the Walnut Street Jail, Newgate, and the prison at Charlestown. His profound faith commitment came to be channeled and directed by means of a vow he made, that his life would be spent in seeking a form of "prison discipline" that would promote religious conversion and remove inmates from the squalor in which they were forced to dwell: "I had rather be the honored instrument of turning a single soul free from the error of his ways, than to be the proud monarch of the universe" (Jenks 1856, 28-29).

> When I shall bring before the Church of Christ a statement of what my eyes have seen, there will be a united and powerful effort to alleviate the miseries of the prisons . . . I only know that these prisoners are the most miserable and degraded of the human race, and that no one in the country is doing anything for their relief (Jenks 1856, 23).

The model that would provide a humane and salvific discipline was discovered when his travels took him to the new penitentiary at Auburn, and the experiment in silence and work being inaugurated there. In a letter to the treasurer of the American Bible Society in October 1825 he recorded these remarks concerning the institution: "it will be in Prison discipline like the application of the steam engine in navigation–an incalculable good to the world" (PDS 1843, 34-35).

With missionary fervor, Dwight undertook to promote the Auburn system. He resigned his position with the Bible society, and in June 1825 formed the Boston Prison Discipline Society whose first comprehensive report on the state of America's prisons was published the following year. He stated the goal of the society in classic Calvinist phrases that were laced with an evangelical tone.

> A more wise and effectual system of Prison Discipline, in the United States, than can be found in any other country: till Christianity has done what its authority requires it to do for prisoners; not to screen them from merited punishment; but to protect society from their depredations; to save them, if possible, from further contamination; and more than this, to preach to them, 'CHRIST AND HIM CRUCIFIED' (PDS 1827, 39).

His tireless dedication was matched only by the success of his efforts. By the year 1833, Dwight, virtually singlehanded, had pioneered the adoption of the Auburn system in the new penitentiaries in Maine, New Hampshire, Vermont, Connecticut, the District of Columbia, Virginia, Tennessee, Louisiana, Missouri, Illinois, Ohio, and Upper Canada (W. D. Lewis 1965, 109-10).

Writing in 1831, Dwight said of the penitentiaries he had helped to establish:

> We can now begin to look upon many of them with complacency, as places of separation at night, supervision, silence, order, neatness, hard labor, economy and good government; and, connected with all these improvements, we see, in each of the reformed Prisons, the Bible, the resident chaplain, the chapel, the Sabbath school, the private admonition, counsel and instruction; in one word, in some degree, what we may suppose the Lord Jesus Christ would require a community, calling itself Christian, to make its Prisons (PDS 1831, 82-83).

Of particular importance to Dwight was that the local penitentiary at Charlestown provide an exemplary witness of the reformative and financial success of the Auburn approach. He was instrumental in creating the architectural and organizational plan that was the basis of the reorganized facility where a building with 300 solitary cells was opened in October 1829 (PDS 1829, 69; MA Sen. Doc. 10 1853, 1-2).

Dwight was, as Orlando Lewis of the New York Prison Association called him, "the high national expert on prisons" (Orlando Lewis 1967, 227). Gideon Haynes, a reform-minded warden at Charlestown, said that he "did more to ameliorate the condition of prisoners and improve the discipline of prisons than anyone in the state or country. He's the 'Howard of America'" (Haynes 1869, 217).

The combination of his boundless missionary fervor, his thorough surveys and analysis of the prison programs in each state, and the fact that he was the only national figure writing on the subject, gave him enormous influence over the development of the penal system in this country. He was the conduit through which information on correctional experiments was disseminated, and virtually every local and state government, as well as many national governments, came to be dependent upon his accounts. His frequent and extended tours of facilities throughout the nation were marked by an empirical and statistical analysis that was quite comprehensive for its time. He used the yearly reports of the society, however, to communicate more than information to his readers. They were the platform from which he could participate in the evangelization of his audience and of the penal system in general. The following description of a visit to a prisoner in the Madison County Jail in New York reveals his deepest reason for engaging in prison reform, as well as an interesting psychological profile.

I found him weeping, and crying for mercy and the forgiveness of his
sins; urged upon him the necessity of confession, as well as prayer
. . . He groaned aloud, wept much, and cried, 'God be merciful to me
a sinner.' I told him I did not think he had any reason to expect
mercy from God, if he had been guilty of murder, and denied it; that,
if he wished to obtain forgiveness, he should first confess his guilt
. . . He still groaned under the weight of his sorrows, but did not say
if he was guilty or not. I prayed with him, that he might confess his
guilt if he was guilty, and that he might find mercy; and bade him
farewell. He did confess his guilt before his execution (PDS 1840,
51).

Another revelatory profile is provided in this portion of a letter
written to his wife: "Let us hope that your self-denial in giving me up, to
continue my efforts in that which is bidden me to do, may result in
salvation to those who would otherwise die in their sins" (Jenks 1856, 29).

His formation in the Edwardsian concept of benevolence to all being
was a constant motif that translated into a spirited needling of state and
local officials on behalf of the voiceless inmates. He pioneered many of
the basic humane provisions accepted as standard within penal
institutions, as well as the movement to build special asylums for the
criminally insane. His checklist of items to be evaluated in each facility
shows the comprehensive approach that sought to create a holistic
environment aimed at the prisoner's body, mind, and soul: divine service,
bibles in each room, prison libraries, water for bathing, sheets changed,
materials with which cells are constructed ("timber and plank . . . harbor
vermin"), evil communication, employment of prisoners, classification of
prisoners, ventilation, and cleanliness (PDS 1849, 18-20).

Auburn, and subsequently the penitentiary built by Lynds at Sing
Sing, became almost an obsession with Dwight. To the degree he
applauded the New York system, he degraded the penal methods being
practiced in Pennsylvania. The rigorous Calvinist approach of New York
not only featured the emphasis on obedience and discipline; it made
substantial provision to see that the penitentiaries were economically
viable. This seminal factor in the American religious psyche had lodged
itself in Dwight's mind. It led him to frequently overlook not only the
documented brutality of the Auburn-style experiments, but to exaggerate
their fiscal health. His comment on the penitentiary at Wethersfield in
Connecticut reveals that economic concerns were seen as central to penal
reform: "This institution . . . is in a state of progressive improvement.
Nothing can show this more clearly, than a comparison of the earnings and
expenditures, during the whole period" (PDS 1831, 41). In a letter to the
commissioners of the Albany Penitentiary, he praised the fiscal astuteness

of the prospective warden, Amos Pilsbury. Such a trait, he argued, gives proof of "wisdom, industry, economy, caution, energy, activity and faithfulness" (Dyer 1867, 63).

Everything that he upheld concerning Auburn and its imitators, he disparaged in regard to Pennsylvania. The Quaker institutions, reflecting a less utilitarian social and economic framework, placed less emphasis on profitability. This principle was cast in negative terms by Dwight, as was the solitary confinement of prisoners. Dwight may or may not have developed the contention that suicides and insanity were rife at the Eastern State Penitentiary, but he did nothing to dispel the rumor. He wrote of the place: "its bill of mortality, reconvictions and pecuniary results are not favorable" (PDS 1837, 50). He asserted that it was not nearly as mild as its proponents claimed, that communication was an ongoing problem (PDS 1835, 21-23) and, finally, that he was "almost sick of the experiment; it fails so much in health, in reformation, in earnings, and in moral and religious instruction" (PDS 1836, 40).

One of his most influential insights was that statistical data, however he may have filtered it through his theological paradigm, be prominently featured in his reports. "Facts are stubborn things," he once wrote after critically analyzing a financial statement from the Walnut Street Jail (PDS 1830, 30-32). This method of analysis was instituted in many of the new penitentiaries by way of the chaplaincy. Dwight and the society paid, either in part or in full, the salaries of chaplains in the penitentiaries that were unable to afford a minister in residence (PDS 1828, 44, 46). Not only did this insure that the religious presence in the institutions was theologically compatible with the ideas of Dwight, but also that the chaplains' yearly reports included the presentation of statistical data (PDS 1849, 167). This development was to have far-reaching consequences. It signaled the inauguration of a way of doing theology grounded in the basic sociological technique of the interview. The method was to become a basic component of the chaplains' ministerial approach and provided many of their operative assumptions about prisoners and their relation to the social environment. This approach, like Dwight himself, would have a profound effect on the development of the penal system in the United States.

Having delineated the religious and social foundations upon which the two great penitentiary systems were built, we must look in detail at the inner workings of these two institutional attempts to further the reign of God in America.

CHAPTER 3

DIFFERENT ROADS TO THE KINGDOM: NEW YORK AND PENNSYLVANIA

H. R. Niebuhr once wrote: "The idea of the Kingdom of God had indeed been the dominant idea in American Christianity but it had not always meant the same thing"(1937, x). This chapter will analyze data provided by the two systems of penitentiary discipline, New York and Pennsylvania, each representing a distinct road to the Kingdom of God. The task at hand is to show how the particular theological and ethical assumptions of Calvinism and Quakerism continued to inform and direct the evolution of these correctional experiments. The period to be studied begins with the opening of the first penitentiary in 1824 and concludes at the dawn of the Progressive Era. Although it is always a tenuous exercise to approximate the beginning of a historical period, the first National Penal Congress held at Cincinnati in 1870 provided a powerful source of energy and justification for the inauguration of "progressive" reforms. The roots of this phenomenon, however, can be traced to events that occurred before the Civil War.

The different approaches to the treatment of offenders revealed distinct models of punishment. In an ideal typical sense they were a deterrent, obedience model in New York and an individual treatment model in Pennsylvania. Durkheim's evolutionary pattern of societal development offers a possible way of differentiating the two approaches. He states that traditional "mechanical" societies employed repressive forms of penal sanction, while modern "organic" societies feature restitutive forms of control. Repressive law is a show of force "shocked by the crime" that reacts against the slightest weakening in social cohesion. Restitutive sanctions, on the other hand, seek to restore the balance in the social order that existed prior to the offense. They are a means of "putting back the clock so as to restore the past, so far as possible, to its normal state" (Durkheim 1984, 60-61; 68-69). The catalyst in stimulating the movement from a philosophy of "expiation" to one of restoration is population growth and density that stimulate greater economic and social interdependence (Durkheim 1984, 200-205).

Durkheim, especially in his later work, believed that whatever the expression of criminal law, it always emanates from the deep religious impulses of a people, revealing a common belief that crime is an "outrage to morality" (1984, 47).[1]

Graeme Newman, in a somewhat different approach, insists that all models of punishment are based either on obedience, which is collective and demands submission of the offender to rules and institutions, or on reciprocity, punishment between equals, which concentrates on the individuality of the offender and is retributive (Newman 1978, 6-7). He explains the movement from sanguinary to more humane variations of punishment in terms of the increased rationalism of the Enlightenment and, specifically, the ideas of the Utilitarians.[2] Newman, like Durkheim, argues that the factor that drives the societal need to punish is embedded in the symbolic and mythic elements of culture. I cannot accept his Freudian basis for the origin of penal law: the manifestation of guilt over the death of the primal father, all within a Hobbesian view of social formation. However, I formally concur that societies derive justifications for punishment out of their particular symbolic and ethical resources, and that they have tended to express themselves in either a repressive or reciprocal model.

The moral and religious conversion of the inmate was a mainstay in the rhetoric of both penal systems, reflecting the common Calvinist heritage of both Puritans and Quakers. "The prisoner in the United States breathes in the penitentiary a religious atmosphere," said de Beaumont and de Tocqueville (1833, 94). However, the specific attributes of orthodox Calvinism—obedience and discipline—as well as the identification of moral worth with pragmatic economic concerns, were critical factors that often came to govern the content of penal legislation and institutional practice in the Auburn model. New England Congregationalists and New York Presbyterians, despite tensions between "old light" and "new light" theological viewpoints, were prone to resurrect a more traditional theology when the heat and fervor of the revivals fell into the necessary period of routinization. Harsh disciplinarians like Elam Lynds, who held out small hope for conversion among the "Godforsaken" inmates, were in constant conflict with the more reform minded evangelicals. The chaplains, more than any other social group, carried the spirit of evangelical and social reform into the facilities. They would pioneer the incorporation of treatment-oriented programs but, in the end, the Auburn system, with its traditional theological roots, was largely unable to extricate itself from a "repressive," obedience-centered model.

The historical development of Quakerism was, on the other hand, focused from the beginning on the inherent goodness of the individual. There was little disparity between this organizational principle and the subjective evangelical emphasis of the early nineteenth century. Thus, one finds a more reciprocal penal philosophy emphasizing reformation within a "just deserts" or retributive format.

The more consistent thrust of the Pennsylvania system was aided by the fact that the Philadelphia Prison Society continued to exercise a guiding influence on the state's penal institutions. Its members were often the wardens and inspectors at the Eastern State Penitentiary, and to a lesser degree at the Western Penitentiary. This leadership would continue throughout the century although, under the influence of one of the Society's members, Richard Vaux, it would not escape the lure of Progressivism and the specific treatment programs and expanded government power that were its hallmarks.

In summary, the reader will see evidence of the religious community steering the development of both penal systems in this pre-progressive period according to specific theological visions. Commenting on these different approaches, de Beaumont and de Tocqueville remarked that Pennsylvania produced "more honest" men and women while New York produced "more obedient citizens" (1833, 60).

Common Elements

By the end of the nineteenth century American penal philosophy would be decidedly homogeneous. Despite the lively and substantive debate between the two strategies throughout the century, there were, from the beginning, notable areas of mutual agreement encouraged by religious ancestry, evangelical receptivity, and national identity.[3]

The fact that both Walnut Street and Auburn took the first step toward a complete cellular arrangement by placing habitual offenders in solitary confinement points to the fact that there initially existed a common appreciation of this rudimentary form of classification. When Theodore Parker spoke of the "dangerous class" of offenders he was articulating a widely held sentiment: that there are born criminals "who have a bad nature." They must be distinguished and separated from those who are led by the circumstances of the moment and are consequently as much victims of their shortsightedness and frivolity as they are perpetrators of evil (Parker 1867, 296, 305, 321).

Neither the silent, congregate system of New York nor the separate, solitary plan of Pennsylvania allowed any form of communication between the inmates.   This was done for the positive reason of concentrating on moral reform, and for the negative reason that without radical separation all agreed that the institutions became schools in which every kind of depravity was learned. The French delegation wrote of this common commitment to isolation:

> Whosoever has studied the interior of prisons and the moral state of
> their inmates, has become convinced that communication between
> these persons renders their moral reformation impossible, and
> becomes even for them the inevitable cause of an alarming corruption
> (de Beaumont and de Tocqueville 1833, 21-22).

Both New York and Pennsylvania seemed intent on concentrating on those inmates who would open themselves to the discipline of the penitentiary and prove its reformative value, recognizing that some individuals are simply incorrigible.   The inspectors of the Eastern Penitentiary wrote concerning the prisoner:

> He has had offered to him, all the necessary and approved means of
> the amendment of his condition, both moral, spiritual and social, and
> if he does not embrace them, it is not to be attributed to the system of
> Prison discipline, but to the entire absence of the material on which
> this system could operate (Eastern Penitentiary [E. Pen.]1846, 18).

Although the religious discourse throughout the nation promoted the evangelical belief that the final cause of criminal activity was an unconverted heart, few were unaware of the corrupting social conditions that were the target of the frequent moral crusades of the era. The renowned reformer, Dorthea Dix, spoke of the perilous environmental influences that mitigated the work of the penitentiaries:

> It is granted that no endeavor on the part of the teacher, however assiduous, will secure radical reform in the majority of convicts. Against these results we have the almost insurmountable antagonisms of debased habits, low views, lives formed on bad and corrupting influences, a vicious parentage, and an evil neighborhood, naturally weak understandings with many, and ignorance with a yet larger number (Dix 1967, 63-64).

There was still another commonly held belief that the incarcerated could only become as virtuous as the staff that was appointed to oversee them. There is irony in this statement for anyone who has studied the violence and corruption that have been the stark companions of penal development, whether in the nineteenth century or in our own day. Such elevated ideals, however, were taken seriously, even in periods of bureaucratization, obsession with economic solvency, and general cynicism concerning the reformation of the residents. There were not only legislative investigations, dismissals, and prosecutions of prison officials who brutalized inmates or absconded with state funds, there were notable conversions of prison inspectors who came to insist on a more humane and Christian approach on the part of their employees. The liberal Unitarian, Theodore Parker, urged that the head of the prison be "the most Christian man in the state" (Parker 1867, 322). A. G. Salisbury, a warden at Auburn wrote:

> Officers in such an institution as this, ought at least to be <u>entirely free</u> from all those habits and vices which have caused the ruin of so many of the convicts, such as profanity, Sabbath desecration, drunkenness, etc., etc., and until such is the case, we cannot <u>reasonably</u> expect our prisons to be very reformatory (NY Sen. Doc. 71 1869, 154).

A common theme in the penal discourse of the day was that the state systems must be consistent in their philosophy of confinement. As long as conversion of the wrongdoer was of paramount importance, it was senseless and inhumane to allow the wretched and counter-reformative conditions of the jails and county prisons to continue. In the jails, the inmates were indolent, in constant communication, grouped together without concern for classification, and often bereft of religious guidance. Most felt that if the penitentiary discipline was to be effective, it would need to be accompanied by similar plans in every facility of detention. John Duer, Chair of the Committee on Prison Discipline of the Prison

Association of New York (NYPA), wrote for many reformers when he stated:

> We know that the abuses exist in our prisons,–I speak more especially of our city prisons:–the foul and loathsome Penitentiary [in New York City]; the still more foul and loathsome Tombs;–we know that these abuses are frightful, appalling, almost unexampled, and in all their atrocity, quite unutterable; and now, that these abuses are exposed and known, *if they are still to be tolerated in a Christian community*, everyone who is silent and passive, who fails to denounce and resist, to expose and counteract them, *will share the guilt of their continuance* (NYPA 1846, 76).

The expense of imposing the silent or separate system on every local jail would have been economically infeasible, whatever one's religious heritage or economic philosophy. There were institutional conversions along these lines, most notably the Philadelphia County Prison, but in large part the municipal and county facilities remained an eyesore and a troubling reminder that the millennial kingdom was not to be built without heroic social and financial cost.

Finally, the penitentiaries at Auburn, Philadelphia, and their imitators were engaged together in the great evangelical enterprise. Roberts Vaux, in summarizing points of mutual agreement, believed "that the benign precepts and sacred obligations of Christianity, must influence and control all successful exertions to restore to virtue this class of our erring fellow men, as well as rule every other availing endeavor for promoting the security and happiness of human society" (Roberts Vaux 1827, 5-6). Gershom Powers was another of the principal architects of the penitentiary who accentuated this mission:

> . . . where every movement, privilege and deprivation tends to produce a moral action upon the mind and to soften the feelings and affections—where the reproofs and consolations of religion are daily administered, and especially on the Sabbath—and where the resident Chaplain and principal officer habitually visit their solitary cells and personally admonish with kindness and pungency—what cheerful hopes may not the Christian, the Philanthropist and Statesman indulge (Powers 1826, 78).

Such high ideals may not have been foremost in the minds of individuals like Elam Lynds. There were skeptics and "old light" Calvinists who derided the optimism of the age. There were conflicts over ideology that surfaced and eventually guided the institutions in altogether new directions. These factors, however, do not alter the fact that the religious movements sweeping the country in the Jacksonian era were the seminal influences in the creation and propagation of the belief that the penitentiary could restore the criminal to society with mind and spirit renewed.

The Pennsylvania System

The decisive factor that distinguished the approach to penology in Pennsylvania was the concentration on each inmate's particular reformation. The founders of the Eastern Penitentiary fervently argued, not without foundation, that the separate system reformed those consigned to its care and did so much more effectively than the Auburn method. The benefits of this emphasis on inner renewal were frequently sounded in the official yearly reports of the prison inspectors to the state legislature.[4] The congeniality of Quaker and evangelical principles is clearly evident in this report:

> The inspectors can never forget that the persons committed to their charge are men, and although fallen, debased and convict, yet they possess feelings susceptible to kindness, and minds capable of improvement . . . The inspectors hope that the language "return, repent and live," is heard in the prisoner's solitude; and through that aid *which alone* can produce the change, many a prisoner can regard his cell as the "beautiful gate of the temple" leading to a happy life, and by a peaceful end, to heaven (E. Pen. 1842, 4, 6).

This evangelical emphasis continued throughout the antebellum period and with it the belief that despite the sinful effects of environment, the dominant malady of the convicted resulted from a personal rejection of the means leading to virtue and holiness. The Philadelphia Prison Society's Journal reacted to those minimizing the impact of free will in favor of the "sensationalist" environmental theories proposed in the post-Lockean world:

> In all weary walks of Christian visitors, tract distributors, Sunday-school teachers, friends of temperance, and ministers of religion, it is scarcely credible that such a statement can truly be made of one in a hundred of those who stand in the "felon's dock." Their own lips will almost always confess . . . that they have deliberately spurned every restraint which the good will of others would have imposed on them, perversely turned their backs on the means of instruction and safety,

and voluntarily plunged into the dark abyss of pollution and guilt
(The Pennsylvania Journal Jan 1849, 35).

The determining influence of these basic evangelical principles on
the reconfiguration of the Quaker penal code in Pennsylvania has already
been noted. We have also observed the Philadelphia Prison Society's
early experiment with silence and separation that planted the seed of
penitentiary discipline in the United States, and its successful campaign
to inaugurate the separate system in the Eastern and Western
Penitentiaries. These were by no means the final contributions the Society
was to make to the shape of penology in Pennsylvania. Virtually every
major expansion in the state's prison philosophy can be traced to its
efforts, including the movement to progressive principles. These
accomplishments occurred not only because the Society furnished many
of the wardens and inspectors during the early decades of the Penitentiary
Era, but also because the Quakers held positions of power within the state
and had controlling influence in the legislature.

When the Eastern State Penitentiary opened in 1829, one of the most
influential voices in the inauguration of the separate system, Samuel
Wood, was chosen as warden. The inspectors had this to say about him:

> [A] gentleman attached to the Society of Friends . . . long been
> distinguished as a member of the Philadelphia Society for the
> Alleviation of the Miseries of Public Prisons . . . In the opinion of this
> board, a better opportunity can never occur of testing the excellence
> of the penitentiary system of solitary confinement at labour, with
> moral and religious instruction, than under his government (E. Pen.
> 1831, 7).

The institution over which Wood assumed control was an imposing
stone structure. The French observers described it thus: "Gigantic walls,
gothic towers, a wide iron gate, give to this prison the appearance of a
fortified castle of the middle ages" (de Beaumont and de Tocqueville
1833, 103-04). The edifice was designed by John Haviland who based it
on the early penitentiary experiments at Rome and later at Ghent. The
massive outside walls were thirty feet high and twelve feet thick at the
base. In the middle of the compound was an octagon-shaped central
building opening onto a series of corridors. Its form may be likened to the
hub of a wheel from which radiated the spokes, representing the banks of
cells. The solitary cells, 8 by 12 feet with ceilings 16 feet at their highest,
were each equipped with an exercise yard that was 8 by 20 feet (Roberts
Vaux 1827, 7; Teeters and Shearer 1957, 65-67). The quarters were much

larger than those at Auburn since the prisoner spent his or her entire institutional life within them. The only circumstances that permitted one to leave the cell once it was entered was expiration of sentence, sickness, or death.

The Quakers spared no expense in constructing the penitentiary, much to the disdain of Louis Dwight, for they believed that a relatively spacious environment would contribute to the process of spiritual reform. The separation of the prisoner from the world and from all contact with other inmates was accorded the highest importance.[5] In such an atmosphere the truth lodged deep in the soul could present itself, aided by the encouragement of the Bible and the words of the minister. The founders were confident that even those less attuned to religious input, or more obstinate in the face of the reformative philosophy, would eventually embrace a daily biblical devotion since that volume, for many years, was the only book inmates were allowed to possess. If they would not instinctively seek the comfort of religion, the weight of endless hours of isolation would drive them to spiritual matters.

The intensity of the enforced seclusion was symbolized by the blindfold incoming prisoners were forced to wear lest they be subjected for even a few brief moments to a corrupting influence (Wines and Dwight 1867, 140). Samuel Wood offered a theological reflection on the solitude the prisoner was meant to endure:

> In what manner can man be placed, where the works of the gospel would be more impressive than in their situation sitting alone, without seeing or being seen by any human being; nothing to distract their thoughts, or divert them, from the truths delivered to them; alone when they hear, and left alone when the minister has finished, to ponder and reflect (Barnes 1927, 59).

An early commentator on prison life, George W. Smith, expressed the retributive philosophy in this way: "each individual will necessarily be made the instrument of his own punishment—his conscience will be the avenger of society" (1833, 71).

The Quakers insisted that this method of incarceration would tame the most rebellious spirit. Then, in the wake of spiritual rebirth, the inmate would come to see work not as an extension of the punishment process but as "a privilege and a blessing" (The Pennsylvania Journal Jan. 1862, 29).

> [W]hen the prisoner has once experienced the operation of the principles of this Institution on a broken spirit and contrite heart, he

learns, and he feels, that moral and religious instruction, relieved by
industrious occupation at his trade, comfort and support his mental
and physical power, divest his solitary cell of its horrors, and his
punishment of much of its severity (E. Pen. 1831, 10).

The leading voices in the penitentiary movement were not blind to
the economic cost of the new facilities, and it was pragmatically hoped
that the labor performed in the cells would compensate the state for its
formidable financial commitment. However, the atmosphere in Quaker
Pennsylvania possessed little of the anxiety such expenditures provoked
in New York and Massachusetts. The religious philosophy was not
encumbered by the pressures Ascetic Protestantism placed on its adherents
as well as on its institutions. Franklin Bache, the first physician at the
Eastern Penitentiary, and a great grandson of Benjamin Franklin, evoked
the prevailing optimistic sentiment that seemed to carry even the more
cautious citizens in its sway. This is a passage from a letter he wrote to
Roberts Vaux:

> The expensiveness of any system of prison discipline is certainly an
> objection to it, when its advantages over other systems, which may be
> adopted at less cost, are problematical; but if any system can be
> shown to be vastly superior to every other, I think the expense of
> carrying it into existence should not weigh a feather. Believing, as I
> sincerely do, that the separate confinement of criminals is the true
> system, I, of course, apply the above remark to it; and I feel prepared
> to advocate a full and fair experiment of this plan, at almost any
> expense. But if it should prove to be the fact, that the expense of this
> system has been greatly overrated, you can easily imagine that my
> preference of it would be still more confirmed (The National Gazette
> 1829, 49).

Each inmate passed the day alone working in trades or industries
suitable to private employment. At year's end, 1833, the large percentage
of the one hundred fifty four prisoners was employed in these industries:
weaving (38), dying and spooling in the cotton department (21),
shoemaking (52), carpenters (5), blacksmiths (5), making and mending
clothes (5) (E. Pen. 1834, 7).

The reformers felt they were recognizing their most cherished
dreams for the new facilities. The original economic returns were
encouraging and, in creating an atmosphere in which the prisoner viewed
work as a privilege and not a punishment, they were undercutting the
indolence aggravated by evil association that had initially contributed to

the criminal act. But despite the promise of economic solvency, early reports were eager to restate their more noble objective:

> The profits derived from the labor of prisoners in the Western Penitentiary for the last year, will more than defray their whole expense in victuals and clothing . . . but even were it otherwise, humanity to the prisoner and justice to society would admonish us to pursue the remedy most likely to work a moral reformation, even if attended with great additional cost (Report of Committee to the Western Pen. 1838, 4).

The commitment to reformation at any price would be sorely tested in the years to come. Individual labor was less profitable than supervised communal labor, the expansive facilities were much more costly to maintain, and expenses dramatically escalated due to a steadily increasing inmate population and inflationary pressures stemming from recessions in the 1830s and 1850s. The defenders of the system became more defensive as internal pressures mounted, and they openly attacked the mercenary attitude they witnessed in the congregate penitentiaries. The inspectors attacked as "sordid" and "selfish," the attitude of their New York and New England counterparts who preferred a "false doctrine" that "idolizes gain, and denies to man the inherent right, even in his worst condition, to every beneficial influence which Christianity or civilization has in its power to bestow" (E. Pen. 1866, 17).

Religious and Moral Reform

The founders of the Pennsylvania prison system created institutions that echoed Calvin's commitment to a political order based on the covenant, with justice and punishment accorded a necessary place, while still remaining faithful to the theology and spirituality of Quakerism. Here, punishment was not sought for its own end, or as a stern reminder to onlookers, but as an extension of the belief in the fundamental goodness of the person and the irresistible connection between environment and grace. The soul, in Quaker theology, hungers for stillness in order to perceive the inner voice. Spirituality was thus at the core of both individual and institutional life. As one history of the Eastern Penitentiary remarked, religious matters "were advocated by the founders of the institution to an almost fanatical degree" (Teeters and Shearer 1957, 70).

What may at first appear baffling is that there was no full time chaplain, or moral instructor, in the Eastern Penitentiary until 1839 when a Baptist minister, Thomas Larcombe, assumed that role.[6] There are two explanations for this apparent contradiction. The first is that the Philadelphia Prison Society was, and continued to be, the "de facto" chaplain. The members conducted thousands of visits each year to every person in the facility. As Samuel Wood testified, they looked upon the confined "as a part of the great human family with ourselves, and we consider it a duty incumbent upon us to use mild and persuasive measures, and endeavor by precepts of virtue, morality and religion to wean them from their vicious course" (Tidyman et al 1835, 14). In one representative year, nine thousand interviews were conducted by society members averaging fifteen minutes in duration (Barnes 1927, 352). Ministry was also conducted by the Prison Association of Women Friends, founded in Philadelphia by Mary Wistar in 1823, the first organization to recognize the special needs and problems of women prisoners.[7] The dedication of these women went arm in arm with an evangelical intensity revealed in this report:

> But it is not only in teaching them to read the Bible for themselves that we feel interested; we are concerned, as ability is afforded, to set before them their sinful condition in the sight of a just and holy God, and to exhort them to flee from the wrath to come by repentance and faith in the Lord Jesus Christ. Their attention is directed to the Lamb of God who taketh away the sin of the world, and to his Spirit, inwardly revealed, which is a "discerner of the thoughts and intents of the heart," and a swift witness against all evil (The Pennsylvania Journal April 1845, 116).

The second reason why there was a delay in hiring a full time moral instructor was the Quaker fear and disdain of sectarianism. The relative consistency of the Pennsylvania approach to penology was largely due to the comprehensive religious and philosophical influence of the Quakers. Although noted for their tolerance of other faith communities, there was little evidence of pluralism in the antebellum pronouncements and policy of the inspectors and wardens of the state penitentiaries. Only Quakers, or those religious figures exhibiting an affinity to Quaker theology, would be given license to preach and counsel the inmates. Even though he received the support of the Quaker leadership, the appointment of the Baptist Larcombe set off a storm of controversy. The legislature was besieged with petitions from citizens urging that the office be discontinued for fear of proselytizing (Teeters and Shearer 1957, 151). One of the many foreign visitors who wrote of the struggle to define the American penal experience, Harriet Martineau, shared the prevailing preoccupation that inmates might become the prey of "proselytizing religionists"

(Martineau 1838, 137). Larcombe was, of course, not unaware of the controversial nature of his appointment. He stated: "[I teach] the simplest, plainest truths, divested of all sectarian taint or bias" (E. Pen. 1853, 32).

When Samuel Wood was investigated for alleged wrongdoing in 1834, he raged that his accusers were "Deists" and that one was "a strong sectarian who was busy inculcating among the prisoners his own notions." In his trial some alleged Deists were not allowed to testify and the testimony of those whose religious views were considered unorthodox was struck from the record. Not surprisingly, Wood was acquitted of all charges (Report of the Joint Committee 1835, 3-24).

The inauguration of the chaplaincy, despite the tensions it revealed, was yet another reminder that religious forces profoundly affected the content of both political thinking and social praxis in the Penitentiary Era.

The state inspectors and legislators constantly invoked religious themes and insisted that the two state penitentiaries express the evangelical mission. In 1835 a legislative committee was sent to investigate the Eastern facility. They had this to say concerning the religious component of convict discipline:

> We place him in the "locus penitentiae," and we seek to present to him motives to return to the paths of virtue. While he is made to feel the vengeance of the law, he is taught to know its mercy, and to learn to sin no more. A judicious religious instructor is very important in this work of reformation. Christian instruction, bringing to the deluded sons of vice, in the solitude of their cells, the wisdom of the purest morals and the consolations of religion, must always prove a powerful auxiliary (if indeed it can be at all accomplished without it,) in bringing the convict back to a proper regard for the obligations which rest upon him (Report of Joint Committee 1835, 17).

A group of legislators visiting the Western Penitentiary said the confined individual needs much more than "a formal sermon, preached occasionally" if the goal of a "change of heart" is to be accomplished (Select Committee 1838, 5). The inspectors equated the "dark and desolate period" in prison history with the time when there were "no prayers—no Sabbath service—no copy of the Holy Scriptures—no minister of the gospel or moral instructor to administer the 'Word of Life' to their wounded and immortal being" (W. Pen. 1845, 4).

In the aftermath of the Civil War, those elected to these positions would begin to adopt the secular language of Progressivism with the same intensity that they employed the devotional language of religion. References to science and progress would come to replace grace and providence. I hope to show, however, that the veil of science could disguise but not eradicate the deeply ingrained religious impulse at the center of penal life.

Many of the wardens similarly exhibited a deep spiritual commitment in their yearly reports. Besides the aforementioned Wood, the third warden, Thomas Scattergood, also a Quaker member of the Philadelphia Prison Society, concluded his reflections on the state of the penitentiary in 1848 in this way: "With feelings of gratitude to the Giver of all Good, the acknowledgment is due—that if any progress has been made in the work to him belongeth the praise—and that to him alone must we look for a blessing upon our efforts" (E. Pen. 1848, 33). Louis Dwight, rarely found to have a positive word for anyone so connected to the separate system, made this remark about him: "Friend, thou art rightly named; for I perceive thy mission in the penitentiary is to Scatter Good" (Teeters and Shearer 1957, 215). Throughout the ensuing decades and even into the twentieth century, such wardens as Edward Townsend and Michael Cassidy continued to embellish their reports with public manifestations of their religious devotion.

The moral instructors were, of course, the primary figures in the religious life of the institution. As evangelicals in the spirit of the Second Great Awakening, they were continually waging war on social evil and calling the sinner to conversion: "I find human nature to be the same in a prison cell as it is in the more favored circumstances of life," said John Ruth, "and fully believe in the universality of the only remedy for a depraved life—the power of grace in the Gospel of Christ" (E. Pen. 1866, 97).

Their ministerial endeavors fully complemented the tenets of Quaker theology that shaped the separate system. Since prisoners were forbidden to see or hear one another, there was no provision for congregational worship. The two forms of contact between chaplain and inmate were the personal visit, which occupied the bulk of the chaplain's day, and the weekly sermon conducted in the corridors outside the prisoners' cells. Inmates, with their doors open, could hear but not see those who exhorted them to spiritual renewal.

The chaplains were involved in the education of the inmates to a lesser extent than their counterparts in the silent system but, like them, had full responsibility for the educational process throughout the early decades of the history of the penitentiary. The appropriation of this and other obligations aimed at addressing the social factors related to crime confirms the unique social analytical skills the chaplains developed as an inseparable part of their evangelical faith with its emphasis on societal reform. They also prefigured the sociological dynamic in the thousands of interviews they conducted over the course of a year. Their experiences prompted them to establish a comprehensive tutoring program to complement their duty of promoting spiritual reformation. Chaplains in both penal contexts were among the first to illustrate the immediate connection between criminal activity and educational underdevelopment.

The Prison Association of Women Friends gave distinct emphasis to the instruction of female prisoners,[8] while Nathaniel Callender typified moral instructors who made literacy training a basic component of the pastoral visit. He sought to "aid those who require assistance in their studies" and "visit those who are learning to read" (W. Pen. 1843, 19). It was not until 1854, with the appointment of Abraham Boyer, that the Eastern Penitentiary officially implemented an educational program as part of the prison routine (E. Pen. 1855, 35).

The continual exposure of the moral instructors to the stories and testimonies of the prisoners, revealing the wellspring of temptation and crime, helped to formulate a ministerial strategy of which the call for systematic educational procedures was only a part. They became the first prison librarians and often dedicated themselves to creating programs for the discharged inmates. Although such programs were emphasized to a greater degree among chaplains in the Auburn institutions, there was a pattern that also manifested itself in Pennsylvania. The chaplains had daily exposure to the inmates and their self-revelations, they drew up charts to concretize the frequency of specific connections between environment and crime, and they appealed to the legislature and the wider religious community on behalf of the prisoners. Early in his appointment, Larcombe wrote that his first desire was to "make some classification," to "systematize as far as possible my future exertions." He followed this statement with a statistical analysis of the new prisoners according to geographical origin, crime, education, marital status, habits (especially regarding temperance), race, number of convictions, age, and sentence (E. Pen. 1839, 25-28). This is an important legacy of the chaplains to the development of the American penal system, and it is from this rudimentary social analysis that the Progressive Movement in penology was born.

Discipline

In June 1833, during the administration of Samuel Wood, Matthias Maccumsey, "in whose mouth an iron bar or gag was so forcibly fastened, that his blood collected or suffused upon his brain . . . suddenly died under the treatment" (Report of Joint Committee to the Legislature 1835, 6). He was a prisoner from Lancaster County serving a twelve-year sentence for murder. Wood's journal states:

Maccumsey having on several occasions got the man next to him
talking and being detected in the act last evening, I ordered the
straight jacket . . . and the gag . . . This I saw put on about 8 o'clock.
About 9 o'clock I was informed by Wm. Griffiths that they had found
him in a lifeless state. I immediately went to him and found him
warm but with no pulse. We tried to bleed him and used ammonia and
many other things but life was extinct. Dr. Bache went to see him but
could do nothing (Teeters and Shearer 1957, 103).

The incident points to one of the troubling realities in penal life. Any
regimen, especially one based on absolute silence, will become completely
ineffective if recalcitrant inmates disregard it.   Conversely, what is
portrayed as the work of a reformative philosophy is no more than a
cynical charade if repression and not conversion becomes its most
recognizable trait.

While some might celebrate the rough justice so vividly portrayed
in the Maccumsey incident in light of the antisocial activities of the
convict population, penal history reveals that punishment requires a theory
of human nature and of social life. It must have a defined meaning both
for those being punished and those inflicting the punishment. Moreover,
the right to punish, while philosophically defensible, must be implemented
in a structural setting consistent with the stated aim.

Such theoretical questions are essential for the operation of any
institution. Failure to create a unified symbolic framework makes any
show of force meaningless. On the other hand, a coherence between the
justification for punishment, the end it is meant to achieve, and the setting
in which it is to be enforced can lead the one being punished to view the
action in a meaningful light.

The architects and defenders of the Pennsylvania system intuited this
connection, at least initially, and were similarly convinced that religion
has a singularly important function at each level of this process. Only
such an interchange between institutional activity and the elements of
culture, laden with moral meaning, can create a penal setting where
discipline can be understood and even embraced by the residents. The
ability of Pennsylvania, or any other penal system, to effect reformation
was and, for that matter, will be directly dependent on whether such
coherence can be accomplished.

The transcripts relating to the Maccumsey incident reveal several of
the means used by prison officials to subdue those unwilling to submit to
penitentiary discipline. Other common forms of punishment were the
shower bath, in which buckets of cold water were poured over the head,
often with a trough-like device attached around the neck,[9] and the

"tranquilizing chair," invented by Benjamin Rush for the purpose of subduing incorrigible mental cases at the Pennsylvania Hospital.

Despite these harsh procedures the Maccumsey case was apparently a rare occurrence in the Pennsylvania prisons. For the most part officials had little need to resort to such tactics as the enforced solitude obviated many possible infractions and the threat of removing the tools of daily labor curbed still others. After her visit to the Eastern Penitentiary, Harriet Martineau stated: "they spoke (such as were qualified) of other prisons with horror, and with approbation approaching thankfulness of the treatment they met with in this, where they were not degraded . . . as if they were not still men" (1838, 132). In similar fashion Dr. Philip Tidyman wrote:

> They all agreed that although this mode of punishment was painfully irksome to them for the first few months of their confinement, yet they were reconciled under a full persuasion that it was intended to improve both their moral and physical condition, by placing them beyond the reach of the society of the most abandoned villains, and afforded them time to reflect and repent, whilst most rigid regard is paid to their health, their Diet, and personal cleanliness, and the greatest humanity exercised towards them (Tidyman et al 1835, 5).

Whatever the level of repression in the Pennsylvania prisons, far fewer violent incidents were reported there than in the rival facilities. This testimony of A. Beckham, warden of the Western Penitentiary, though not lacking in rhetorical fervor, seems consistent with the available source material:

> We have passed another year, without the necessity of resorting to that cruelty so much practiced in the congregate system. We have scarcely had occasion for the slightest punishment, and if under the system of solitary confinement, with mildness, firmness, kindness and justice, there will seldom, indeed, be occasion to resort to such cruelty (W. Pen. 1840, 4).

As the nation moved into the era of sentimentalism and romanticism that will be discussed in the next chapter, coupled with the shocking abuses revealed at the penitentiary at Sing Sing, a general movement occurred to relax the more corporal forms of punishment. Warden Halloway noted in one of his reports: "General good order has prevailed," incidents of punishment have "not been numerous," and have consisted of confinement in a "dark cell on bread and water" (E. Pen. 1859, 12).

Reactions to the System

The Quakers were a rather small sect within the expansive family of American Protestantism. This fact probably insured that the beliefs so central to their treatment of the offender would not capture the imagination of many Americans formed under a different image of God. Their reliance on mysticism and a subdued cultic experience as the catalyst for social change would be quite foreign to the theologies dominating the world-view of New Englanders and New Yorkers. Nevertheless, their approach to penology was adopted by many of the nations that sent delegations to study the boisterous debate over penitentiary discipline.

One possible explanation for this affinity is that the first written formulation of penitentiary logic surfaced with the writings of Dom Jean Mabillon, a Benedictine monk writing in the seventeenth century. His work reveals that the Quakers had indeed intuited, or borrowed, ideas that had their roots in Catholic Europe and that had been practiced in monastic prisons dating back to the Reformation, if not before.[10] Note the similarity between Mabillon's penal vision and the regimen adopted at the Eastern Penitentiary:

> In this place there would be several cells similar to those of the Carthusian monks, with a workshop to exercise them in some useful labor. One could also add to each cell a little garden which would be open to them at certain hours and where they could be made to work or walk. They would be present at Divine Offices, to begin with, locked in some separate gallery . . . Their food would be simpler and coarser and the fasts more frequent than in other Communities. They should be frequently exhorted and the superior or some one in his place should take care to visit them separately and console and fortify them form time to time . . . I am sure that all this will pass for an idea from a new world but whatever is thought and said about the matter, it will be easy whenever the desire arises, to make these prisons both more useful and more easy to endure (Sellin 1927, 592).

It would not be surprising, therefore, that representatives of Catholic countries, including de Beaumont and de Tocqueville, would find greater sympathy with the justification and structure of the separate system.

Many reformers in the United States also echoed the international preference for the Quaker approach. Francis Lieber, a scholar and confidant of the French delegation, wrote: "uninterrupted solitary confinement at labor is the preferable, because the most humane, yet most effective mode, to which society can resort in punishing its unfortunate numbers" (Lieber 1838, 6). Dorthea Dix said in reference to the Eastern Penitentiary: "I consider the moral, religious and mental instruction in this prison, which is officially provided, and voluntarily and regularly imparted, more thorough and complete than is supplied to the convicts of any prison in the United States" (Dix 1967, 60). Samuel Gridley Howe, a member of the Boston Prison Discipline Society, united with Horace Mann and Charles Sumner, also members, to criticize Louis Dwight publicly for his denunciations of the separate system: "The spirit of our Reports was so partial, the praises of the Auburn system were so warm, and the censure of the Pennsylvania prisons were so severe, that one could not help suspecting the existence of violent party feeling" (Howe 1846, iii).   They carried out an independent investigation of the Eastern Penitentiary and filed several minority reports as addenda to the official publications of the society. This selection from Howe responds to the frequent criticism that inmates were deprived of the basic human need of social interaction:

> [N]ot only many individuals, but entire classes of men, at different times and in different countries, have voluntarily secluded themselves, to the extent of entire separation from the world and its inhabitants. They were moved to this act by the wish to do penance for their sins, or to resist temptation, or by a belief that they could purify themselves by a life of meditation and prayer. A little reflection, moreover, will soon convince us, even without historical precedent, that the best lessons for man's guidance in his ever-difficult career, are obtained through seclusion, and the frame of mind and soul which it induces (The Pennsylvania Journal Jan. 1849, 1).

There were others, of course, who were less sanguine about the effects of separation on the individual so confined. Generally, these critics did not question the sincerity of the Quaker experiment, but its lack of appreciation for the human reality. As one journalist commented: "it showed a touching faith in human nature, although precious little knowledge of it" (Barnes 1927, 291).

With the onset of the Civil War, and the increased urbanization and industrial growth in its aftermath, Pennsylvania moved quickly to embrace a more positivist approach to the correctional experience. The seeds of this development, whatever the intentions of the founders, were already in place. A methodical, routinized environment with a concentration on the individual, would lead to more pragmatic economic strategies and an unfolding of the progressive thinking that would come to dominate American penal philosophy.

Perhaps the most appropriate statement of the optimism and moral righteousness that characterized penology in Pennsylvania in the pre-bellum period is found in this report of the inspectors of the Western Penitentiary:

> Pennsylvania broke the dark night of suffering which for ages brooded over that unhappy portion of the family of man, and was the first sovereignty which, by legal enactments, illustrated the divine principle of the Saviour, that the depth of their guilt does not diminish a regard for their well-being . . . They [penal officials] forget not that he has an immortal spirit–that he is still an object of God's regard. The soft and soothing sounds of affection and sympathy, of instruction and prayer, fall upon his ear "whether he will hear or whether he will forbear"; useful and salutary labor, clean and wholesome apartments, a comfortable place to lay his aching head or wearied limbs, air and water, ample sustenance, the light of Heaven, and the Holy Scriptures to guide his heart to God. Such is the spirit of the Pennsylvania system (W. Pen. 1845, 4).

The Auburn System

The Great Awakening initiated a powerful movement in America toward religious pluralism. Puritan theology, through influential figures such as Jonathan Edwards, mediated the establishment of new religious ideas that had a significant impact upon the social environment and the American ethos. The ensuing differentiation was keenly felt, as seen in chapter two, in areas whose roots were deeply implanted in Calvinist soil. Fundamental emphases of that tradition: democratic polity, "ascetic" economics, obedience, civic voluntarism, and a basic sense of human sinfulness, underwent transformation as they blended with revivalism, Arminianism, and millennial optimism. In New York and Massachusetts, evangelicals formed an uneasy but socially significant alliance with traditional Calvinists in the early decades of the nineteenth century.

In the correctional arena, these variations in religious practice would express themselves in the turbulent history of the penitentiaries patterned after Auburn. Elam Lynds, recognized by most historians as the principal force in the development of the silent system, is a central figure in the pre-progressive era. Deeply distrustful of the fallen creatures under his care at both Auburn and Sing Sing, he stressed the Calvinist virtues of strict discipline and work. He was controversial, many believed criminal, scoffed at the optimism of the evangelicals, and was discredited both in his personal comportment and in his penal methods. Yet it was his philosophy that set an unfettered tone in those penitentiaries at least until the Civil War. He told De Beaumont and De Tocqueville:

> [A]ccording to my experience, it is necessary that the director of a prison, particularly if he establish a new discipline, should be invested with an absolute and certain power . . . The point is, to maintain uninterrupted silence and uninterrupted labor; to obtain this, it is equally necessary to watch incessantly the keepers, as well as the prisoners; to be at once inflexible and just . . . I consider it impossible to govern a large prison without a whip . . . Nothing, in my opinion, is rarer than to see a convict of mature age become a religious and virtuous man (1833, 162-64).

The philosophy Lynds propagated was "old light" severity laced with Utilitarianism. The strict order of the penitentiary would not reform the prisoners but, in conjunction with the habits of industry gained from confinement, it would make the prospect of crime and possible reimprisonment a terrifying check on their rebellious natures. Lynds banked on the fact, correctly I suggest, that the public, in the long run, would support a controversial and even brutal penal discipline as long as it did not severely strain the state budget. Evangelical and humanitarian activists fought him and his followers throughout his tempestuous career. They succeeded in modifying disciplinary codes and introducing expanded reformative programs in the 1840s, and again when the revivals resurfaced in the 1850s. Despite these gains, however, the issues of slavery, economic recession, and the inevitable cooling of the fires of charismatic religion served to distract public interest and enthusiasm for the easily forgotten souls in the penitentiaries. The one group who would prove to be the most influential in deposing Lynds and steering the institutions in new directions were the chaplains.

The alliance between conventional New England theology and that of the evangelicals was made possible because all formally agreed on the conceptual format of the silent system: silence, work, discipline, and spiritual instruction. The final ingredient needed to maximize the desired effects of these common concerns was the structural environment.

The novel architectural addition at Auburn was the work of William Britten, the first agent. He built what was to become the most frequently copied prison design in the United States, as well as a model for the prisons of many countries, imitated into the twentieth century. In the center of the new wing was an island of cells five tiers high and surrounded on all four sides by a vacant area eleven feet wide. The individual cells were seven feet long, three and one-half feet wide and seven feet high. Each tier consisted of two rows of these cubicles placed back to back. The walls separating the individual compartments were a foot thick and extended outward two feet beyond the cell doorways, thus greatly diminishing the ability of the inmates to communicate by word of mouth or by the use of signals. These outward projections created the recesses in which the chaplains could stand while counseling the prisoners. The extensions also made it impossible for the convicts to know where the constantly patrolling guards, walking silently, were located.[11]

> Turnkeys are enjoined to keep constantly moving around the galleries
> . . . having socks on their feet, walking so noiselessly, that each
> convict does not know but that he is at the very door of his cell, ready
> to discover and report, the next morning, for punishment, the slightest
> breach of silence or order (Powers 1826, 7).

Behavioral conformity was maintained in the workshops not only by officers armed with the dreaded "cat" (cat-o'-nine-tails),[12] but also each workshop was surrounded by a hidden gallery where the unseen keepers constantly observed the labor process.[13]

The prisoners marched to and from work in lockstep, single file, hand on the shoulder of the one in front, no lip movement, eyes turned toward their keepers. The spectator, as Powers remarked, was given "similar feelings to those excited by a military funeral" and the convicts were given "impressions not entirely dissimilar to those of culprits marching to the gallows" (1826, 4). Martineau commented: "Some of the prisoners turned their heads every possible way to avoid meeting our eyes, and were in an agony of shame" (1838, 124).

They worked from sunup to sundown and ate their meals in their cells in silence. After the evening meal, the residents waited for a signal to undress and go to bed. Until this occurred, they were positively forbidden to lie down. If light permitted, they could read the Bible or await a visit from the chaplain. The only change in the schedule was on Sunday when all were marched to chapel for services.[14] De Beaumont and De Tocqueville vividly described the mood at the close of the day.

> But when the day is finished, and the prisoners have retired to their
> cells, the silence within these vast walls, which contain so many
> prisoners, is that of death. We have often trod during the night those
> monotonous and dumb galleries, where a lamp is always burning: we

felt as if we traversed catacombs; there were a thousand living beings, and yet it was a desert solitude (1833, 65).

Discipline and obedience were the essential components in this routine. The evangelicals were practically unanimous, at this historical juncture, that corporal punishment was a necessary element in penal administration. The convict needed to feel the wrath of God as a pretext for conversion.[15] The views of chaplains like Jonathan Dickerson at Sing Sing helped justify the exacting regimen of the institution: "the many favorable circumstances of solitude, privations, and even punishment itself, if it does not press so hard as to sink the man in a state of despondence, place him in an attitude for advantageous reception of every gospel invitation, promise and consolation" (Sen. Doc. 23 1836, 19).

Similarly, the Congregational chaplain, B. C. Smith, expressed how the structure of Auburn struck an alliance between evangelicals and more traditional Calvinists:

> Without the checks and constraints of its admirable police organization, the religious instructions, I am fully aware, would be of little or no avail; and I am as thoroughly convinced that, without the aid of religious influences, the other part of your system would fail to produce any radical or permanent changes in the character of its subjects. In the combination of both lies the secret of their power. The one, by coercion, suspends the operation of vicious influences upon their minds, and holds them in a favorable posture to be acted upon by moral motives; while the other pours in upon them the light of truth, and brings to bear the great and commanding motives of the Gospel, which never fail, when once they gain access, to affect and amend the heart (PDS 1835, 17).

Whatever the prevalence of abuses, and there were abuses indeed, particularly at Sing Sing, as long as Louis Dwight publicized the humanity and effectiveness of the Auburn approach, it continued to win support in the correctional community and throughout society. Dwight spoke of the Lynds administration in glowing terms representative of the traditional Calvinist social ethic:

> By those who have witnessed the power and wisdom of this government, the order, and industry, and silence of these convicts, it is believed that here is a specimen of authority and vigilance on the one hand, and obedience on the other, which to a great extent prevent evil communication among prisoners (PDS 1827, 66).

Dwight's mind reflected the harmony of utilitarian thinking with the concepts of both individual and collective deterrence. This ethical foundation was alluded to often in the writings of the Auburn advocates and provided the necessary moral defense for the violence of the system. Dwight showed familiarity and agreement with the writings of Beccaria and Bentham in this cost/benefit justification of the use of "stripes":

> If the efficacy of these different modes of punishment were to be judged . . . punishment by stripes, as at Auburn, would be preferred . . . it requires less time; the mind of the prisoner does not brood over it, and settle down in a deliberate resentment and malignity; it is in some case more effectual; it is less severe; it can be more easily proportioned to the offense (PDS 1827, 17).

Regardless of how one chooses to judge Dwight's ideological preoccupation, by the late 1830s it became clear to virtually everyone concerned with the state of the penitentiaries, including Dwight himself, that Lynds and his successor at Sing Sing, Robert Wiltse, had gone too far.

Discipline and Punishment

When Auburn was converted to the silent system in 1824 there were not enough single cells to accommodate all the prisoners. The legislature, having despaired of the Newgate facility, called for the creation of a new state penitentiary at Sing Sing (Mount Pleasant), located on the Hudson River some thirty miles north of New York City on the site of a marble quarry.[16] Lynds was appointed to govern the institution and given the task of overseeing its construction. He left Auburn in 1825 with one hundred convicts, "having no other means to keep them in obedience, than the firmness of his character and the energy of his will" (de Beaumont and de Tocqueville 1833, 43). As the reader may have already surmised, that "will" was formidable indeed. Warden Charles Sutton described the expedition and the remarkable dominance of Lynds:

> [The inmates] were in the open fields, guarded by less than one tenth of their own number, and yet from the day they left the cells at Auburn until the day they had finished the cells that were to entomb them at Sing Sing, there was not one attempt at escape, and no infraction of discipline . . . The moral energy of that one man was sufficient to awe into subjection the most turbulent, while the most desperate were hardly rash enough to provoke a contest which they knew would be "short, sharp and decisive" (Sutton 1874, 585).

By May 1828, the prisoners from Newgate were moved to the new penitentiary, entirely constructed by convict labor. It formally began operation in 1829 with eight hundred solitary cells (another two hundred were added within several years).

The legislative team that supervised the building of Mount Pleasant–Samuel Hopkins, George Tibbits, and Stephen Allen (later a mayor of New York)–were of a like mind with Lynds. They felt the penitentiary idea would succeed only with severity. They also concurred that the evangelicals had placed too much faith in the capacity of inmates to reform. Allen had written that those convicted of "rape, highway robbery, burglary, &c." were "DEAD IN LAW" and consequently were "without any rights natural or political" (Roscoe 1827, 4). Furthermore, he wrote that "however desirable it may be to reform a confirmed villain, it is, to say the least of it, A FORLORN HOPE" (1827, 10).

Despite such dire warnings, the architectural shape of the new facility was not marked by the security devices Britten had built into Auburn. The cells, for example, were not recessed and therefore inmates could talk more easily and were able to watch the movement of the patrolling guards. Added to this was the shear size of the edifice, creating a much larger space to patrol. The expanded possibilities for conversation were met with expanded use of physical punishment by the keepers and by the agent. Chaplain Dickerson once stated that the agent was similar to "a man who had tamed a tiger that one day may devour him" (W. D. Lewis 1965, 145).

Reports of cruelty and corruption began to emanate from Sing Sing in its very first year of operation. Aside from the beatings of the prisoners, the insistence of Lynds on financial stability, coupled with the same intent on the part of the contractors who supervised the work of the inmates, led to drastic reductions in food, heat, and winter clothing. Levi S. Burr, a war hero of 1812, who had been convicted of perjury, reportedly under suspicious circumstances, spent three years at Sing Sing during this time. He later addressed a joint session of the state legislature on his experiences:

> A man may go half fed for a short time—say a few days, and not feel a sensible diminution of his strength: but when there is a daily deficiency in food, and the stomach has not once been satisfied for weeks together, the subject is in continual distress; and that such has been the case, I am a suffering witness. And it is true, that I have suffered to that degree, that I have gladly eaten the roots of shrubs and trees that I dug from the ground in which I labored. I was not alone

in this extremity. I saw no exceptions in the individuals around me. The cry of hunger was general, but greater with some than with others. There were some who told me, they eat the clay they worked in. They would secrete it in their bosoms, and carry large pieces into their rooms with them at night, and eat it with their mush (Burr 1833, 24).

The event that finally triggered an investigation was the dismissal of the Chaplain, Gerrish Barrett, who was a critic of the harsh state of affairs. Hopkins and Tibbits were sent to gather testimony. They reported: "Barrett and Lynds had an altercation in the prison yard, in sight of the convicts; that Lynds appeared angry and Barrett provoking; Lynds threatened to strike, and Barrett appeared to invite it; and immediately after Lynds discharged him" (Sen. Doc. 60 1831, 26-27).

The altercation with the chaplain was significant in several respects. The authority of a self-described autocrat, revered by the penal community and legislature for the measure of order and fiscal responsibility he achieved within the prison, was publicly challenged by a religious figure. The legislature, wary to criticize Lynds, dispatched two of his allies to conduct the investigation in an apparent attempt to gloss over the incident. Neither Hopkins nor Lynds were to emerge quite the same as a result. Despite the fact that the investigation produced neither censure nor indictment, Lynds was miffed that the inquest occurred in the first place. He resigned in frustration in 1830.[17] Hopkins, for his part, although predisposed to support the agent, was deeply distressed at the affair and the general tone being set at Sing Sing. He began to insist that "moral discipline" was of equal value to obedience based on fear of the lash. He described the episode as both "an insult, and a personal humiliation."[18]

There are many matters in the conduct of Mr. Lynds, which have only appeared of late, and which show him to be a different man, in his present temper and conduct from what he was, and unfit to govern a prison. There are unanswerable instances of cruelty to prisoners; his harsh and violent speeches regarding them are justly offensive to public feeling; he has given orders for indiscriminate punishment . . . as in the case of his effort to stop the loud and universal clamor for food: his conduct to the Reverend Mr. Barrett was a series of insults, and is the second instance of bad temper shown to an excellent prison chaplain (PDS 1830, 12-13).

The legislators apparently were more disposed to side with Lynds than with Hopkins. The new agent summoned to administer Sing Sing, Robert Wiltse, was cast in the mold of his predecessor. He once said, "the best prison is that which the inmates find worst" (W. D. Lewis 1965, 142). He operated under the strategy of strict obedience and financial stability. Yearly reports throughout his tenure were dedicated to a review of profits and expenditures resulting from the contract system. It was left to the chaplains and, infrequently, to the inspectors to lead efforts to insure that humane and reformative treatment be emphasized in the life of the institution.[19]

As tensions continued unabated at Sing Sing, Elam Lynds was about to reenter the correctional arena. In 1838 he was reappointed agent at Auburn and was almost immediately embroiled in renewed controversy.

When word of the reported abuses in the two prisons reached Dwight, he decided to embark on a tour of the facilities to determine the accuracy of the claims. His visit left him horrified at the neglect of the reformative programs he had fought so hard to establish. Not only was he angered by the violence he witnessed; he was also appalled at the decision by Lynds to disband the Sabbath school program. As mentioned earlier, the chaplains had been the catalysts for the formation of Sabbath schools in which inmates were given basic educational skills as well as taught to read and memorize passages from the Bible. The students at the Auburn seminary were the instructors supervised by the chaplains.[20]   The following are sections of the report Dwight filed which triggered a swift and concerted response. The first quote concerns Lynds, the second is in reference to the situation at Sing Sing.

> The keeper, in accordance with his views of the comparative inefficiency of moral means with physical, has dispensed with the Sabbath school. If there is any one thing, in our opinion, in the history of this Prison, for the first ten years, clearly good, and only good, and that continually, it is the Sabbath school (PDS 1839, 39).

> The secretary of this Society made a short visit to the Prison at Sing Sing, last autumn, and saw himself enough to satisfy his mind that the punishments were odious and detestable, both in manner and degree. He saw a convict beaten with a staff over his head, by an officer, in a violent passion, without any provocation . . . He also saw evidence to satisfy his mind that the convicts were not properly fed . . . And the state of the hospital showed a want of proper attention to the sick . . . It was therefore no surprise to him that thirty-three prisoners died last year in the Prison at Sing Sing (PDS 1839, 42-43).

The year Dwight's report was published both institutions were under investigation. Lynds was accused of five violations: the death of two inmates, abbreviated rations, "whipping, beating and otherwise ill-treating convicts;" and "the freezing and other suffering of the convicts for want of sufficient fire" (Sen. Doc. 37 1840, 5). One of the committee members, Henry Livingston, reported from the testimony he had taken that a contractor's agent, Mr. Bruce, had "screwed a man's hand in an iron vise, and when in that situation lacerated his back with the instrument used in the prison called a cat" (Sen. Doc. 38 1840, 5). Depositions taken in reference to Lynds included this statement regarding the legally imposed six lash limit: "the agent told several of his keepers that six blows with a cat were only an aggravation, that he must have keepers who could not count six, or did not know how to count." In reference to a disturbance on one of the tiers Lynds reportedly remarked: "There is no difficulty at all; ascertain the gallery they are in, and the place, as near as you can; then take out fifteen, twenty or twenty-five and flog them all, and you will be sure to get the right one" (Sen. Doc. 38 1840, 9).[21]

At Sing Sing, Wiltse was accused of fifty-five violations, among them: fraud in contracts and impropriety in fiscal matters, cruelty and short rations, inmate suicides buried before the coroner could examine them, and the frequent scourging of female convicts (Sen. Doc. 37 1840, 47ff). The Prison Association of New York (NYPA), in its first report, reproduced the suicide note left by a resident before drowning himself in the Hudson:

> To whom it may concern. I can't stand to be flogged. Today I Die.
> First Farewell all my friends now am unwilling to own that such a
> vile outcast you never knew I would not [be] but for the flogging that
> I can't take. I am sorry for what has happened but alas it is too late.
> I thank Mr___ for his kindness to me since I have been here. tell Mr
> ___ not to be so fond of punishing his fellow creatures he will have
> to give an account sometime. Feed the molatters and show mercy.
> A. Judson (NYPA 1844, 25)

The most influential chaplain in both penal systems during this era, John Luckey, described the situation among the inmates when he assumed his position at Sing Sing in 1839:

> Labor was an exceedingly irksome task to the convicts, and as a
> matter of course, no interest was taken in its performance. Escapes,
> or attempts to escape, were of almost weekly occurrence; the convicts
> choosing, as they have frequently told me, to run the risk of being
> shot down by the guard than remain to be killed by inches (Luckey
> 1860, 25).

Although most of the charges against Lynds and Wiltse were dropped, and neither official was indicted, the outcry from the religious community once again proved to be effective. Both men were forced to resign. They were replaced by more humane and evangelical administrators, intent on upholding the reformative aspect of the silent approach. This change of affairs represented a general movement in the state toward "the restoration of the inmate for a renewed trial in the bosom of society" (Sen. Doc. 16 1850, 7).

A leading figure in the evangelical reclamation of the prison was Governor William H. Seward, a confidant of Luckey, who supported him in a number of his reformative suggestions. Seward addressed an inmate on one occasion: "You are right . . . the blessed Saviour is rich in mercy unto all who truly repent of their sins, and call upon him" (Luckey 1860, 89).

The new agent at Sing Sing, D. L. Seymour, not only attended religious services with the inmates, he "went from cell to cell on the Sabbath, delivering tracts" (Luckey 1860, 89). Such public signs of religious devotion were a frequent characteristic of the agents of both the men's and the new women's facility (opened in 1838) while Luckey was chaplain.

At Auburn, the inspectors were also giving witness to a more rehabilitative approach to New York's penal philosophy. Monetary concerns, however, retained their importance:

> Having reformation for its object, it seeks the end by kind treatment, and wholesome moral instruction, separate confinement, non-intercourse and the silent and social labor required for health of body and mind to the convict, and which may reimburse to the community the expenses of his necessary imprisonment (Sen. Doc. 18 1844, 6).

Although twice placed under investigation for his relentless and violent disposition, and despite the more humane turn in penal discourse, the Lynds saga was still not over. In 1842 he was appointed principal keeper at Sing Sing. Although this last appointment was brief in tenure, it was once again characterized by his trademark of rough justice. Luckey was bitter over the reinstatement of Lynds and made it clear in his writings. The following event concerned an inmate, understood by the chaplain to be making progress in his religious awakening, who continually ran afoul of the new keeper:

> When the "reign of terror" was fully initiated under Capt. L.'s command, it was, by Jim and his compeers, resisted with the same

fierce, determined, "don't-care-what-becomes-of-me" spirit that the officials manifested in swaying their "knock-down-and-drag-out" scepters (Luckey 1860, 158).

Luckey sarcastically related the rest of the incident: "He was, of course, flogged almost to death, and 'laid aside' with the threat that as soon as his lacerated back was sufficiently healed to render it exquisitely sensible to 'another hundred lashes,' he should have them" (1860, 159).

Luckey was more than a concerned chaplain, however, he was a most formidable and influential figure. The episode moved him to petition directly to the head of the Board of Inspectors, Judge John Edmonds (later the president of the Prison Association of New York) "who, I knew, was beginning to have his eyes opened to the cruel, unjust, brutalizing 'discipline' then in full operation" (Luckey 1860, 160). Edmonds invited Luckey to his home. There the chaplain related that he had formed clandestine agreements with various overseers at the prison who had agreed to test the effects of a more lenient work regimen. He contended that inmates worked more efficiently, were actually "industrious and cheerful," in a more moderate environment. Edmonds was convinced and "at once determined upon a return to the former mild course" (1860, 32-33). Not only was the particular inmate exonerated of his charges, Lynds was once again forced to depart, closing one of the most controversial chapters in the history of American penology.

Lynds was toppled on three different occasions by religiously motivated leaders. They upheld a vision of the penitentiary grounded in an ethos that was meant to permeate each sector of the institution. This enabled them to evaluate the day to day reality of a large organization against a set of behavioral and structural images that provided the basis for an ongoing critique. The work of Max Weber reveals that as officials assume clearly defined roles and spheres of influence, they gain competence and learn to outlast the periodic reshuffling of high level administrators (Weber 1978, 956ff). Luckey and, to some extent, Barrett were able to turn bureaucratic stratification to their own advantage. Luckey, for example, conspired with shop overseers and guards to circumvent the "reign of terror" and, eventually, to overthrow a key administrator. The same dynamic works in reverse, as well. Humane legislation can also be sidestepped. While the lapse into routine and the seduction of power are a part of all institutions, including those that are religious in nature, the need to ground institutions in moral soil that has a consistent and transcendent quality remains essential. Such a teleological framework can pierce the walls of bureaucratic apathy and routine at times when the future viability of the organization is called into question.

New York and Massachusetts moved to abandon all forms of sanguinary punishment in the 1840s. In 1847, the New York legislature formally enacted what had been the growing practice since the removal of Lynds: the prohibition of any beatings whatsoever unless in self-defense or to suppress a revolt or insurrection (NYPA 1849, 314). The shower bath and shortened rations became the punishments sanctioned by law but, as Luckey attests, "whether the substitution of the shower-bath is any less degrading or more humane, is a question on which there is a diversity of opinion" (1860, 17).

Massachusetts had adopted the Auburn system at its Charlestown facility but, being under the watchful eye of Dwight and his associates at the prison society, was not subjected to distressing scandals with the frequency of its neighbor to the west. Francis Gray toured the American penitentiaries and reported to his English associates in penal reform that Charlestown was the outstanding representative of the silent system: "The prison at Charlestown resembles a great manual-labor school. The prisoners are not required to keep their eyes fixed upon their work and never look up, as at Auburn, but simply to attend to their task as in school. As in school, also, silence is required" (Gray 1848, 47).

The events surrounding the investigation of Lynds and Wiltse convinced the Massachusetts General Court also to move to suspend corporal punishments, save the shower bath. Chaplain Charles Cleveland urged the residents to respond happily and obediently to the new policy:

> In many prisons the infliction of stripes is resorted to, with a view to benefit the delinquent, and warn others against transgressing the laws of the prison. Praise God, that you are not placed under the task-masters of Egyptian mold. Your officers are indeed discreet and kind, and would sooner take punishments upon their own persons, than complain of you without cause—subjecting you to the operation of the shower bath. You are well clad, well fed, have comfortable cells and cozy lodgings. You are allotted the kind of labor which, in the judgment of the master, is best suited to your several capacities and physical strength. Again I say, be thankful, conduct well, and you will enjoy peace (Cleveland, 3).

The more benevolent legislation, although a welcome sight to both evangelicals and inmates, served to underscore the hard and contradictory reality of the silent system: idle inmates would undermine reformation by neglecting rules of silence and comportment; while inmates who were forced to labor often did so only under the threat of coercion. Furthermore, a controversy over the use of convict labor prompted the New York legislature to pass a law in 1835 banning prison industries "injurious to the interests of those of our fellow-citizens engaged in similar pursuits" (Sen. Doc. 91 1841, 1). The results of this act were felt at the penitentiaries at the same time that they were moving to a less repressive mode of operation. In their 1843 report the inspectors of Sing Sing stated:

> It had been found difficult to provide employment for all the men, and the consequence was, that very many were idle, straying about the yards and collecting in groups, where conversation could not be prevented . . . the board endeavored to remedy. The convicts did not abandon their indulgences and return to a state of strict discipline without a struggle. This involved the necessity of inflicting a good deal of punishment (Sen. Doc. 20 1844, 21).

It was apparent that the two New York penitentiaries were too overcrowded to accomplish either discipline or reformation. The legislature hoped to remedy this shortcoming by authorizing the construction of a new facility at Clinton, in the northern part of the state. The site, opened in 1846, was located near a deposit of iron ore, providing hope in the legislature that the prison would be self-supporting. The new prison, however, simply aggravated a nagging tension in the Auburn system. Its construction intensified the already sizable correctional budget and, to everyone's dismay, never once produced a balanced annual financial report.

Prison Economics

Economic matters often informed the institutional directions invoked by the leading voices of the Auburn system. Those heirs of the Yankee heritage never conceived of the penal system simply as a place for reform. Calvinist psychology was too complex to allow for such single mindedness. However little Calvin may have stressed it, ethical behavior in what Weber called the "disenchanted" Protestant world sought the steady assurance of personal and corporate financial accountability. Louis Dwight repeated time and time again this central belief among the descendants of the Puritans:

> We have seen from facts, that in those Prisons, in which there is the most moral improvement, there is the least expense, and believing as we do, that the enormous expense of Penitentiaries in past years has been the result of odious and detestable abuses, we are at a loss to know from what motive a sentiment was ever advanced so fraught

with mischief as this, that economy and moral improvement are adverse principles in the government of a Prison (PDS 1828, 14).

Rusche and Kirchheimer argue that the mode of production provides the outer structural limits in which penal thinkers select their institutional options, and that a survey of local economic conditions will always reveal the existing penal logic (1968, 5).[22] I am suggesting that the religious system, in this instance one whose roots were deeply embedded in Calvinist theology, provided the initial foundation from which economic policies were conceived. That does not diminish, however, the significant influence those economic policies, once sanctioned by the guiding theological paradigm, have on the evolution of institutional life.

New York and Massachusetts chose the particular organization of the silent system because the diverse variations of Calvinism operating in the early nineteenth century were amenable to its two precepts: a silent discipline widely believed to be the fertile ground in which a religious conversion could take place, and a congregate labor arrangement. The latter element further satisfied two fundamental criteria of the Calvinist heritage: a social, corporate focus as opposed to the strict individualism of the Quakers, and an environment in which a productive economic arrangement could be implanted. David Foot, a keeper at Auburn, unwittingly explained a pivotal component in the logic that governed so many of the developments in the silent system, not the least of which was the type of punishment:

> The public ought to know that most of the able bodied convicts are hired out to contractors at a given sum per day, and that when for any cause they cease to labor, their wages stop. A man shut up in the dungeon for punishment cannot, in the meantime, earn anything for the state; and so a man deprived of necessary food, can hardly be expected to earn daily wages (Report of Auburn Inspectors 1848, 9).

Similarly, we have this statement from the inspectors of Charlestown:

> The salutary restraint and compulsion to labor of such men as are sentenced to the Penitentiary, necessarily demands the application of occasional punishments. These punishments must be either internal by starvation, or external by corporal Infliction of Stripes. The latter of these modes has been adopted in this Prison, as being less cruel and injurious to the health of the Offender, producing a more prompt and cheerful obedience, and preserving his labor for the benefit of himself and the community (Inspectors of the MA State Prison 1832, 17).

This important element of the prevalent social and moral structure explains why figures such as Lynds and Wiltse could not be abruptly dismissed, however violent they may have been. They were symbolic personages who, whatever their religious practice, clearly embodied a major tenet of the religious value system.[23] They were witnessing to Dwight's claim that moral transformation is incongruous in a financially troubled institution. They effectively balanced the books. When the investigators from Albany came to receive testimony from the battered residents, there was a hermeneutic operating that enabled committee members to deflect most of the patently obvious blame away from the agents. One such committee, as noted, had been sent to investigate the death of several inmates and other alleged abuses. They included the following revelatory section in their report to the legislature:

> Much praise is due to the agent and the inspectors of the prison who have been instrumental in effecting contracts, not only for the supply of this prison, but also for mechanical labor, on such advantageous terms. They have, in the judgment of the majority of the committee, vigilantly pursued a course of economy in the management of the affairs of the prison highly commendable, and furnishing strong proof that they have faithfully discharged the duties of their respective offices . . . This prison, at the time the new board was appointed, and when Captain Lynds was called to the agency in 1838, was in embarrassed circumstances, and from the amount of its receipts for convict labor was unable to defray its ordinary expenses. The manner in which the prison has been managed under the agency of Captain Lynds, has enabled it, from the avails of contract labor, to meet its ordinary expenses, and leave a surplus on hand when he left it (Sen. Doc. 37 1840, 23-24).

The downfall of Lynds and Wiltse was caused, therefore, not by their abusive treatment of the inmates but, as shown earlier, by their disregard of the authority and ministerial freedom of the chaplains.

Clearly, the strategy of both evangelicals and more secular reformers could not simply be reduced to either a mercenary concern for profit or a one-dimensional focus on reformation. Luckey, among others, railed against the contract system as "miniature slavery" in which the contractor's "pecuniary interest" drove the inmates "to the last inch of their strength" and provoked them either to insanity or rebellion (1860, 50-51). On the other hand, he demanded both industriousness and a "mild but firm discipline" (1860, 41). Dwight may have been correct after all, that an effective penitentiary would need both financial and reformative success. Unfortunately, history proved that the choice of one curtailed the accomplishment of the other.   When, for example, the aggravated violations of the contract system were diminished, particularly when outside labor interests succeeded in proscribing competitive prison industries, the silent system fell into a state of lethargy and decay that signaled its downfall and contributed to the birth of the reformatory.

It is apparent from the history of these institutions that the "reign of terror" often produced financially stable structures that did not reform; while the separate strategy often led to reformatory environments that were fiscally unstable. In a discipline fraught with ironies, the one that stands out most clearly in this era is that New York wisely would not settle for terror as a cost-cutting strategy and the result was the effective demise of the Auburn plan. Pennsylvania would not abide by reformation at an inflated price, and, in so doing, signaled the eventual downfall of the system it fought so hard to establish.

Religious and Moral Instruction

The penitentiaries in Pennsylvania and New York were different because the latter were imaged and constructed by people steeped in the austerity of the "old light" tradition amid the evangelical fervor of the Second Great Awakening. The Pennsylvania approach, on the other hand, presented a more congenial relationship with the evangelical character of American religion.   The conversion of the prisoner was never a contentious issue at the Eastern Penitentiary. Quaker and like-minded Protestant leaders in the legislature, boards of inspectors, and among the wardens complemented and extended the work of the chaplains and the Philadelphia Prison Society.

The Auburn system had no such coherence.   From the days of Thomas Eddy it mirrored the uneven fit between traditional and revisionist strains within the Calvinist family.   There were certainly periods in which a harmony of vision was shared between state officials, the prison administration, and the chaplaincy, but those periods were short-lived. The coercive nature of congregate labor and persistent fiscal pressures produced a predictable internal strain. Chaplains were often embroiled in controversy with legislative committees, with agents and keepers, and ultimately with the traditional religious assumption that criminals were the cause of their own misery. The violence that they witnessed, especially in Luckey's case, led many to question time-honored theological suppositions and to focus on what might be called sociological concerns. Instead of the revivalist credo that personal conversion must precede and accompany social and moral reform, they helped to turn Evangelicalism and Arminianism in a new direction. Good people go astray due to the environments in which they are raised, and due to the penal environments in which they are confined. These chaplains were more socially involved and ultimately far more influential than their Pennsylvania counterparts. Although it turned out that religious leaders in each context were guiding their institutions in the same direction.

In the pre-bellum era virtually all chaplains were evangelicals and emulated their associates in Pennsylvania in zealously seeking the redemption of the sinner. B. C. Smith, at Auburn, wrote: "The state of feeling in the Prison at large, and particularly in the Sabbath school, is certainly remarkable . . . It seems to be a revival feeling . . . They labor and pray as if they expected a blessing, and could not be denied" (PDS 1840, 28). At Charlestown, Charles Cleveland preached in this way:

> O that you may as heartily welcome the King of glory to the heart, as the footsteps of your chaplain are welcome to your door. Repent, I beseech you, without delay . . . Tomorrow the door of hope may be forever closed against you, should you procrastinate the momentous business of preparation for eternity (Cleveland, 1).

The bulk of the chaplains' work was done in the evening after the inmates concluded their long hours of labor. The daily tasks were to stand in strategic locations in the vast cell blocks and read passages from the Bible accompanied by a short sermon and prayer. At the conclusion of the prayer, the chaplains would then visit with particular inmates at their cells. Jonathan Dickerson claimed in 1835 that he had "literally broken down" from six years of such daily preaching (Sen. Doc. 23 1836, 20-21). Gerrish Barrett gives a vivid description of this ritual at Sing Sing:

> [A] little after 7 o'clock, every evening, I commence reading the scripture to the convicts, afterwards make some remarks, and then offer a prayer on each side of the Prison. I have found by experience, that to stand as near the centre of the Prison as possible, on the pavement below, is far better, for the purpose of being easily heard, than to stand upon the gallery. I am persuaded, that, of all the methods which have been used for fastening divine truth upon the minds of convicts, this daily reading of the scriptures and prayer is most likely to succeed. The truth strikes upon the ear, when the men are sobered by the labors of the day, when no mortal eye sees them, and when the twilight, and the silence, and the loneliness combine in causing it to make a deep impression. They can then reflect on what they have heard till they fall asleep (PDS 1828, 67).

The effects of the conversion experience among the inmates are subject to a multitude of interpretations. The statistics offered by the chaplains, and later by penitentiary officials, not surprisingly revealed a low rate of recidivism. This can be explained in several ways: the most serious problems did not occur in the facilities until they began to feel the effects of overcrowding, and the unscientific and probable ideological nature of the surveys missed or neglected to account for variables that would have otherwise contravened them. Of course, one could also conclude that the inmates actually did undergo a renewal that produced a resolve to conform to religious and institutional norms. I am disposed to accept the middle account but neither do I exclude the probability of the last explanation. Institutions whose regimen is coherent, with a unified symbolic framework, can produce telling social and psychological effects.[24] Furthermore, the power of the evangelical movement in the nation at that time, and its spiritual and social consequences, were simply too significant to deny their impact. Statements such as this one from Chaplain Dickerson were common and ought not be dismissed too casually: "it is an extremely rare occurrence, that a person who has given good evangelical evidence that he has been born again is found recommitted to this prison or to any other" (Sen. Doc. 8 1835, 27).[25]

The most significant quality of the chaplaincy was its conversational nature. It featured an encounter between the individual inmate and a religious guide concerned with leading him or her to repentance and conversion. This dynamic constantly surfaced themes concerning the contributing factors to the criminal act. It led to a consistent list of activities and programs that were felt to be elemental to the reformative process. This was true in both systems, but due to the organizational instability of the congregate penitentiaries, and their periodic conflicts with advocates of moral reform, chaplains in those venues assumed greater prominence in the initiation of programs intended to magnify the religious presence.

The basic tool of the chaplain's art was the basic tool of sociological inquiry, the interview. Edward Shils sees the birth of sociology in a sympathetic exploration of the causes of social problems. Sociology for him is primarily a moral science that seeks to achieve a consensual relationship with the interviewee. He says that a sociologist "becomes a part of any society of living persons that he studies" and that he or she seeks "the elevation of the public life of society by improving the citizen's understanding of the collective life . . . and by improving the quality of discussion among citizens" (Shils 1980, 88, 92).

Many of the chaplains probably approached the daily routine of visiting prisoners with a determined sense that a personal spiritual rebirth was the remedy for what ailed them. But the result of religion entering into an honest exchange with the nonreligious world is, as Ernst Troeltsch argues, compromise. The sense of "humane detachment" that Shils describes as fundamental to the sociologist planted the seed for a future set of understandings concerning the nature of crime and reformation that would not come to complete fruition until the Progressive Age. However, in the pre-bellum era, such interviews did lead first to a systematization of contributing factors to crime, followed by an insistence on necessary programmatic adjustments in penitentiary organization, as well as necessary social modifications to combat these negative influences. Consequently, chaplains throughout the period assumed responsibility for the education of inmates, the establishment and administration of libraries, temperance revivals, the organization of philanthropic movements to aid the discharged convict, and, as previously noted, the defense of prisoners against maltreatment. They clung tenaciously to these programs, engineering the removal of powerful figures such as Lynds and Wiltse who attempted to abrogate them.

In their report for the year 1831, the inspectors of Charlestown praised chaplain Curtis not only for his ministerial skills but also "for the interesting accumulation of facts which he has obtained in regard to the early history and habits of convicts" (MA Sen. Doc. 7 1832, 20). Curtis, himself, related this description of his method and its accommodation to the specific details of the inmate's life:

> The chaplain has also devoted a large portion of his time to private conversation with the Convicts;–obtaining a knowledge of their history, studying their character and disposition–giving them individually such instruction, counsel and advice, and administering such reproof, as their several cases seem peculiarly to demand (Sen. Doc. 2 1834, 26-27).

Curtis also employed the technique of the interview, with the subsequent accumulation of statistics, in his work with recidivists. He established three sets of questions with those who had been reconvicted: the relation between alcohol consumption and crime, the effect of employment or unemployment on criminal behavior, and the amount of association with former prisoners and its influence on lawlessness (Sen. Doc. 2 1838, 27ff).

Orlando Lewis of the New York Prison Association was one observer who did not underestimate the importance for subsequent penal history of what the chaplains were inaugurating:

> We find, in 1832, the chaplain [Curtis] issuing in the annual of the board of inspectors some social statistics regarding the prisoners. This is noteworthy, not because of the intrinsic value of the collated facts, but because they are "published" facts, gathered with the evident design of knowing more about the men in the prison. The prison is emerging from the period when the inmates were treated as so many human beings consigned to oblivion and requiring no study. It is an effort, in a simple way, to understand the problem of the inmate. It is the birth, in Massachusetts, of the statistical method, applied to prisoners with the sanction of the board of inspectors and the warden (1967, 162).

The approach of Curtis was duplicated by most chaplains in the congregate prisons. Alonzo Wood presented his array of statistics to the inspectors at Auburn with this preface: "The following table, made up principally from statistics collected with great care from the men, at their cells, exhibits, it is believed, as true a statement as can be made, considering that for much of the details the convict's own account is all we have to rely on (Sen. Doc. 46 1846, 83).

The fact that so many of these religious figures were engaged in such analytical concerns can be partially explained by the fact that many were, at least in the early years of the penitentiary period, receiving a subsidy from the Boston Prison Discipline Society. Dwight elicited such data that it might be published in his yearly reports. He also was a powerful advocate for the programs that the chaplains, aided by insights from their interviews, sought to establish.[26]

The troubled histories of the prisoners made a deep impression on the chaplains and prompted them to call repeatedly for expanded institutional aid for the discharged inmate. The traditional practice was to give the departing resident three dollars and a graduated sum (three cents a mile) to enable him or her transportation to their family locale (Sen. Doc. 30 1853, 23-24).[27] Aware of the easy temptation to crime on such minimal subsistence, the chaplains made recurring pleas to the churches for "Christian benevolence and charity" to these unfortunates. Luckey was at the center of the effort to prod the inspectors to increase state aid in this matter. In his 1845 report he thanked them for granting his request for greater material assistance to the newly released prisoners (Sen. Doc. 9 1845, 38-39).

Sabbath schools were an attempt to evangelize the inmates and provide rudimentary education at the same time. The state did not initially make provision for schooling and no books were provided by the institution. The Bible thus became both spiritual guide and textbook. Classes were held after the mandatory attendance at Sabbath services. Barrett, at Sing Sing, would teach his charges to memorize the biblical verses that they read, once claiming that his thirty-five students memorized 770 chapters in an eighteen-week period (PDS 1829, 25). Chaplain Morrill, at Auburn, called the Sabbath school "a gentle shower upon a thirsty land" (Sen. Doc. 8 1845, 86). Throughout the first twenty years after the opening of the penitentiaries, the schools continued only with the interruptions periodically ordered by penal officials. All the while the chaplains continued to advance their concern that the state begin to "provide some means of teaching the ignorant to read" (Sen. Doc. 7 1838). They supported their proposals with the formidable evidence, discovered in their pastoral visits, linking ignorance and crime. By 1846 the Auburn inspectors were similarly convinced and successfully petitioned the state government to release funds for education:

> In our last annual report we recommended, and the Legislature has authorized, an appropriation from the funds of the prison, for the purpose of instructing the convicts in the rudiments of learning. It appears from the reports now and heretofore made by the chaplains, that about one-fourth of the convicts received in this prison can neither read nor write (Inspectors of Auburn 1848, 3).

The original vision of the penitentiaries provided for long hours of labor punctuated by hours of silence at the end of the day, and a Sabbath given to the purposes of prayer, reflection, and Bible reading. Evangelicals were at first adamant that only the Bible and religious tracts be made available to the prisoners. Dickerson expressed this view as he quoted the words of a reborn Christian: "Ah, said he, my mind was so full of Tom Paine, Voltaire, and such other writings, that I had no room when I first came here for this blessed book" (Sen. Doc. 13 1834, 18).

As many of the chaplains, through their exposure to the personal histories of the inmates, came to embrace new understandings concerning crime, they concluded that education was central to good citizenship and a moral life. This commitment led to the establishment of prison libraries. Once again, this development originated within the religious community and only much later, and reluctantly, was it accepted by the state. Luckey wrote Governor Seward in 1839 in this regard:

It appears evident to me that while punishment of crime is rendered necessary for the peace and safety of society, and it is therefore consistent with the principles of Christianity, humanity and religion require that such punishment be not unnecessarily aggravated by withholding from the delinquents the means of moral and intellectual improvement (Luckey 1860, 21-22).

Seward was most positive in his reply:

I have great pleasure in saying that all its suggestions seem to me both wise and benevolent. It is my purpose to call the attention of the Legislature to the expediency of making some legislative provision for the instruction of convicts in the prisons, and I find myself sustained and enlightened by your communication (Luckey 1860, 23).

It took a year to secure state funding for the project. In the meantime, Seward personally financed the initial library acquisitions.[28]

Disunity in the Protestant Empire

The libraries, as it turned out, were to become centers of controversy on several occasions, previewing an irreversible chasm within American Protestantism. Chaplains saw it as their duty to evaluate the books to be read in terms of their accommodation to the religious focus of the institution. Chaplain Parmelee at Clinton inspected the cells of the inmates each week "removing improper books" (Sen. Doc. 16 1850, 331). Chaplain Cooke at Auburn wrote: "In the selection of the Library, care has been taken to exclude works of a sectarian character, while at the same time the best practical treatises of the different evangelical Christian denominations have been indiscriminately admitted" (Sen. Doc. 16 1850, 122).

Sentimentalism began to demonstrate its influence on social relations during the 1840s and its central vehicle was the novel. Evangelical chaplains adamantly opposed the introduction of such romantic literature into the prisons, no one more so than Luckey. He engaged in a heated confrontation with the matron of the women's facility at Sing Sing over her startling innovations in penitentiary discipline, among them the reading of popular novels.

Eliza Farnham began her controversial tenure as matron in 1844 after a series of disorderly outbursts among the female prisoners.[29] An atheist by upbringing and a Protestant by profession, she was committed to the school of thought popular during that time called Phrenology. The

Phrenologists believed that the brain was divided into four compartments: the animal propensities, the moral sentiments, the intellectual faculty, and the reflective element. Simply stated, they held that convicts were those with an inordinately expanded section of the brain's animal propensities. This could be verified by an examination of the skull.[30] Charles Caldwell, an early advocate, expressed the theory in this way:

> [S]earch the records of public executions, and it will be found, that where one individual, of good moral developments, has suffered capital punishment, fifty, at least, with ruffian heads, have surrendered their lives to offended justice. On the truth of this, the friends of Phrenology might safely hazard the fate of science. Observation confirms it (Caldwell 1829, 25).

The important consequence of this theory was that the criminal was involuntarily motivated to deviant behavior. Farnham believed that some, by gentle influence, could be nurtured into health. She also held, to the further dismay of Luckey, that some were incapable of reform and must, reluctantly, be subject to chains, straight jackets, and mouthgaps (W. D. Lewis 1965, 239).

Although Luckey was among those with a growing appreciation of the power of social facts to influence human behavior, he was still molded in the revivalist tradition. The eradication of problems in the social environment was never intended to circumvent the need for conversion by means of divine power. The dispute over control of the library came to symbolize the rift within Protestantism. It was fought over the role of religion in an era of expanded government control of institutions, and increased rational regulation of the social milieu.

Farnham and her assistant, Georgiana Bruce Kirby, wrested control of the library from Luckey and Miss Knox, the evangelical assistant matron. Kirby related that Knox would read aloud to the women from "some dry evangelical book" and "was bent on converting them, and saving their souls from hell in the next world, while we worked to help them to lead better lives in this" (Kirby 1971, 199-200).

Farnham instituted the reading of popular novels and works of Phrenology during meals. Luckey's wife, a volunteer in the women's section, reported that works such as Nicholas Nickelby, Oliver Twist, and The Wandering Heiress were being read while the Bible was only recited on "funeral occasions" (NYPA 1847, 51).[31]

To make matters even more alarming for traditionalists, Farnham greatly softened the strict environment of the penitentiary and, finally, dispensed with the rule of absolute silence in January 1846.[32]

The dispute between the two figures grew into a statewide debate over the continued authority of the evangelical understanding that social analysis was never meant to replace the central role of religious conversion.   In the confrontation that followed the inspectors fully supported the chaplain while the influential New York Prison Association, headed by Luckey's former ally, John Edmonds, took up the cause of the matron.[33] In the final showdown with the inspectors, the appointment of Farnham was maintained and the embittered Luckey was released.

The new chaplain, Matthew Gordon, a Presbyterian and a recent graduate of Union Theological Seminary in New York City, was hardly prepared to fathom the ministerial demands of the penitentiary, let alone the upheaval that had left much of the staff demoralized and resentful. The principal keeper, Harmon Eldridge, smarting over the removal of Luckey and particularly resistant to his replacement, unexpectedly resigned.   Gordon was now forced temporarily to assume the responsibilities of Eldridge as well (Sen. Doc. 153 1847, 4).

The inspectors publicly bemoaned the "feeble state of discipline" and the mounting resistance to the rule of silence "heretofore strictly observed" but now "almost entirely disregarded when the convicts are together, and not much observed in the workshops" (Sen. Doc. 153 1847, 4). They laid the blame directly at the feet of Farnham and called for the reinstatement of the former religious discipline:

> The matron has spent much time during her stay there in the examination of heads . . . We regret that this element should have been introduced into the government of the prison. We hope it may not be permitted any longer to interfere with holy endeavors to be merciful and kind to the prisoner. We trust that the old fashioned wisdom, founded on the word of God, may soon take the place of the "sublime" truths of phrenology (Sen. Doc.153 1847, .5).

The altercation that surfaced two sharply divergent trends in the philosophy of penology finally ended when Farnham resigned in 1848.

In this most revelatory confrontation there were numerous portents of the coming Progressive Era. Farnham and her supporters maintained that her innovative programs had their origin in Christian principles. They believed that the inmate was a victim of circumstance and needed gentle and personal rehabilitation. Luckey, an advocate of both free will and what might be termed supra-rational forces, advocated firm discipline as well as institutional and social programs aimed at spiritual renewal and eradicating environmental defects. Still others, like Gordon's successor, J. Green, retained the evangelical demand for conversion but were beginning to evoke the socially conservative "pre-millenialism" that would later evolve into Fundamentalism. Green said it was the prisoners' "own wrong" that convicted them and "not that of the law or the courts." His mission was to proclaim "the only and all-sufficient atonement of the Lamb of God who taketh away the sin of the world, and whose blood cleanseth from all sin" (Sen. Doc. 16 1850, 260).

It was becoming apparent that the original vision of behavioral uniformity, silent congregate labor, spiritual renewal, and an institution that paid its own bills was an impossible illusion. After the enactment of legislation banning corporal punishment, the inspectors at Auburn seemed to indicate a more realistic understanding of the enormity of their task:

> Our great effort has been to rescue and preserve this institution from debt, while maintaining in letter and spirit the restrictions and limitations of the act of 1842, in relation to the prisoners, and at the same time to take care that the system of discipline which has been an example to others, should not fail in our hands (Sen. Doc. 8 1845, 6).

The two roads to the Kingdom of God that have been presented in this chapter reveal the overwhelming influence of the Pennsylvania Quakers, and the heirs of Calvinism in New York and Massachusetts, on the development of the penal system. While the Quakers proceeded with much greater singleness of purpose, their emphasis on individual treatment, coupled with impending financial and administrative difficulties rendered by the Civil War, would propel their penal philosophy in dramatically new directions. Meanwhile, the reform-minded New York Prison Association, aided by the return of Luckey to Sing Sing in 1855, would begin to look elsewhere for a restorative environment to replace the once-proud penitentiaries. The rival systems, it turned out, were to agree that the hope of American penology was to be found in the reformatory.

CHAPTER 4

SENTIMENTALISM, SCIENCE, AND
THE PROGRESSIVE MOVEMENT

Prisons are isolated places. Their affairs and the anguish of their inhabitants are designed to be hidden from the law-abiding populace. As the frequency of public punishments began to decline during the Enlightenment, psychological and social conformity had to be instilled by other means. The era of treatment began to replace the reign of terror. Foucault commented on this shift of emphasis from affliction of the body to refashioning the soul of the offender:

> The old partners of the spectacle of punishment, the body and the blood, gave way. A new character came on the scene, masked. It was the end of a certain kind of tragedy; comedy began, with shadow play, faceless voices, impalpable entities. The apparatus of punitive justice must now bite into this bodiless reality (1979, 16-17).

Despite the contagious spirit of civic renewal often generated by social movements, the enclosed architecture and restricted nature of the prison, coupled with the weight of the personal pursuits of the average citizen, inevitably distance the affairs of these institutions from the mind of the public. Judge Gershom Powers once told a new inmate at Auburn:

[I]nstead of now enjoying the inestimable privileges of a free American citizen, of social intercourse, and the endearments of home and friends, you appear in culprit robes, doomed to the gloomy solitude of a prison, where the smiles of kindred and friends can never cheer your gloomy abode ... You are to be literally buried from the world (W. D. Lewis 1965, 114-15).

This shadowy environment is suddenly brought into the light, however, when the scale of social calm and self-absorption is tipped by a rise in the rate of crime. John Stuart Mill argued that self-interest, as well as benevolence toward the innocent victim, unite to form a common demand for justice when social deviance increases (Mill 1957, 64-65). Public cries for safety and order reanimate the debates over punishment, the nature of crime, and the shape of its cure. If the public outcry leads to increased arrests and commitments to penal institutions, there is an inevitable strain on accommodations, resources, and often the operating philosophy of the institutions. This proved to be particularly true for the American penitentiaries with a ruling logic based on silence, separate housing, and the attempt to implement a cost-effective discipline.

The number of crimes began to increase dramatically during the 1860s. Urban growth, expanded industry with consequent class antagonisms, the large number of veterans returning from the war,[1] and multitudes of freed slaves added to the basic and enduring social problems of poverty, poor education, and mental and emotional instability that traditionally generate the highest percentage of the prison population. Together, these factors overwhelmed penal facilities. On October 1, 1860 there were 2,659 inhabitants in the New York State penitentiaries, 237 more than the number of cells (Sen. Doc. 25 1861, 7). This disparity increased noticeably as the decade progressed.

Although the following report of the Massachusetts Board of State Charities was unable to account for the growth in the criminal population, it echoed a common theme within the prison reform community that something new must be undertaken:

With the large expenditures made for the criminal class, with our great advantages of education and Christianity, should not crime decrease? While confining and punishing the criminal, cannot something more be done to improve his morals and effect a permanent reformation in his character? (1878, xlix)

Perhaps the most telling harbinger of a new age in penal philosophy occurred in 1867. In that year, the Pennsylvania General Assembly denied a request by the inspectors of the Eastern Penitentiary for the construction of new cell blocks to accommodate the rising number of commitments (E. Pen. 1868, 26). If separate cells were to be sacrificed for the sake of economy, or any other reason, the entire philosophy and organization of the Pennsylvania system was being jarred at its foundations. The days of internal cohesion between the Quakers of the Philadelphia Prison Society and their counterparts in the legislature had come to an end. A new organizational logic was about to emerge and Richard Vaux, the son of Roberts Vaux (who had laid the cornerstone of the Eastern Penitentiary), was to be the chief voice in providing it. Indeed, by the 1870s there would be but few hints of the penitentiary systems heretofore described but, as in the prior period, it would be the religious community that would originate the new developments.

Sentiment and the Age of Romanticism

We saw in the last chapter that there was a humanitarian and evangelical backlash in the 1840s to the brutalizing discipline that had characterized the institutions based on the silent system. The reaction was triggered in part by a movement of sentimentalism that originated during that time and slowly came to govern the thinking of much of the Protestant community, and hence much of the nation, in the ensuing decades. Besides a continuation of the evangelical focus on benevolent social activity, the delicate virtues came to be extolled in literature and social intercourse.   The most cogent sociological explanation for the phenomenon was that the churches, which are powerful mediators of new information and social change, were in large part dominated by women. One writer viewed the era as a "feminization" of American culture. It was perhaps the final nail in the coffin of traditional Puritanism, a time in which the "Pink and White Tyranny," characterized in the writing of Harriet Beecher Stowe, captured the imagination of the country while the more sober, Calvinist-flavored compositions of Thoreau and Melville were largely ignored (Douglas 1977, 8).

This turn to romanticism had been an element in the sharp dispute between John Luckey and Eliza Farnham at Sing Sing. That controversy bore witness to a widening fault in what was, for the most part, a united evangelical domain.   The threads holding the religious community together would continue to unravel and create several disparate, if not hostile, camps.

The figure of Lyman Beecher looms large in tracing the origins of this trend. The reader will recall that Beecher was a lifelong enemy of liberalism in general, and the Unitarians in particular, who had moved to

Boston in 1826 to instill the revival spirit in that city. He promoted the Arminian idea of "sameness," that the heart's natural longing for God would be the basis of creating an evangelical empire in America that was democratic and virtuous. He advanced "the renewed dream of an organic and tightly-knit community made up of like-minded people who worshiped the same God the same way and who imparted to one another a sense of wholeness" (Marty 1984, 234). This dream of the organic unity of humankind, predicated on the emotional expression of deeply held religious values, was at the heart of the sentimentalist movement, the leading figure of which was Beecher's daughter, Harriet Beecher Stowe.[2]

Despite its benevolent leanings the movement was fundamentally conservative. The educated middle class women who dominated the churches of the Northeast lacked social power and, therefore, asserted themselves chiefly through the one medium of communication society had opened to them, literature. These admirers of Stowe's Little Eva were to express influence "through the exploration of their feminine identity as their society defined it" (Douglas 1977, 8). Thus the matriarchal values of nurture, generosity, and acceptance came to prominence in public discourse, leading to the creation of a "culture of feelings." Douglas adds: "They inevitably confused theology with religiosity, religiosity with literature, and literature with self-justification" (1977, 8).

Such an ethic was incapable of mounting a serious challenge to, or providing an adequate explanation of, the growing social problems facing the nation in the Civil War era. It led its adherents to forego the more critical socio-political analysis of traditional Calvinism in favor of an exoneration of the prevailing distribution of power and wealth.

Among the many publications that orchestrated this new understanding was *The Presbyterian Sabbath School Visitor*. In one issue the children were warned of the danger of "bad boys" and reminded of the Bible teaching that "evil communication corrupts good manners":

> By disregarding this important Bible truth, Tom Wilson very gradually came to be, notwithstanding his mother's teachings, and those he received in the Sabbath-school, a bad boy like those with whom he played . . . Boys! Avoid wicked playmates. Shun them as you would shun savage wild beasts (Feb. 1866, 6).[3]

Whereas the preaching of Lyman Beecher and Finney was exhortatory and aimed at bringing the sinner to an immediate decision, the revivals of the 1850s featured a more optimistic and genial tone. The Reverend DeWitt Talmage defined religion in terms that revealed how far romantic sentiment had progressed: "Religion is sweetness, and perfume, and spikenard, and saffron, and cinnamon, and cassia, and frankincense, and all sweet spices together" (Weisberger 1958, 172).

Henry Ward Beecher, Lyman's son, was a leading figure in the revivals during this period.   The flames of hell and the profound seriousness of conversion to the Christian life, that had dominated revival preaching from Jonathan Edwards to Charles Finney, were seldom found in his sermons:

> We are come by virtue of our Christian life, my dear brethren, not to self-denial, and to pain, and to repentance, and to sorrow, and to limitation . . . There are thousands that say, "How can I become a Christian? How can I give up my husband? How can I give up my children? How can I give up my occupation!" Who asks you to give them up? "But do not you tell me that I must give up every thing for Christ?" No, I do not tell you any such thing as that. I tell you that you must *keep* every thing for Christ (Henry Ward Beecher 1869, 153-154).

Clearly, the new ideas of progressive evolution, science, and critical social analysis embraced, and in some cases pioneered, by a segment of the religious community would find little acceptance among the devotees of sentimentalism.

Positivist Science and Progressivism

The leading voices in penal reform in the last half of the nineteenth century: John Luckey, Richard Vaux, Enoch Wines of the New York Prison Association, Franklin B. Sanborn of the Massachusetts State Board of Charities, and Zebulon Brockway, superintendent of the Elmira Reformatory, were all influenced by the evangelical movements of the pre-bellum era. Each came to embrace a more detached, and scientific approach to penology as Positivism and sociology grew in influence. Although many criminologists and historians interpret this shift as a decline in the influence of religious ideas and the ethical, "holistic" approach of evangelicals such as Lyman Beecher, the use of an analytical methodology to study social phenomena was often spearheaded by the religious community, particularly the chaplains.

The irony of liberal Protestantism is that it receded in vocal and visible influence to the degree that it was successful in accomplishing its ends. Indeed, the ideology of Progressivism, with its confident belief in a harmonious future, actualized by the application of reason, expanded government, and scientific method to the problems of the individual, was, to a great extent, a secular metaphor for the evangelical millennial kingdom. Millennial energies were being redirected in terms of the very ideals that the political philosophy of Calvinism had always upheld: moral government, equality, democratic participation, a covenanted public life, and a trust in the providential hand of God guiding the course of human history. As H. Richard Niebuhr said: "Protestantism could not fail to draw the conclusion that renunciation of power by the church was the inescapable corollary of its acknowledgment of the sovereignty of God" (1937, 33). He also stated: "Insofar as the Kingdom was conceived in social terms the faith in its coming was transformed into a belief in progress" (1937, 83).[4]

In this environment of secular confidence, linguistic expressions, that both reflect and define reality, inevitably began to change. The term "manhood" became a popular referent for "Christian." Repeatedly, chaplains and penal officials in the Progressive Age would use the term as the goal of the correctional and social project. The New York State Commission of Prisons said of the inmates that not only must their bodies be kept in good condition, but their moral and mental attributes should be strengthened thus "stirring in those men, in whom it has never been stirred before, the spirit of manhood" (NY Sen. Doc. 15 1898, 68). Alvah S. Barker, the evangelical superintendent of the Concord Reformatory, saw this difference between the reformatory and the penitentiary: "The purpose has been to maintain discipline by appealing to the manhood of the prisoner, rather than enforcing obedience to rules through fear of punishment" (MA Prison Commissioners 1908).[5]

The state became for the liberal Protestants the predominant agent in the creation of the reign of God. It was the visible symbol of the faith of the Puritan founders, refined in the fires of the revivals. The term "Christian civilization" was commonly employed by the progressives, reflecting the earlier influence of millennial thinking. Instead of the need to create institutions that would call society to conversion, as in the Jacksonian era, the new optimism insisted that there was nothing fundamentally wrong with American society, and therefore penal facilities should be modeled on the social environment, emulating its individualist orientation. Charles A. Collin, an instructor at Elmira, gave this testimony to the beneficence of the state and its necessary usurping of the role once claimed by the churches that have now become "invisible":

> The church has lost this machinery and will never regain it. But behold the State has already done this work better than the church ever could. Here and now, the State has seized these sinners, has

cleaned them up, is giving them the requisite physical diet and discipline, and is to-day calling to the invisible church: We have cleared away the entrance, come in and feed these famished souls with the bread of life (NY Sen. Doc. 9 1886, 31).

Edward Townsend, warden at the Eastern Penitentiary, said in his report for 1870 that legislation (not religious conversion) was "now undoubtedly necessary for the changing condition of our social system" (E. Pen. 1871, 6).[6] In like manner, Richard Vaux insisted that the "moral power wanting in society" is education, "moral, mental, mechanical and scientific" (1862, 22).

Positivism, once maligned by both Unitarians and strict evangelicals, was now understood to be eminently compatible with the religiously grounded social optimism fed by social scientific analysis. A Unitarian journal defined the system is these terms: "Its design is nothing less than the *recasting of the whole system of modern thought and knowledge on the basis given in the method of the natural sciences*" (The Christian Examiner March 1851, 178-79). Its founder, Comte, and its leading spokesperson, Herbert Spencer, believed that with the advancement of knowledge, the authority once given to religion would be accorded to science. Parsons asserts that it was a natural extension of Utilitarianism, replacing the subjective, pleasure-oriented explanation of action with the non-subjective correlates of heredity and environment (1968, 67).[7]

Positivism, when applied to criminology, notably in the Italian school, was expressed in several major theorems. First, punishment of the inmate was fruitless since he or she was reacting to either hereditary or environmental defects. Therefore, crime must be attacked at the genetic level (sterilization and state control over sexual reproduction, particularly among deviants), and/or at the environmental level (concern with poverty, education, and familial surroundings, as well as creating a penal environment where the inmate could be molded to the beneficial and industrious habits of the good society).   Second, the Positivists emphasized that criminals must be treated individually, on a case by case basis, since each one manifested the particular stamp of supra-rational influences.

David Rothman declared, "in effect, all Progressive programs assumed one outstanding feature: they required discretionary responses to each case" (1980, 6). For those who disdained or were simply incapable of responding to treatment programs, the only hope was to provide for the defense of society by keeping them incarcerated. Andrew von Hirsch explains the positivist ideology in this way:

> Its aim was to prevent further crimes by convicted offenders, when those crimes might be forestalled through rehabilitative efforts, treatment programs should be tried. But to the extent that the success of such programs was uncertain, the offenders who were bad risks could always be restrained (1985, 5).

The growing involvement of key religious figures in the analysis and elevation of environmental factors as a catalyst for criminal behavior, coupled with the enduring inheritance of millennial optimism, provided the necessary intellectual and social channel through which the previously disparaged positivist theory could find acceptance within the American cultural and social milieu. Formerly strict evangelicals, galvanized by the vacuous social interpretation of their sentimental counterparts, and invigorated by the new analytical insights, paved the way for the appearance of liberal Protestantism and the Social Gospel movement.

D. G. Mayhew, moral instructor at Elmira, gave a clear statement of the positivist, progressive mentality in this 1881 plea to the New York legislature:

> Oh, Empire State, yield not your claim! Foremost now among earth's governments in the idea of reform and restoration of the criminal, made criminal by heredity and environment, which means State neglect; falter not in your march! Make louder your cry—"give me back my children" (Sen. Doc. 26 1882, 7).

Pennsylvania

A number of factors coincided to insure the inevitable triumph of the progressive agenda within the state institutions: the resistance to classification and the consequent individual emphasis of the separate system, the early recognition on the part of officials and church leaders of the significant impact of the social milieu on misconduct, the more concentrated employment of statistical analysis,[8] and the inability of the legislature to economically sustain the deficit-ridden penitentiaries.

Officials turned their creative attention to possible new penal arrangements in an effort to ascertain how an effective system could be constructed, given the constraints of the architecture and general philosophy of the Eastern Penitentiary. The inspectors of the Western Penitentiary had already decided that the financial limitations placed on prison industry by the separate system, as well as the impossibility of maintaining an individual cellular format in view of the increased inmate population, were simply too compelling to warrant the continuance of that approach.[9] In 1869 the prison was reorganized along the Auburn model to allow for the congregation of prisoners in workshops. The Eastern Penitentiary was now the only institution in the United States governed under the separate strategy.

The case of the Western Penitentiary revealed the dilemmas the inspectors in Philadelphia were soon to discover. Their yearly reports throughout the 1860s continued to lament the profit motive of the rival penitentiaries, even as Vaux and his associates grew more methodical and scientific in their analysis.

Weber maintained that the progress of rationalization in the West inevitably favored the expansion of capitalism. This theory was validated in the ascent of Progressivism in the United States, and Pennsylvania was no exception. To accept an ideology that points to an American Christian civilization as the model in which the inmate must be socialized, and consistently to uphold the individual as the central focus of penal efforts, establishes the cultural conditions receptive to rational economic methods. The long resistance of the Eastern Penitentiary to automation was simply an anachronism as the institution lost one element after another of the system envisioned by Roberts Vaux. It may be appropriate to consider a psychological factor underlying the prolonged resistance to labor in common: Richard Vaux may have been compelled by an unarticulated familial allegiance to retain the skeleton of the separate system (work and silence within the cells) even as overcrowding forced the end of single housing and undermined the spiritual significance of isolation.

The Role of the Religious Community

Since the religious community, so fully represented at each level of institutional decision making, had embraced the factors instrumental in the development of Progressivism, it showed little resistance to the sweeping changes that were to come in its wake. The decided sociological orientation of many of its public figures enabled the largely evangelical membership to resist the trend toward romanticism and quickly reflect the growing liberal religious perspective. There were, of course, some who were hesitant to accept the growing fascination with criminal anthropology and criminal sociology. Chaplain Joseph Welch stated that viewing ignorance or poverty "as the efficient cause or causes of crime, seems the merest child's play" in the presence of the reality of "inherent depravity" (E. Pen. 1892, 97-98). J. Y. Ashton also revealed a Calvinist leaning in his reports. He once stated:

> Others think that a man once in a felon's cell must be reformed before the Gospel can reach him. He is expected to overcome his besetting sin by his own volition . . . This is a species of Pharisaism that could say 'You must become as good as I am before you can look for the advantages of grace' (E. Pen. 1888, 150).

These orthodox views, however, so common a generation earlier, seemed strangely misplaced amid the rapid advance of the new penology. Moral instructors like John Ruth, who presided over the institution during its years of revision, were avid proponents of the new developments. Note how progressive language, laden with environmental references, was utilized over the previous emphasis on conversion:

> It is a sad comment upon Christian civilization, when prison science is evoked to perform the work which parents and guardians have so sadly neglected. Nevertheless, it is a source of rejoicing to those who are interested in these youthful criminals, whose crimes have been superinduced by the neglect of their natural protectors, to know that they are placed under competent instructors immediately on their entrance into prison (E. Pen. 1865, 71)

The Philadelphia Society, too, the strategic force behind virtually all reforms in penal practice from the revising of the criminal code to the establishment of the Huntingdon Reformatory, was imbued with progressive optimism:

> It is often truly said that progress 'is the order of the day'. No one who notes the characteristics of the age we live in can doubt it . . . All things are manifestly tending with a rapidity unknown before toward their final consummation, the full development of their capacities, and their largest influence upon the condition and destiny of our race . . . The past is a picture of darkness, and error, and corruption, and moral death, from which the eye turns instinctively to the brighter picture of the present and the future (The Pennsylvania Journal 1894-1895, 9).

Richard Vaux

Richard Vaux became an inspector of the Eastern Penitentiary in 1842. He remained an inspector for 53 years, nine as secretary of the Board, and 43 years as its president. Among his notable accomplishments during that span was his election as mayor of Philadelphia (1855). Yet, throughout his tenure, he never relinquished firm control over the leadership of the prison. He oversaw the appointment of the wardens and used his influence and intellect to reshape the state's penal philosophy. Michael Cassidy, warden from 1881-1900, wrote of him:

> Mr. Vaux was the exponent of the [separate] system, and the Eastern Penitentiary will never be mentioned or remembered without associating his name with it. He has stamped it with his own individuality and characteristics. To serve continuously for fifty-three years for the good and uplifting of unfortunate human beings, and that without pay, reward, or advantage, is such a noble self-sacrifice that it should enshrine the name and memory of Mr. Vaux as a great benefactor of his race (Cassidy 1897, 6).

Vaux was a Quaker and in later life a Mason. He exemplified the movement among many Protestants from evangelicalism to a liberal, ethical Christian stance. He said in 1864 that progress was the result of the united action of "science, philosophy, and Christianity" under the influence of "the developed powers of mind, knowledge and experience," all leading to a "better and more exact" civilization (E. Pen. 1864, 6, 8-9). Truth was no longer opaque but clearly revealed in scientific method: "these statistics held like a mirror before the face of veneered civilization, will show what manner of face it really has" (E. Pen. 1864, 13).

Like many of his liberal counterparts, his revival-centered faith was slowly transformed by the appeal of factual data which provided a novel and seemingly crystalline portrait of the nature of crime and the prescription for its remedy. He said such evidence "partakes of the character of truth, is derived from no theory, is the result of no misconception" (E. Pen. 1862, 7). Penal methods had to change not in a rebuke to Christianity but as an extension of its mission. The evolution of civilization from one phase to another would be augmented by the conjunction of church and state, aided by the sure revelations of statistical analysis, and not, as formerly, by "platitudes in the garb of official language." This would enable the creation of penal and social environments capable of influencing the felon into sociability:

> Indeed the question becomes significant how many criminals has society itself made by its peculiar phase of civilization, as it is called. And then it becomes material to inquire and determine what system of prison treatment will re-educate those vicious and criminal from such causes (E. Pen. 1864, 11).

The answer for Vaux was to be found in the combination of the individual emphasis of the original system, coupled with the practice of granting primacy to the environmental causes of crime. His dedication to the individual approach, so central to the progressive methods about to appear, marks him as a key figure in championing the new methodology:

> [Pennsylvania] preserves, cultivates, teaches the individuality of the convicts; their personal relations to society and their fellow man, and the God of that newer dispensation which seeks for the soul of man, not that of a class, and proclaimed that it were better, individually, to receive the whole promise of the gospel, than to gain the world without it (E. Pen. 1865, 6).

He was an early representative of the Social Gospel movement that would exercise great influence in liberal Protestant circles. Crime would be erased, and the reign of God would be hastened, by analysis of systemic shortcomings and the application of government-sponsored programs to eradicate them. He called for liberality in public expenditure, but always preceded by a thorough investigation "of the social structure and its defects, errors, evils, vices, crimes, and their causes, and that which would tend to remove or change them" (E. Pen. 1871, 9).

Years before the opening of the Reformatory at Elmira, Vaux had already adopted much of the language and many of the ideas that would define that most influential institution. He gave energetic attention and emphasis to the problems and needs of young offenders–the segment of the population most vulnerable to corrupting social influences. As a result, he and his associates in the Philadelphia Prison Society lobbied for the enactment of a commutation law, a form of the indeterminate sentence, in which good conduct by a prisoner would enable him or her to be discharged prior to completion of their term. "Time is no true element in punishment by imprisonment," he stated. The effort was successful and an important progressive innovation was signed into law (E. Pen. 1871, 25-26).[10]

Classification, unneeded before the penitentiary became overcrowded, and long reviled by former inspectors, was being practiced by 1874: "the whole number of convicts is divided into primary divisions—crimes against persons and crimes against property. Then each is again subdivided, by age, education, social relations, cause of crime, and term of sentence" (E. Pen. 1875, 48).

This statement in his report for the year 1861 again foreshadowed many of the basic elements that would later define the American penological approach:

Crime then, in it social aspect, embraces the treatment of the criminal during his imprisonment, as a science. It involves in this science, the consideration of the causes of crime, as discovered by the operations of its reformatory regimen. It devolves on the legislative authority, the duty of applying remedies for these causes. What these remedies may be, can only be determined by the most careful examination of the aggregate of crimes over an extended period of time (E. Pen. 1862, 42).

The method he was advancing would enable Vaux to utilize the physical structure of the Eastern Penitentiary, while at the same time amending its time-honored tradition of individual quartering, in the face of the expanded criminal population and the refusal of the legislature to allocate funds for either expansion or a new facility. The optimism that once filled the reports of the inspectors over the moral conversions being wrought in the silence of the cell was replaced with a new optimism, one concerning the discovery and treatment of the unique problems of the individual inmates:

As the Pennsylvania system is the separate treatment of convicts, its character is maintained in all its relations to the prisoner. His individuality is never merged nor mitigated. His habits, youth-training, education, industrial, social and communital relations; crime-cause; mental, moral and physical healthiness, each, like his personal identity, stand alone (E. Pen. 1863, 8).

As with his contemporaries in the Progressive movement, Vaux's faith was most deeply present in the manner in which he invoked a profound hope for the future, manifested in expanded bureaucratic programs. Rational, secular institutions gave new shape to the old evangelical optimism and social concern. Yet religious faith and imagery formed a secondary language which, as Robert Bellah and his colleagues claim, lies beneath the primary language of American individualism (Bellah et al 1985, 154). The religiously motivated socio-political assumptions that preceded and shaped Progressivism frequently unveiled themselves in the midst of scientific language and analysis. The earlier Calvinist and revivalist belief that some were simply ontologically or environmentally incapable of receiving the grace of salvation had been translated into an affection for the Italian theorist Lombroso's popular belief that hereditary factors made certain inmates incapable of reform: "Hereditary crime-cause makes it next to impossible to prevent those who are afflicted by it from committing crime" (E. Pen. 1887, 16).[11] Yet, in describing the constitutionally defective inmates, he once reflected that in time they may try to form better associations, for with God "all things are possible" (E. Pen. 1880, 86). He would on occasion fall back on his biblical upbringing when attempting to explain a particular occurrence. Describing the effects of congregate prisons on former Pennsylvania inmates, he stated: "Then goeth he and taketh to him seven other spirits more wicked than himself, and they enter in and dwell there, and the last state of that man is worse than the first" (E. Pen. 1878, 28).

The shape of Vaux's commitment to Positivism and Progressivism enabled the Eastern Penitentiary to continue for another half century, embracing elements of both the past and the present. Since the facility never experienced the severe scandals and pronounced failures of some of the penitentiaries based on the silent system, and probably because of Vaux's own personal attachment to the institution, it was both unnecessary and physically impossible for it to incorporate all of the particular programs of reformatory discipline. That task was left to the reformers in the New York Prison Association.

New York and Massachusetts

The combination of humanitarian sentiment and revulsion at the violent regimes of the 1830s led to a more relaxed atmosphere in the penitentiaries of these states in the decades preceding the Civil War. Romanticism invaded the New York penal system, reflecting the state's more polarized religious landscape, and setting the stage for a concerted response from the developing modernist faction. Warden Throop, at the Clinton penitentiary, spoke of the inmate in a manner that would make the children of Lyman Beecher proud:

> [S]mile upon that iron heart with words of love, patiently, unweariedly, until we should feel some pulse of good throbbing yet, perhaps with the mystic beatings which it learned in some departed mother's arms. Holy memories of childhood shall rush upon that long shrouded soul--voices of early innocence shall ring like Sabbath-church bells long forgotten, calling him back to innocence and peace (NY Sen. Doc. 30 1849).

Warden Salisbury, at Auburn, was another evangelical given to sentimental musings. He spoke thus of the chapel services:

> 'Tis here that the thoughts are sent careening *back* upon the past, *in* upon the yearning necessities of the inner life, and *on* to the stern realities of the coming future. 'Tis here that the faces of the absent

and loved ones are made to put on a *beauty* and *distinctness* of outline which art cannot imitate. 'Tis here, and in *their* presence, that the heart is moved by the rush of memories that bind them to the *innocent* and the *long-ago* (Sen. Doc. 16 1869, 93).

Among the chaplains, P. G. Cooke, at Auburn, was particularly fond of the tract, "A dying Mother's Counsels to her Son," in his evangelical labors.

Despite these examples of sentimentality, the main pursuits of the officials of the New York and Massachusetts penitentiaries remained fairly constant. Inspectors, and the wardens they appointed, still subject to the whims of, and pressures placed on, newly elected administrations, continued to concentrate on financial affairs. As mentioned in the last chapter, however, the restrictions placed on corporal discipline were not conducive to the requirement of enforced labor. The persistent demand for self-supporting institutions only exacerbated internal pressures. For example, in 1854 and 1855, all of the reports filed by the inspectors and wardens were concerned with lawsuits filed by contractors for loss of property due to willful damage and fires caused by inmates resisting the work imposed upon them.

The violent reaction of the inmates was not surprising given the conditions within the workshops. By 1856 the "miniature slavery" that characterized the administrations of Lynds and Wiltse had largely been abrogated, yet inmates at Auburn still averaged 10 hours 23 minutes of daily labor, Sing Sing, 9 hours 47 minutes, and Clinton, 10 hours 30 minutes (Sen. Doc. 110 1857, 7). Punishments were common and the fixtures of the silent system–the lockstep, striped uniforms, the downcast eyes, and strict silence were still being imposed on the reluctant convicts.

As financial losses mounted and disciplinary infractions increased, the officials of New York, for different reasons than Pennsylvania, were also looking for a new penal configuration to offset the problems they faced.

While the wardens and inspectors concentrated on their immediate problems, the chaplains, by and large, continued to fill their reports with statistical charts seeking to explain the rush of new prisoners into the already crowded institutions. In the same report in which Warden Throop indulged in Christian sentimentalism, Chaplain Green, at Sing Sing, provided statistics on the county of conviction, occupation, place of birth, term of sentence, age, race, recidivism, and marital status of the inmate population (Sen. Doc. 30 1849, 255ff).

Chaplain Luckey continued to be a dominant presence in his second tenure at Sing Sing (1855-64), as he had been in his first. A sentimental encomium was offered by warden G. B. Hubbell that reveals something of the reputation the chaplain had established: "Other ministers may wear resplendent stars in the crown of their glory, but few, like him, will wear such stars, not only in their crowns, but studding all over their robes of purest white" (Sen. Doc. 9 1864, 44).

The historian, W. D. Lewis, mentions that Luckey's objective was to understand the criminal mind by a thorough study of the backgrounds of convicts. This was not only to become a basic tenet of progressive philosophy, it would also be a staple technique of social work in general, and probation and parole departments in particular. Lewis calls him "New York's pioneer penal caseworker" (1965, 212).

Luckey followed a daily routine of "making diligent inquiries of sheriffs and other visitors, concerning the character and habits of convicts previous to their coming here, as well as after their discharge." He studied all the letters sent to the inmates "which contain much data from which can be inferred the predominant propensities of those to whom they are addressed." He also spent much time and money "visiting the families and friends of those convicts who are now in prison, as well as those who have left" (Sen. Doc. 99 1843, 82).

His sociological imagination produced this striking analysis well before his contemporaries saw its importance:

> The simple fact, for instance, that your prison district includes the city of New York—a place affording, necessarily, as many facilities for pollution and crime as it does for mercantile and mechanical pursuits—demands at our hands the most thorough investigation of the causes and modes of preventing crime (Sen. Doc. 39 1842, 24-25).

He was not a simple environmental determinist. His evangelical nature, coupled with another of the later criminological emphases, inquiry into the psychological derivations of criminal behavior, produced an interest in uncovering the inner compulsions that drive the offender. He said his analysis helped him gain "a thorough knowledge of those *characteristic* passions, affections, propensities and imbecilities which gave being to their misfortunes" (Doc. 99 1843, 83). This combination of heredity and environment was the basic interpretive device used by the progressives and a central feature of the positivist movement in penology that he helped inaugurate.

Other chaplains were gaining similar insights as a result of their labors with the prisoners and from their reflection on the state of the penal system. J. A. Canfield's program at Clinton was particularly visionary. He said the chief aim of the penitentiary was "making *men* instead of *money*." He called for a graded system of classification, renewed the call to "place our prisons beyond the deadly influence of partizan politics," advocated a system based on intellectual, moral, physical, and manual "training," and sought a "thorough revision of our whole criminal code" with special emphasis on the "total abolition of time sentences" (Sen. Doc. 9 1867, 384-85). Each one of the above suggestions was implemented during the reformatory era.

The first serious recognition on the part of New York officials of the need to ascertain a clearer portrait of the background of offenders as a complement to a reform program came in the 1856 report of the Secretary of State (Sen. Doc. 111). Although there had been several analytical presentations in earlier reports of inspectors (e.g., Sing Sing in 1853), the 1856 account presented 223 pages of statistics. It was an important development and a silent tribute to the influential contribution that the chaplains had made to the evolution of penal theory in the United States.

The religious sociology of Massachusetts provided less constraint in the movement toward progressive thinking and the construction of a reformatory. It was, of course, the base of operations of Dwight and the Prison Discipline Society, as well as the cradle of liberal religious thinking in America. Both Dwight (who had died in 1854) and the chaplains at Charlestown had been tireless advocates of the type of analysis that would eventually give birth to the reformatory. Their influence, combined with the instrumental factor of overcrowding that has consistently instigated structural revision, resulted in early appeals for the construction of a new facility exemplifying the important value of classification. A state commission reported in 1853: "A division of the convicts into two classes, and their confinement in separate prisons would . . . tend greatly to improve both the physical and moral condition of this class of our unfortunate fellow beings" (MA Sen. Doc. 60, 3).

Figures such as Warden Gideon Haynes at Charlestown and Franklin Sanborn of the Massachusetts Board of State Charities, in concert with Enoch Wines and the New York Prison Association, began to press for a radically new approach to the penitentiary experience.

Sanborn, while at Harvard, became a fervent disciple of the Unitarian preacher, Theodore Parker, and an avid abolitionist. He had collaborated with John Brown and reluctantly supported the raid on the federal arsenal at Harper's Ferry; a decision that forced him to flee twice to Quebec and eventually resulted in his incarceration. So admired was he by his neighbors in Concord that initial attempts to apprehend him resulted in the arresting party being driven from the town. The Massachusetts Supreme

Court soon dropped the charge and, in 1863, he was appointed secretary of the Board of Charities, the first office of its kind in the United States (Malone 1936, 326).

He had once asked the rhetorical question: "But do our prisons work reformation of the criminal?" and had responded, "Go to our prisons as I have done . . . inquire of the officers, hear the story of the convicts, watch the workings of the system and you will see that instead of reforming they harden the criminal" (E. Pen. 1866, 23). He became the leading voice in Massachusetts on behalf of the programs that would come to fruition at Elmira, advocating initiatives introduced in Europe and Australia: a system of rewards built into the structure of the prison (the "mark" system), the indeterminate sentence, and parole (MA Bd. of Charities 1866, 117).[12]

Sanborn and Haynes, along with many legislators, continued to press for a new facility but the movement was delayed largely for financial reasons. Charlestown may have been dilapidated and overcrowded, but it was "contiguous to the business parts of the city of Boston, thereby facilitating the procurement of supplies and the general business transactions of the prison" (MA Sen. Doc. 16 1873, 1). A frustrated committee reported in 1873:

> Under encouragement of the state authorities the governing policy of this prison seems to have been to "make the institution pay." The *reformatory* element has entered but slightly into its management. Proceeds from the labor of the convicts, and punishment for their crimes, are the considerations which appear to receive decidedly the most attention (Sen. Doc. 244, 3).

Although in the year that Elmira opened, 1876, the state prison commissioners lauded the work of Wines and the reformatory's superintendent Brockway, Massachusetts seemed destined, as it had with the penitentiary, to await the example of New York before it changed its penal structure.

The New York Prison Association

From its inception in 1844, the Prison Association of New York (NYPA) was less partisan than its counterparts in Massachusetts and Pennsylvania. Its founders were well aware of the substance of the debates between the separate and silent systems. They were intent, however, on finding a third way that would incorporate the best elements of each, as well as other penal ideas, and thus substantially effect the reform of the criminal population:

> This Association is not pledged or committed to either of the systems of prison discipline, which have originated in this country . . . but is disposed rather to advocate a plan combined of both, avoiding the evils of each, adopting their respective advantages, and attempting to mold from them a system which shall receive the sanction of all humane persons, and be emphatically national in its character (NYPA 1846, 32).

The goals of the association were three: amelioration of the physical condition of penal facilities, improvement of administrative and disciplinary functions, and aid for discharged convicts (NYPA 1844, 3).

The independent outlook of the organization was manifested from the beginning. Standing apart from the insistence of both systems on enforced silence as the preventive for contamination, it was more disposed to a wider use of classification. It also mirrored the energetic involvement of the chaplains in seeking to provide secular as well as religious education in the penitentiaries:

> The further reforms demanded, and which would require legislative aid, could be comprehended in two words—CLASSIFICATION AND INSTRUCTION; not the imperfect classification attempted in some of the British prisons, according to the crimes committed, nor instruction confined merely to their moral and religious duties, but that which should separate the hopeful from the incorrigible, and elevate the mind and improve the understanding (NYPA 1844, 26).

The society also turned a sympathetic eye to the issues being raised by Louis Dwight and many of the chaplains as to the importance of "recording and reporting prison statistics," as well as the impact of the communal environment on the development of deviancy (NYPA 1849, 50). It recorded the conviction, "fast becoming general, that the community is itself, by its neglects and bad usages, in part responsible for the sins of its children" (NYPA 1844, 30).

The persons responsible for the philosophy of the association were religious but in a less evangelical sense. Liberal religion was beginning to tear itself away from its evangelical moorings. Presbyterian and Unitarian ministers, always the most educated representatives of the clergy, having received their ministerial training at schools such as Yale, Princeton, Harvard, and Union Theological Seminary, were, like Luckey, incapable of sacrificing their intellect to a purely romantic understanding of society. The secretary of the NYPA was William H. Channing, a Unitarian minister. Reverend Dr. Gardiner Spring was a vice president,[13] as was John Edmonds, the former inspector and associate of Luckey. Edmonds showed a more intellectual and ethical approach to religion; the same approach that characterized liberal Protestantism as it developed in the last half of the century:[14]

> But the hour is on the wing when the great truth will be practically acknowledged, that the Author of Nature has constituted human affairs in relation to the supremacy of the moral part of man over the animal—of the law in the mind over the law in the members . . . the essence of Christianity: Good will to man (NYPA 1844, 29-30).

Similarly, John Duer, Chair of the Committee on Prison Discipline, offered a rationale for the association that demonstrated how the traditional Calvinist belief in providence, which had evolved into the image of the millennial kingdom, could again be reworked to prefigure the progressive mentality:

> Let it not be said, Mr. President, that the hopes on which our Association is built . . . are visionary and delusive . . . It is, indeed, a libel on Providence, a practical denial of the moral government of the world, to assert that the efforts of benevolence—of consistent, enlightened, and systematic benevolence—of benevolence, acting under the guidance of calm reason and sober judgment, can ever prove entirely abortive (NYPA 1846, 75).

This liberal and independent vision was to accompany the association throughout the rest of the century.

Apart from its nonpartisan dedication to penal reform, the NYPA had another significant advantage over the prison associations in Pennsylvania and Massachusetts. Whereas the Philadelphia society played a powerful role in the development of the separate system, and the Boston society a comparable role in the spread of the silent system, the NYPA, in 1846, was officially designated the independent inspector of the state prisons. Its yearly report was to be part of the legislative record. As an established state corporation, it could convey its agenda with greater formal ease. This privilege was granted probably as a result of several factors: the disarray of the New York penitentiaries was both a state and national scandal and needed the supervision of an outside agency; and the members of the association were highly regarded. Edmonds, for example, was former chief inspector of the state penitentiaries, and Governor Seward, who approved the group's official status, was a committed evangelical who would have sanctioned the fusion of rational analysis with religious conviction. Seward had written the association in December 1846:

> Our holy religion makes no distinction among the prisoners whom it enjoins us to visit. Your experience has taught you that such ministrations bless those who render them even more than those who receive them, and you are sure of your ultimate vindication (NYPA 1847, 18).

The work of the association was controversial from its inception. Professing no ideological allegiance to the Auburn program, and given the protection of legislative sanction, its thorough inspections amplified the natural ambiguities that accompany the world of the prison. The insistence on humane treatment over the institutional requirements of order and economy produced instant friction between the membership and penal officials. This tension was captured in an early report concerning the operation of the penitentiary at Clinton: "The exhibition of passion, and the application of brute force, will transform the image of the Maker into the likeness of a wild beast" (NYPA 1849, 213).

The inspection committees uncovered abuses in the facilities and publicized them in the reports to the legislature. After detailing the violent mistreatment of a recalcitrant prisoner who was beaten, shot, stabbed, lashed, and then confined on bread and water for eight months, the narrative concluded: "not one word of this affair ever reached the public eye except through our report" (NYPA 1849, 14). Investigators excoriated penal officials for the use of the shower bath which they deemed to be "equally cruel and degrading" as the "cat" (NYPA 1849, 213).

Besides the affair at Sing Sing, in which they supported the matron, Eliza Farnham, their vocal denunciations of prison conditions triggered a particularly vehement conflict concerning their right to inspect the institutions without accompaniment by prison administrators. Both wardens and inspectors had ordered that all activities of the association be open to scrutiny by the prison staff. The Executive Committee of the NYPA protested: "Our three State Prison Inspectors thrust themselves upon the public gaze, as the sole monopolists of secret and irresponsible power" (1851, 20). They mourned that the prisons of the state might "become the sport of unprincipled and unfeeling men" (1855, 21).

Given its liberal religious dynamism, and its designated role as a controversial advocate for reform, the association was the natural place from which a powerful new direction for the New York prison system could emanate. The frustrations engendered by the outmoded organizational principle of silence, balanced books, and a still prevalent corporal discipline, not to mention the stubborn resistance of penal officials to their investigations, were stirring the energies of the members away from confrontation over abuses to proposals for systemic reorganization.

Abraham Beale, a fervent evangelical who became the chair of the Committee on Discharged Prisoners, was moving in a positivist direction similar to that of his contemporary, Luckey. He said in 1856 that convicts should be regarded as "diseased patients" who needed care exercised by "moral physicians" (NYPA 1857, 65). Joseph Stanton Gould, the Corresponding Secretary, assured the Christian community that while the association did not deny that "the power of cleansing the depravity of the human heart from its pollutions belongs wholly to God," it still maintained that it was the conjoined action of government and citizenry that must be the vehicle for the suppression of crime (NYPA 1855, 54-55).

The report of the association for 1854 was of special interest. It began to investigate the innovations of several European prison reformers whose ideas proved significant to the reformatory movement.

Captain Alexander Maconochie was a British penal official who oversaw a colony of transported felons in Australia.[15] Ironically, the reformatory schema was to draw inspiration from the experiment whose inception was a crushing personal, and ultimately fatal, defeat for the great voice of prison reform, John Howard. Howard felt that the British were shunning the opportunity to concentrate on developing a humane and exemplary penal system by banishing convicts to the unregulated and often cruelly administered colonial outposts. Maconochie, however, developed a novel system of "marks" and other incentives whereby convicts could progress to levels of expanded freedom and privileges. He was, according to Wines, "placing the prisoner's fate measurably in his own hands, and thereby enabling him, through industry and obedience, to raise himself step by step to positions of increased freedom, privilege and comfort" (NYPA 1854, 32-33).

Whereas both the Auburn and Pennsylvania systems were based on the deprivation of contact between inmates, Maconochie sought to develop a communal sense of responsibility among his charges:

> As I would . . . never punish an individual apart from his party, so neither would I ever reward one. No exertion, no favor, no degree of individual merit, should carry a man through without his fellows; for on the absolute community of interest among the individuals of each

party, I would rely more than on anything to make the system efficient (NYPA 1856, 75).

While Maconochie's insights were to suffer the same fate as those of Farnham, his concept that penal officials should employ rewards, and not simply punishments, in seeking to influence the reformation of the convict had a profound impact on the American reform community, particularly Wines and the NYPA.

The association favored the new approach, particularly in allowing the fruits of extra labor, traditionally called "overstint," to be saved for the inmate on his or her discharge: "A system of marks or merits for good conduct, tending to mitigate punishment, or to reward in some way at the end of the term of imprisonment, would be a strong incentive to reformation, and a powerful incentive to general good conduct" (NYPA 1857, 22). The group was able to convince both Governor Seymour and his successor, Myron H. Clark, to endorse the idea (NYPA 1856, 21). This innovation became a feature of the Elmira Reformatory under Brockway who spoke thus of it:

> When it was seen that the ideal of simple merit and demerit befogged these men, that mere time value was ineffective, an important change was made by translating time values into monetary terms. This was more tangible and, joined as it soon was to the wage-earning system, brought and kept the men in touch with the essential thing—the economies of personal earning, expending, and saving for future needs (Brockway 1912, 321).

Although the inclination was present to study and adopt the methods of the European reformers, the principal motivating force was absent until Enoch Wines assumed control of the organization.

Enoch Wines

Reverend Doctor Enoch C. Wines was for several critical years the Corresponding Secretary of the association. This powerful position (similar to that of Dwight at the Boston Prison Discipline Society), coupled with his broad educational background, his burning interest in reforming the penal system, and his "progressive" evangelical theology, provided the platform from which he could substantially affect the thinking and practice of the American penal community.

He was born in 1806 and much of his life was spent in educational pursuits. After graduating from Middlebury College in 1827, he founded several schools based on the classical educational model. He was briefly the editor of the *American Journal of Education* and, prior to accepting the position at the prison association in 1862, he served for several years as president of the City University of St. Louis. He published a work, *Commentaries on the Laws of the Ancient Hebrews* (1853), that bore witness to the principles of liberal democracy. The volume attempted to demonstrate the biblical foundations of the principles of civil liberty and popular government (Malone 1936, 385).

In 1849 he entered into the first of several pastorates, as a Congregational minister in Vermont, followed by service in a Presbyterian church in Long Island. For all his scholarly inclination and penchant for critical thinking, his son Frederick once stated that he "never had a religious doubt" (McKelvey 1977, 66). He once described the work of the NYPA in this way: "Our work is mainly a work of humanity and benevolence . . . It is a philanthropy akin to that divine benevolence that calls backsliders to repent" (NYPA 1863, 51). This mixture of evangelicalism with the modern methods of the social sciences mark him as one of the key figures in leading the religious community into a new theological self-understanding.[16]

As secretary, he used his connections with both the church and the state government to increase the revenues of the society and thus expand its efforts. The financial assistance, joined with his avid study of the early reports of the various state prison societies, prompted him to undertake a thorough inspection of the state penal facilities. When his visits revealed desperate overcrowding and the political instability of which we have spoken, he proposed that the association initiate a study of the current system in order to make substantive recommendations at the forthcoming state constitutional convention. He personally felt that novel insights were demanded and he was not reluctant to investigate national and international institutions in order to obtain them.

Thus, in 1865, he and Theodore Dwight commenced an extended visitation of all the penitentiaries and detention facilities in the United States and Canada, save those in the far west, producing the *Report on the Prisons and Reformatories of the United States and Canada* (1867). The undertaking did nothing to diminish Wines' uneasiness with the state of penal institutions. While he and Dwight steadfastly held that the goal of the correctional enterprise was, and should always be, reformation, precious few facilities had manifested the coherence at each level of institutional life necessary for such a lofty aim to be reached:

Upon the whole . . . we are constrained to avow the opinion that there is not a state prison in America in which the reformation of the convicts is the one supreme object of the discipline, to which everything else is made to bend, and which the whole administration, in all its arrangements, is intended to advance. The eastern penitentiary at Philadelphia, comes nearest to that design, considering not only what is done by the prison authorities themselves, but also the official connection of the Pennsylvania Prison Society with the institution and its systematic and earnest labors for moral amendment of the prisoners (Wines and Dwight 1867, 287-88).

The authors contended that substantive changes were called for at each level of both social and penal organization. As preventive measures, compulsory education, nursery schools, and industrial schools were recommended (1867, 62-64). Juvenile reformatories were seen as essential for wayward youth and were to be financed, in part, by the parents of the offenders (65-66). At the adult level, the indeterminate sentence and the "mark" system were viewed as preferable to the time sentence (281), and much praise was lavished on Sir Walter Crofton in Ireland for his modernizing procedures (72-75).

Wines and Dwight also continued their assault on partisan politics as a devastating hindrance to a consistent penal philosophy. They called for the termination of the contract system in favor of industries geared toward "reforming prisoners and restoring them to society" (72).

Finally, religion was highlighted as the principal agent of reformation: "This, undoubtedly, is first in importance, and the most potent in its action" (263). One way to encourage this, they argued, was to make the interview between the incoming inmate and the chaplain "a matter of fixed regulation" (143).[17]

At the same time, Wines commenced a mammoth study of all known prisons and "child-saving institutions" in the world, a work completed just before his death in 1879. While compiling the manuscript, he published portions of the data in the yearly reports of the NYPA. These insights not only brought to the American criminological community the basic tenets of the reformatory program, they also formed much of the agenda for the first National Prison Congress in 1870 which was a turning point in American penal history.

Wines was the most influential representative of the new liberalism among evangelicals: providence was guiding the nation and its expanding institutional base, ethical behavior, in conformity to the immutable laws of nature, was the proper public expression of the religious life, and the disobedient were being molded individually to social conformity by reformatory institutions:

Such a [penal] system must work with nature, not against it; and this is its first essential basis. The Creator has impressed indelibly upon the human soul certain great principles. Of these the most deeply rooted . . . are hope and sociability. We must not crush out of the man by our modes of penal discipline these primal and essential elements of humanity, but rather seek to guide, control and mould them to our purpose (Wines 1880, 613).

Wines continued to praise the work of Maconochie but also lauded the important innovations of Colonel Montesinos in Spain and, especially, Sir Walter Crofton in Ireland. Montesinos completely reorganized a prison in Valencia. He initiated a more humane discipline, instituted a system of rewards and levels of privilege, and introduced a wide variety of trades from which the prisoners could freely choose.

Colonel Montesinos did not attempt to repeal the laws of nature. He seized those great principles which the Creator has impressed upon the human soul, and molded them to his purpose. He aimed to develop manhood, not crush it; to gain the will, not simply to coerce the body. He employed the law of love, and found it the most powerful of laws . . . He excited them to diligence by allowing them a by no means inconsiderable portion of their earnings. He enabled them to raise their position step by step, by their own industry and good conduct (Wines 1880, 30-31).

Crofton introduced several important innovations which, like those of Maconochie and Montesinos, were to become key elements in progressive penal discipline. He established a minimum sentence of five years for each felon, accompanied by a discretionary power to shorten the sentence for good conduct. His three grades of penal organization, corresponding to different levels of responsibility and personal progress, were established in three different facilities, and he initiated a "ticket-of-leave" or conditional liberation, the forerunner of parole.

By 1866, the reports of the NYPA were filled with references to the work of these reformers, particularly Crofton, and Wines was not reticent to castigate the American penal community for failing to appreciate the necessity of such modifications. Much like Louis Dwight a generation earlier, he used the influence of his position to prod the legislature and correctional officials to adopt his point of view.

Wines embarked upon two extraordinary projects in order to implant the new approach. In a report to the legislature in 1867, he and Theodore Dwight proposed that an institution be constructed based on the Irish system: "We believe that in its broad, general principles . . . it may be applied, with entire effect, in our own country and in our own State" (Frederick Wines 1919, 203).

This "reformatory" would serve first-time youthful offenders from 16 to 30 years, would be based on moral, scholastic, and industrial education, and would incorporate both the "mark" system and the indeterminate sentence: "We therefore propose that when the sentence of the criminal is regularly less than five years, the sentence to the reformatory shall be until reformation, not exceeding five years" (NYPA 1870, 229ff). The legislature approved the proposal in 1869. Although financial pressures did not allow the new facility to be completed until 1876, the reformatory was now set to emerge as the dominant structure in American penology.[18]

In describing the birth of this new type of institution, the first superintendent, Zebulon Brockway, gave evidence of the main theme of this study: that religious movements were the catalyst for the development of the penal system:

> A certain diffused, indefinite, religio-philanthropic sentiment had been created by the work and publications of the Prison Association of New York through its very efficient secretary, Rev. E. C. Wines. This was remarked by Senator Schoonmaker, who declared that the influence of the Prison Association had prepared the public mind for even such a radical reform measure (Brockway 1912, 168).

At the same time, Wines sought to capitalize on the openness to reform by calling for and organizing a national convention in 1870. The first National Prison Congress was held in Cincinnati and served to realize not only the original vision of the NYPA, a truly national correctional discipline, but also to galvanize acceptance of the essential principles of progressive penology. The gathering led to the formation of the National Prison Association. Wines was named its first secretary, a post he held until 1877.

At the conference, Wines presented two key addresses, one on the present outlook of prison discipline, and the other on the need for an international prison congress. Brockway, whose work at the Detroit House of Correction had garnered enthusiastic praise from Wines and Dwight, read an influential paper outlining many of the contemporary ideas soon to be incorporated at the Elmira Reformatory. Other speakers bore witness to the extent the religious community dominated progressive penal discourse. The following is a partial list of the lectures given by religious leaders: Rev. B. K. Pierce: "General View of preventive and reformatory institutions in the United States," Rev. C. C. Foote: "The importance and power of religious forces in prisons," Rev. A. G. Byers: "District Prisons under state control for persons convicted of minor offenses," Brother Teilow (Catholic Boys Protectory of Westchester, N.Y.): "Confidence in the inmates of reformatories as an element of success," and Rev. Marcus Ames: "On the desirableness of an increased number of juvenile reformatories" (NYPA 1871, 165).

The resultant set of principles issued by the delegates formally inaugurated the Progressive Era in penology. Among the most important were the following: the reformation of the inmate as the "supreme aim of prison discipline" and not "the infliction of vindictive suffering," the "progressive classification of prisoners," the creation of a "system of rewards for conduct, industry and attention to learning," a resolution that the fate of inmates "should be placed, measurably, in [their] own hands," and the recommendation that time sentences be of "indeterminate length" (Frederick Wines 1919, 205).

Several other items will serve to further attune the reader to the influence of this remarkable person. Following one of his own recommendations at Cincinnati, Wines secured a joint resolution from the U. S. Congress creating a special commission authorized to invite the countries of the world to an international congress on prison reform. As a result of his efforts, twenty-two nations were represented at the first International Penitentiary Congress at London in 1872, from which both an international and several national organizations were created (Malone 1936, 385).

Finally, at the state constitutional convention in 1867, the NYPA presented the recommendation of Wines and Dwight that the administration of New York's prisons be independent of partisan political control. The convention approved the proposal that there be established a superintendent of state prisons, appointed by the governor and the senate, who would serve for a period of ten years. Although the motion was initially defeated, as the voters rejected the particular draft of the constitution, an abridged version with a five-year term of office was finally approved (NYPA 1868, 79; Wines 1880, 149-50).

The first state superintendent, Louis D. Pilsbury, had the task of appointing the director of the new reformatory at Elmira. He chose a man who had served under his father, Amos Pilsbury, at the county penitentiary at Albany, one of the most influential administrators in American penal history, Zebulon Brockway

The Reformatory

The essence of the reformatory, as Brockway defined it, was the "socialization of the anti-social by scientific training under completest government control" (Brockway 1912, 309). The inmate, now seen almost universally as the unwilling product of environmental and hereditary factors beyond his or her control, was a subject to be molded into the values and virtues of the wider community. Brockway expressed the philosophy in his abrupt style:

> The ancient doctrine of the independent freedom of the human will and the correlative belief in unconditioned retributive moral accountability was also put aside as an incomprehensible theory for any human administration. We must invade the will of those committed to our charge and determine their behavior quite outside their own election. The dismissal thus of these old doctrines . . . cleared the field of our endeavor and opened wide to science that which had been dominated by sentiment alone (1912, 85).

The individual, case work approach was to feature what progressives felt was the most reliable component of the socialization process, education: "All agencies of reformation may properly be classed under religion, education, and labor, a trinal unity truly expressed by the term education when used in its most comprehensive sense" (Sen. Doc. 15 1884, 4). The inmate was now a specimen to be studied and reshaped by an army of penal specialists: "each separately must be nourished and trellised until [reformation] is entwined and established" (Sen. Doc. 13 1885, 6).

The programmatic innovations were those urged by the NYPA and orchestrated by Brockway at the 1870 prison congress: the indeterminate sentence, the "mark" system, and, by the early 1880's, release on parole with subsequent absolute discharge (Sen. Doc. 13 1885, 3).

The method, as we saw, was not so much original as it was syncretic and timely. It pulled together several strands of reform thinking at a time of burgeoning hope in scientific and social progress and, consequentially, at a time of growing despair concerning the future of the penitentiaries. Another factor in its appeal may have been the indomitable character of Brockway himself. Wines' son, Frederick, also a leading voice in the progressive movement, stated:

> There is in the organization of this Reformatory, and in the laws by which it is governed, nothing that is absolutely new. The novelty consists rather in the combination of principles whose validity had

been separately recognized, and in the intense earnestness with which they have been here applied by a man whose enthusiasm for the reformation of convicts has in it a quality closely allied to genius (1919, 206-07).

Brockway was something of a mythical figure even before he assumed control of Elmira, which he governed, quite literally with an iron hand, from its inception in 1876 until 1900. He was a Connecticut Yankee by birth, the son of a sober, rational, and intermittently religious father (Congregational originally, Methodist for a time, and finally agnostic), and a mother who became deeply imbued with the evangelical spirit of the Second Great Awakening. "Our home was a hostage for visiting preachers . . . more of the evangelistic type, whose conversation of scriptural prophecy and fulfillment, of milenarianism, and of a spiritual consciousness, served . . . to develop my maternal heritage of mystic tendency" (Brockway 1912, 10).

During a revival at Rochester, New York in the mid 1850s, he heard the renowned evangelist, Charles Finney. Brockway related that he was "profoundly moved" by the experience and subsequently joined an evangelical Congregational church, eventually assuming leadership of the Sunday School. He later surmised that he had fallen prey to the "prevalent mental and moral contagion" (1912, 63).

He had begun his long career in correctional service in 1848 at Wethersfield, Connecticut. Subsequently, he served under Amos Pilsbury at the Albany County Penitentiary.[19] Pilsbury, the son of a notable warden, had an outstanding reputation as a firm administrator and, more importantly, a financially astute one; traits not lost on the eager and intelligent Brockway. Brockway recounted an incident in the life of Pilsbury that left a deep impression. Before his tenure at Albany, the warden had been the director of Wethersfield in the mid 1830s. At that time, the institution was experiencing internal conflict as a result of inmates openly showing contempt for the silent system. On his first day they had refused to return to their cells, and when finally convinced to do so, "marched to the cell-house, singing, shouting, besmearing the walls with the mush in their ration pans . . . It was a fiendish uproar." On a visit to Sing Sing, Robert Wiltse presented Pilsbury with the standard disciplinary tool in the New York prisons, a cat-o-nine-tails. Upon returning to Wethersfield the following morning, he could hear the noise being made by the inmates a mile away. Brockway completes the story:

[H]e summoned his deputy and at once, within the hearing of all, he made use of the instrument he carried on the first disturber he discovered. The effect was magical. From that day the disorder ceased, good order was restored, industrial efficiency returned and salutary discipline was reestablished (1912, 28-29).

Brockway learned well. He came to see what Lynds and Wiltse had discovered in their tenures at Auburn and Sing Sing: that physical force was an essential element in the successful administration of a congregate prison. "The stringency of control maintained at Albany was not so much for safety as it was for the sake of serviceable industrial efficiency, the increase of prison earnings" (Brockway 1912, 46).

He was not, however, a simple reincarnation of either of those infamous figures. He was a complex individual who embodied the evolution of evangelicalism into scientific Progressivism. In a mix of Weberian metaphors, he was patriarchal, charismatic, and a proponent of technical rationality. He was patriarchal in his autocratic disdain for the criminal class, which he once suggested pointed to a misanthropic tendency, coupled with his belief that the reformatory regimen could ransom at least some of them. He was charismatic in his ability to mesmerize state officials, the public, and the inmates under his command. He was rational in his belief that positivist scientific methods were infallibly correct.

He remained avidly "religious" despite his frequent denunciations of the evangelical "sentimentalism" that had once captivated him. Faith in God became a belief in the immanence of the "Infinite-Creative-Formative-Force by which all things are, and move, and have their being" (1912, 64).[20] He was a product of his times, and perhaps the first national penal figure to demonstrate that liberal Protestantism inevitably led its adherents to place their faith in a universal, rational ethic:

In place of previous assent to the inconsistent doctrine of an exclusive anthropomorphic Infinite Being corralled in edifices . . . governing from outside at the insistence of apostolical agents, or adherents of specific dogmas, the Infinite was now conceived as the highest ultimate principle of all existences, absolutely immaterial, the basis of the order of the universe, operating always, everywhere; the divinely purposeful immanence whose ways are to us incomprehensible. Religiousness, which had been accredited only to declared believers . . . now seemed to be the native quality of all humanity (1912, 84-85).

Brockway was invited to become the superintendent of two houses of correction: at Rochester, and subsequently at Detroit. In the years (1854-1872) when the penitentiaries were overwhelmed with financial losses and violent lapses of discipline, Brockway's institutions were governed in an orderly manner and achieved, in his words, "phenomenal" success in financial matters (1912, 61, 79).

This alone may have been enough to warrant the acclaim he received, but his progressive leanings also led him to innovative efforts in these facilities. He was fervently committed to the concept of the indeterminate sentence that he, immodestly, claimed to have pioneered in the United States (1912, 171).[21] He had also come to see the need of a separate facility geared to the reformation of young adult offenders.

The Elmira experiment was an immediate public, if not financial and reformative, success. Weary administrators and legislators in other states saw it as an opportunity to renew calls for similar experiments. All prisons built in the 1890s, for example, were based on Elmira (McKelvey 1977, 163).

Massachusetts had finally made some degree of progress in the stalemate over the construction of a new facility based on the principle of classification. The reticence of the legislature had been modified by the disintegration of the once proud Charlestown facility. Sanborn had stated: "our actual system does not accomplish the ends which the originators of it had desired . . . it does not prevent crime, nor reform the criminal, nor pay its own expenses" (MA Board of State Charities 1866, 113). Of the 683 convicts at the prison in 1874, only 224 were contracted to work. One inspector stated, "the labor system at Charlestown has broken down" (MA Board of State Charities 1875, lvi-lvii).

The state was desperately in need of a complex to accommodate the growing number of incarcerated women. Given the deterioration of Charlestown and the publicity surrounding the construction of Elmira, the Massachusetts legislature decided in 1873 to operate the new institution at Sherborn on the reformatory model.[22] The state prison commissioners had provided the substance of the design:

> Let the prison building be arranged for different grades of offenders and make it possible—a part of the system—that by good behavior a prisoner may advance from a lower to a higher grade, where she shall have less rigorous treatment and more privilege. Let the whole be in the charge of persons having faith in humanity, that however degraded and hardened, it yet never in this life gets beyond the reach of softening, elevating influences; never beyond the power of God's

truth and word; never beyond the scope of His Gospel (House Doc. 30 1872, 29).

The combination of favorable reports received from both Sherborn and Elmira, eventually convinced the state legislature to pass a bill in 1883 establishing a reformatory for men at Concord (Sen. Doc. 369 1884, 3).

Pennsylvania, as described, had already developed the ideological base upon which a reformatory could be constructed. For some time, the reports of the inspectors had kept alive the traditional disparity with New York, emphasizing the difference between the congregate and the individual treatment systems. With the opening of Elmira, however, those distinctions were virtually eliminated. Already the separate system had disappeared to a large degree, save in the nostalgic language of some, as overcrowding had forced double and, in some cases, triple celling. Vaux and the inspectors had originally rejected the Irish system precisely because it was congregate, hence avowal of it would have undermined the last element of the original Quaker vision: "Like all novelties or expedients it is highly estimated. Experience will divest it of all its attractions" (E. Pen. 1869, 80).

The rising number of youthful prisoners, however, led Vaux to change his mind. It had long been apparent to him that a separate institution for first time offenders was a necessity, as was the teaching of trades. By 1877 the population of the Eastern Penitentiary was over 1100, double its capacity, and nearly triple what the institution had been built originally to accommodate. The situation was compounded by the fact that it was impossible to find labor projects to keep so many occupied. With nothing but pride separating the two systems at that point, Vaux began to urge the construction of a reformatory: "Reformatories, or industrial schools, or educational institutions, which teach the hands to work, and the mind to understand how the work is best to be done, are more needed now than prisons, for youths" (E. Pen. 1878, 28-29).

After some years of prodding the legislature, the Huntingdon Reformatory was finally opened in 1889. Perhaps the last obstacle to its inception was lifted when Vaux made a statement cautiously espousing a congregate organization for the complex. The declaration effectively ended the sixty-year debate between Pennsylvania and New York, and inaugurated what Wines and other reformers had desired, a national prison philosophy: "If the evils of association can be lessened, and individualization be made a prominent feature in the administration, the encouragement of Reformatories should be freely accorded" (E. Pen. 1888, 122).

In the same year, 1889, another significant development occurred, bearing witness to the influence of Crofton and the Irish system. The New York legislature enacted the Fasset Law that carried many of the Elmira innovations to the three state prisons, no longer called penitentiaries. Classification was expanded and the indeterminate sentence and parole were introduced (Sen. Doc. 15 1898, 69). Furthermore, the three prisons were to be graded in the following way: Sing Sing would receive inmates convicted of their first offense, Auburn would house those convicted a second time, and Clinton would contain confirmed recidivists. The State Commission of Prisons stated: "It is now practicable to introduce compulsory education in letters and in trades in prisons, with reformatory methods at least, in the prisons of the first and second grades" (1899, 20).

For good or for ill, the hopes of the American penal community had been placed squarely on the shoulders of the reformatory.

Education and Ethics Replace Religion

One of the figures in the history of ideas who had a powerful impact on the development of epistemology and ethics was Immanuel Kant. Although writing at the end of the eighteenth century, Kant came to be a dominant figure in the social ethics of liberal Protestantism. He contended that the phenomenal world provided the parameters in which religious language must express itself. This did not lead to a denial of theology and metaphysics, but to a bracketing of their claims to the realm of faith and belief. In the empirical world, rationally grounded ethical behavior was the only viable expression of religious commitment.

Kant's philosophy was given credence in the rational and humanitarian vision being inculcated at the reformatory. D. R. Ford, a school director at Elmira, outlined the ideas underlying the curriculum that verified the harmonious union of Kantian and liberal Protestant philosophies: "1. To teach those things which are aids to getting an honest living. 2. Those things which show the rights and duties of good citizens under the law. 3. The ethics of truth and obligation. 4. The main facts of science, bearing upon arts, industries and health" (Sen. Doc. 8 1883).

Ethical rationalism dominated the schoolroom and the pulpit at Elmira and Concord.[23] Since truth had become one with certainty, as Descartes had surmised, the more rationally oriented the scholastic or religious presentation, the more it was believed to lead the residents to behold the truth they had been avoiding. It was not seriously considered that the majority of the young men had little or no schooling before they entered the reformatory, and could hardly comprehend the language, let alone the content, of the lectures by professors from nearby Cornell and other universities. This incongruous tribute to the program was written by F. Thornton Macaulay:

> Men familiar only with the novel and the newspaper now gladly made acquaintance with Plato, Dante and Homer. With minds freed from bias and bigotry by the discussions of the morality class, they opened the books of Mill, of Spencer, of Taine, Bentham, Cicero . . . culled from them the arguments and points which they carried into their debates, to stand or fall, without regard to the prestige of name or school, in the light of common sense (Sen. Doc. 9 1886, 30).

There was little difference in orientation when the residents were marched to the chapel for services. Brockway wanted an end to the impractical evangelical preaching he had heard in his home and at the revivals in Rochester:

> The actual value of preaching to prisoners, in its near and ulterior effects, is certainly questionable when subjected to practical tests. All prison preachers do not possess the tact or the subtle design and simplicity of the Vicar of Wakefield . . . It is chiefly through the instrumentality of preaching, as a means of imparting instruction, that any expectation of reformative work can be exercised in the minds of the subjects of prison discipline . . . At the best, it is an adjunct in the plan of prison correction, which bears the semblance but not the reality of a vivifying element intended for edification and moral growth (Sen. Doc. 21 1881, 7-8).

He was not disappointed by the excessively rational and scientific discourses that the inmates continually received. Chaplain McCarthy stated:

> I have given to the two upper grades a course of eight consecutive Sunday afternoon lectures, discussing with great care the general principles of *theism, anti-theism, cause and effect, design in creation, providence,* etc. . . . written examinations were held on these lectures with promising results (Sen. Doc. 8 1883, 47).

Nor was the situation much different at the reformatory in Concord. Chaplain Robert Walker, rector of a Cambridge congregation, intoned similar progressive ideas:

> One who is familiar with the kind of young men who are sent to prison to-day knows that a large majority of them are incapable,

through lack of education, through defective mind, through weak inheritance and through unwholesome environment, of fulfilling their financial obligations. They have fallen behind in the race, and resort to foul means in order to share in the prosperity that results from honest labor, thrift, and obedience to moral and civic duty (Board of Prison Commissioners of MA 1911, 52).

Brockway was correct in pointing out the mere instrumentality of religion in the reformative philosophy. What he failed to realize was that religion had created the system he mistakenly attributed to the influence of scientific method, as well as determined its own fading instrumentality.

Reality Confronts Progress

The same controversies and inherent contradictions that overwhelmed the penitentiaries slowly eroded confidence in the system the progressives had hoped would eradicate the criminal class. As David Rothman claims in his study of the period, prison leaders saw no incongruity between incapacitation and reformation.[24] There was no appreciation for the insight, offered by both Louis Dwight and Enoch Wines, that the imbalance created by these competing forces can only be overcome by the conscious and thorough application of moral and reformative principles throughout the institution.

As with the penitentiaries, a major determinant in exacerbating this inner tension was the increase in the number of felons committed to institutional care. As Durkheim had argued, increased population in a society leads to greater complexity of organization and, consequently, requires greater social cooperation. Without a cooperative infrastructure the social order is reduced to ego-driven individuals and a dominant and destructive apparatus of government control (Durkheim 1984, xxxix ff.). The theory does not lose its validity when applied to penal environments, especially of the congregate variety.

Administrators, of course, had hoped that the graded system of privileges would create the mechanism whereby inmates would readily accede to institutional demands. Although this general cooperation may have been realized in the early years, history and programmatic inconsistencies proved that it could not be sustained.

Meanwhile, the numbers increased. By 1884 there were 580 residents confined in the 504 rooms "with a certainty of 700 by May, 1885" (Sen. Doc. 13 1885, 11). Even as the physical plant was expanded, the criminal population continued to overwhelm its capacity:

[T]he institution has been full, and the pressure of the increasing number of commitments to it has resulted in its being overcrowded every year since 1884. Originally containing 504 cells, the institution has been increased in size until it now contains 1,250 cells, occupied at the close of 1892 by nearly 1,500 prisoners... therefore it has been necessary to double or treble prisoners in a cell, which is objectionable in practice and interferes with the reformatory objects of the institution (Sen. Doc. 6 1893, 45-46).

The rising tensions caused by overpopulation led to heightened conflict between the philosophy based on reformation and the institutional imperative of law and order. Brockway, who remembered the lesson he had learned under Amos Pilsbury, was not one to shy away from the "magical" effects corporal punishment could induce:

The excess of prisoners—the overcrowding—is largely the cause of what has these later years grown to be a very serious fault; namely, superficiality and ineffectiveness of the reformatory regime . . . In 1884-85 we were confronted with another alternative—either to suffer relaxation of requirements and consequent institutional disintegration, or resort to more coercive measures to maintain established standards. The latter of these alternatives was deliberately chosen regardless of the not unforeseen criticisms that subsequently followed (Brockway 1912, 272-73).

Brockway felt no compunction in admitting: "friction occurred as was natural, and in our estimation desirable, for friction in reformatory procedure is proof of effectiveness" (1912, 320). This philosophy, however, was not widely shared by many of his progressive contemporaries, and was in violation of the laws passed in the 1840s to minimize physical mistreatment. The Brockway era was punctuated by several governmental investigations of cruelty to prisoners and other alleged improprieties (1880, 1882, 1893-94). The investigations, not unlike those at Auburn and Sing Sing decades earlier, uncovered collusion on the part of the supervisors appointed by the state to inspect the facility. An interchange between Edward H. Litchfield of the State Board of Charities and W. C. Wey, president of Board of Managers, went as follows:

Q. I am requested to ask you, during the entire ten years that methods of corporal punishment adopted by the superintendent has been in vogue, has it been with the entire approval of the board of managers?

A. Entire approval, sanction and approbation, and has been, as I said before, very often discussed and commented upon (Sen. Doc. 74 1894, 8-9).

The legislature, reluctant to discipline Brockway, accepted the rationale given by the managers. Officials, such as the Catholic Chaplain, Father Bloomer, who publicly criticized the violence of the administration were dismissed as being "hostile to the reformatory and its management" (Sen. Doc. 74 1894, 20).

A final quote of the managers concerning the inquest is tinged with the bitter irony that has often accompanied the American penal experience:

There is no proof anywhere in the entire evidence of blood upon the walls or floor of the bath-room, in the halls or corridors incident to the spanking. There was an occasional nose-bleed . . . Mr. Brockway himself states that upon one occasion, with the strap doubled over in his hand, he lightly tapped an inmate with the handle, producing a slight abrasion perhaps half an inch long. That was an accident and a misadventure (Sen. Doc. 74 1894, 22).

If the reformatory was weakened by the inability to execute its stated non-coercive policy, it was fully deterred as a positive counterforce to criminal behavior by the continuing pressure placed on it by state officials to minimize its financial cost.

The contract system had originally been promoted as the most effective way to realize a cost-free penal arrangement, as well as a reformative device for the often indolent prisoners. But, as we saw, the outcry against the practice had been widespread. It bore responsibility for much of the abusive treatment received by prisoners, as contractors and agents drove the inmates to their physical and emotional limits. Prisons where contracts flourished had been the targets of repeated investigations. They consistently lacked the reformative vision, as wardens filled their yearly reports with receipts and deficits, instead of analysis of the convict and the programs geared to his or her reformation. At the same time, organized labor mounted a series of drives to protect local industry from the goods manufactured in prisons, where the inmates could be forced to work up to fourteen hours a day with minimal cost to the contractor.

Accordingly, both New York (1865) and Massachusetts (1886) abolished the contractors; inaugurating what was known as the state-use system, in which inmates produced goods exclusively for operation by state agencies. This was presented as a foundational element in the progressive method of treatment, with the reformation of the inmate, and not institutional finances, as the focus of incarceration. Brockway, commenting upon the contact period, stated that the "prevailing motive of the prison labor systems with the state government, the prison managers, and the prison contractors became excessively mercenary." He went on to say: "Prevalence of this notion hindered for a time ready acceptance of the reformatory system" (1912, 167).

Despite the checkered history of the practice, it had been occasionally profitable (under Lynds for example), and state governments were never content with a deficit-ridden penal system, no matter how reformative it appeared to be. Economic rationalization, initially rooted in theological anxiety, had become a principal characteristic of American life, especially in the late nineteenth century. By 1880, concern over the financial cost of Elmira prompted an investigation into its affairs. Legislators, disconsolate over monetary losses created by the state-use method, ordered a return to the contract system. This development infuriated both Brockway and the managers of the facility, who rightly saw the explicit affront to the philosophy they had so diligently promoted (Brockway 1912, 227-29).

Although the outcry of the progressive community led the legislature to abolish the system once again, when the contracts expired in 1886, the incident served as a reminder that the Calvinist-oriented approach to penology, at the heart of the American experience, could not rest content with a single-minded emphasis on reformation. The image of Louis Dwight, and the claim that moral and financial effectiveness are interrelated, remained a part of the unconscious mechanism guiding the development of American penology.

The problems of overcrowding, violence, and philosophical uncertainty soon revealed that the new innovations pioneered by Wines and his associates were not producing the expected results. Despite the confident assurances by Brockway and reformatory advocates that the parole figures revealed the reformative benefits of the individual treatment regimen, other analysts disagreed. A legislative committee presented its conclusions concerning the rehabilitative influence of Elmira:

> The investigation does not bear out the claim of estimated reformation among the paroled men. The last annual report declared the percentage to be eighty-four. The facts, sustained by abundant and competent proof . . . show this claim to be greatly exaggerated, as well as that it is arrived at by estimate or guess work, instead of proof or a competent knowledge of the facts (Sen. Doc. 36 1887, 21).

The advent of probation in the early years of the twentieth century, an important development that attempted, among other things, to ease the pressure of overcrowding, was another serious blow to the philosophy of the reformatory. The State Commission of Prisons in New York asserted that "jail life tends to contaminate and debase prisoners, while probation surrounds them with wholesome and healthful influences" (1909, 11). The reality, however, was an implicit admission that many offenders did not need the reformatory; that the best form of treatment was to leave them in the very environments, and psychological trauma, that many progressives argued were the causes of their antisocial behavior.

In an environment where reformation was threatened by overcrowding, coercion, and sometimes brutality, where economic productivity was often considered of equal value to rehabilitation, and where convenience was ultimately more valuable than the programs believed to be regenerative, the reformatory became, all at once, the centerpiece of a national penal system, and a symbol of the seeming futility of corrections.

The progressives had boundless confidence that the inmate would be ransomed from a life of crime by a proper socialization into the American milieu, with its correlative values of hard work, practical ethics, and individualism. In some respects, those hopes were precisely what the institution accomplished, with ambiguous results. In the end, consonant with the American value system, state officials had to appeal to the self-interest of the inmates in order to convince them to work: "With very few exceptions, prisoners are not kept employed to anything like their full capacity. This is not because there is not work enough to be done . . . Perhaps the best whip over a laborer is the whip of self interest" (State Commission of Prisons 1908, 93-95).

Thus did the reformatory establish itself as the hope of the American correctional philosophy in its restless search for the answer to crime. The liberal Protestant community, which had created the conditions that both effectively ended the penitentiary era and inaugurated the reformatory, had become as one educator stated earlier, "invisible." The new system never accomplished what its originators intended. Despite this, the reincarnation of millennial hope, transformed by trust in modern institutions and Positivism, had created a momentum, constantly fed by the "incontrovertible" data of the social sciences, that would carry the American penal experience for the next half century.

CHAPTER 5

RELIGION, PROGRESS, AND THE END OF THE PENITENTIARIES

As we have moved rapidly over the terrain of American penal and religious history, we have seen that Calvinism cast a long shadow. Its sober regard for the virtue of Adam's children, enabled it to coexist with a culture preoccupied with wealth, science, and progress, only as the result of a series of transformations. Yet it was "the bone and flesh of American life" (Weisberger 1958, 268). It continued to inform the development of American social psychology and the evolution of its institutions.

The penitentiary bore witness to the heavy stamp of Calvinist influence in the area of crime and punishment. It developed out of an evangelical strain of Calvinist theology, dominant in the early nineteenth century, that the energetic political activity of the "saints" could embrace an ever-widening army of repentant and reformed men and women. Despite the innovative trajectories for penology established with the emergence of the Progressive movement, the religious forces that shaped the American penal system continued to exercise their influence. Scientific methods, professionalization, and increased governmental programs barely disguised the confident millennial spirit that had characterized the Jacksonian era, and the proud institutions for the reclamation of the sinful that it spawned.

The spirit of reform, albeit disguised in secular metaphors, was now centered in the reformatories. The penitentiaries: Auburn, Sing Sing, Clinton, Charlestown, Pittsburgh and Philadelphia were left with an inherited architecture and internal structure void of meaning. They moved laboriously as the momentum established in the 1820s steadily decreased, until they became a symbol for the progressives of all the errors and misconceptions of the past. Chaplain Batt at Concord stated: "The old-time prison stands condemned" (The Pennsylvania Journal 1894-95, 87-88). As artifacts of the religious culture that gave them life, however, the penitentiaries continued as representations of an inheritance based on a renewed moral community—the foundational principle of American penal history.

The liberal wing of the religious community, so closely identified with Progressivism and the reformatory philosophy, continued to recede in deference to the secular institutions, commonly agreed to be the carriers of the divine plan. Chaplain Stebbins at Charlestown was among the many employing no religious language in their yearly reports. Instead, he worked to instill the reformatory philosophy at that institution. He invited professors, representatives of the building trades, and leaders in commerce to speak to the inmates:

> In this way the men have been instructed in agriculture, steam engineering, machinery, electricity and salesmanship. The results of this experiment the past year encourage the enlarging and broadening of this phase of manhood training during the ensuing year (MA Board of Prison Commissioners 1911, 32).[1]

The acrimonious dispute within Protestant circles had led to the erosion of the involvement of evangelicals in their traditional pursuit of societal and penal reform. The refashioning of Calvinist and millennial beliefs in the Progressive Era had the effect of eliminating social activism, and engendering a new form of quietism, in view of the belief that God was working within America's industrial and democratic context. The most prominent evangelical of the late nineteenth century, Dwight Moody, exemplified the theological movement that originated with Henry Ward Beecher and the revivalists of the 1850s, and continues to this day. It is a fusion of biblical literalism, born-again revivalism, and a belief in the divinely inspired nature of the American economic and political structure.

Moody stated that poverty was virtually impossible for any "consistent member of the Christian church" and that "there would not be a drunkard walking the streets" or "a harlot walking the streets, if it were not for unbelief" (Findlay 1969, 275-76). This philosophy was not only congenial to the expanded industrial and military adventures of the late nineteenth century, it provided their moral and spiritual foundation. Josiah Strong, secretary of the Evangelical Alliance, saw America as the new Rome with the divine mandate to "Anglo-Saxonize" the entire world (Ahlstrom 1972, 8). Although there were still social movements in the areas of temperance and Sunday observance, the province of the evangelical churches was now narrowly focused on individual conversion.

New York and Massachusetts

From their inauguration, the penitentiaries organized under the silent system functioned with the twin images of the moral hospital and the prosperous business enterprise. They reflected the conflict between "old light" and "new light" theological paradigms. As the focus of the religious community shifted to the reformatory, and as officials came to greet the prospect of economically self-sufficient institutions with almost universal skepticism, the original penitentiaries entered a period of resigned gloom and increased chaos. Warden Hubbell provided his impressions of Sing Sing:

> Ten years ago I was warden of this prison. I then considered it a failure, and yet compared with it when I returned here the first day of January 1873, it might be called a model of perfection. One bad practice after another and one loose habit after another had followed each other until the degradation was so low that nothing could be found worthy to be called by the name of discipline (Sen. Doc. 5 1874, 17).

As Hubbell rightly surmised, in the wake of the optimism following the Cincinnati congress and the decision to build Elmira, "this prison, to a large extent, is a mere reservoir to accumulate convicts for the other State prisons" (Sen. Doc. 5 1874, 18).

The press, particularly with the advent of the *Police Gazette* and other sensationalist publications in the 1840s, was often involved in seeking to expose the more vulgar practices of prison life. Now, with little to elevate the tone of conversation concerning these institutions, its portrayals became more graphic and derogatory. Hubbell stated:

> A morbid curiosity has grown up in the mind of the public to learn
> every particular incident in relation to every prisoner of any note, and
> in order to gratify this vicious desire writers often visit this prison,
> sometimes frankly, and at other times in disguise (Sen. Doc. 5 1874,
> 18).[2]

As overcrowding continued, and as the contracts expired, the
penitentiaries regressed to the chaotic conditions of the prisons before the
age of reform. The verbal "contamination," indolence, and violence that
had plagued Walnut Street, Newgate, and Charlestown were once again
evident.[3] One could hear the echo of the inspectors from an earlier era:
"without such a system of strict seclusion and non-intercourse religious
motives would have no power to make bad men better" (Sen. Doc. 20
1833, 16). The New York Prison Association, also recalling words from
the past, called Sing Sing "a vast school of crime" (1874, 25). A report
concerning the New York prisons stated: "Dealers were publicly
supplying the prisoners with almost anything they would pay for" (Sen.
Doc. 49 1877, iii).

Charlestown, almost unanimously claimed to be the finest example
of the silent system, was similarly beset by the disintegration that resulted
from the death of its founding principles. Governor William Russell
described the condition of that institution in his 1891 address to the
legislature:

> There has existed for some time a condition of affairs that is
> unsatisfactory and demands your attention. During the past year there
> has been insubordination, even to the point of riot and rebellion,
> amongst the prisoners; a lack of harmony between the Warden and
> some of the subordinate officers, which is subversive of proper prison
> discipline, and disagreement between the Warden and the Prison
> Commissioners. Public opinion has been aroused by the repeated
> insubordination of the prisoners and their frequent escapes, by the
> finding of keys, saws and other implements, and, in one instance, of
> firearms in their possession, and by other acts which seem to show
> negligence at least on the part of some officers in control (House Doc.
> 275 1891, 1).[4]

Changes in Institutional Structure

The internal structure of the institutions remained legally in force
until the early years of the twentieth century. It is important to remember
that mass criticism of the philosophy of the silent system did not surface

until overcrowding forced the amendment of the ban on communication. New York inspectors, as late as 1887, still bemoaned the "crying evil" and "loathsome practices" associated with inmate fraternization (Sen. Doc. 36, 19). Warden Chamberlain stated in relation to Charlestown: "All this crowding has been harmful to the perfect discipline which would otherwise be maintained" (Sen. Doc. 227 1878, 3-4). However, once the inmates were housed together, and as overcrowding, contract abuses, and outside labor agitation eroded the possibilities of providing work for all, it was only a question of time before the trappings of the old order vanished. The Massachusetts Prison Commissioners noted in 1911: "the discontinuance of the lockstep and the marching of the men in open order has caused no inconvenience" (1911, 9).

The Commission of Prisons in New York recorded in its report for 1904 that the "military step" was now used in place of the lock step "which was abolished in all the prisons some three years ago." Also, the use of striped clothing had been abolished for convicts serving their first term (1905, 21).

In a description of the facility at Clinton in 1905, Lewis Lawes, future warden of Sing Sing, showed, with some animosity, that many of the old regulations were still being enforced:

> Clinton prison was then run, as were all other prisons in the State, on the silent system . . . No talking in shops, or at mess, or during the march to mess or shops; limited rations of tobacco, hardly any recreation and a hundred and one other rules. The striped uniform was then in vogue, except for the first offenders; two stripes for the second, three for the third and subsequent offenders. Incorrigibles, so called, wore four stripes . . . zebras they were called (Lawes 1932, 15).

Lawes commented concerning Auburn and its system: "Silence was the symbol of authority. It was the hush of repression. It countenanced no laugh, no smile" (1932, 34). With his fellow progressive wardens, he would abolish all semblances of the system now almost unanimously deemed the cause of past failures in the correctional arena.

Although stated some years before the official end of the silent system, Franklin Sanborn correctly announced the death of the penitentiary movement as he commented on the changes in organization and discipline at Charlestown: "It must be said, however, that these changes take out the pith and point of the Auburn system" (MA Board of Charities 1866, 88-89).

The term "penitentiary," used to describe the moral hospital of the Jacksonian era, was rarely used after the Civil War. As the former penitentiaries were once again called prisons in the official and popular literature, county houses of detention came to be called penitentiaries.[5] They bore little resemblance to the institutions whose name they bore, but the term has remained a stable part of the penal lexicon ever since.

Pennsylvania

It was noted that the results of overcrowding and shrinking labor opportunities had deteriorated the fabric of the separate system. Richard Vaux had attempted to reconcile these unavoidable realities with the moral and contemplative vision established by his father and the other originators of the Eastern Penitentiary. He had coined the phrase, "individual treatment system," demonstrating the debt the progressives owed to the Pennsylvania approach. At the same time, the phrase effectively breached the barrier that separated the two models of incarceration. With his death in 1895, the last link to the penitentiary philosophy fell away. A new generation of administrators was set to emerge, not only in Pennsylvania but throughout the nation. These individuals, imbued with the progressive, scientific spirit, and removed from the religious forces that shaped it, were to inherit a system they did not fashion, and whose controlling impulses they did not understand. Despite the work of Wines and his allies to free the appointment of inspectors and wardens from the electoral process, they were generally political appointees who lacked the vision, and often the capacity, to grasp the complexities of the penal project.[6]

The formidable problems faced by the Eastern Penitentiary increased in intensity. Idleness—which contradicted every Calvinist and reformist impulse—was exacerbated by the passage of the Muehlbronner Act (1897) which decreed:

> . . . not more than five per centum of the whole number of inmates shall be employed in the manufacture of brooms, brushes or hollow-ware, or ten per centum in the manufacture of any other kind of goods, wares, articles or things that are manufactured elsewhere in the State (E. Pen. 1899, 7).

Thus, a large percentage of the inmates had no labor whatsoever. Warden Cassidy's earlier remark seemed apropos: "it is almost a crime in itself to confine a man or woman in a cell for years and not provide work for him or her to do" (E. Pen. 1896, 6). This act not only spelled the doom of the separate system, but also destroyed the automated, congregate approach now employed at the penitentiaries in the western part of the state.

Inactivity and overcrowding seriously undermined the moral and religious function of incarceration, that was the intent of the founders of the institution. John Ruth commented:

> With two or more in a cell, it is difficult to bring the subject of morals and religion directly to the attention of either personally. It is found rather that the crowding of convicts together furnishes them an opportunity to strengthen each other's hands in crime, and greatly lessens the probability of their reformation (E. Pen. 1876, 186-87).

Ruth's observation was borne out by the facts. Recidivism and violence increased with the elimination of labor opportunity and private accommodation: "Reconvictions have become much more frequent since we have been compelled to place two or three prisoners in the same cell" (E. Pen. 1878, 89). Warden Cassidy, in 1893, reported the death of the third officer "in recent years," stabbed while escorting an unruly convict to another cell (E. Pen. 1893, 118).

With no consistent ethical justification or organizational logic left to uphold, the Eastern Penitentiary inevitably began to move in a congregate direction. Like its counterparts in the other states, this institution was forced to change by social circumstances that state legislators were unwilling or unable to confront. No concerted effort was ever mounted to replace the separate system due to philosophical inconsistencies. The crisis faced by the Eastern Penitentiary was essentially the choice between the alternatives of committing massive resources and ingenuity to a restatement of the original vision, or an acceptance of external pressures and an alteration of the structure to accommodate them. The new leadership chose the latter.

Within a year of the death of Vaux, the chief inspector, Andrew Maloney, stated:

> [W]e believe the three existing State prison buildings afford facilities for a judicious combination of the separate and congregate methods of treatment, which would be advantageous to the State and its convicts, and would commend itself to the public judgment (E. Pen. 1897, 7).

The Pennsylvania Prison Society (formerly the Philadelphia society) saw the reformatory organization as the only viable option for the places of confinement in the state. In that format, it reasoned, a series of trades and programs could be provided, whereas in the traditional arrangement, the prisoners were enduring the very conditions the society was formed to counteract:

> There seems to be no reason why our prisons and jails may not be reconstructed or remodeled, giving the men work to do, that reformatory plans may be installed, seeing that the separate system has been almost obliterated by the overcrowding of the buildings set apart, and especially as our legislature prohibits employment in any manual work of over ten per cent of all those held in Prisons and jails (The Pennsylvania Journal 1900, 2).

These changes, now set in motion at each level of organization, insured the official demise of the separate system. Reports from inspectors, wardens, and chaplains became increasingly less prosaic and more statistical in the early years of the twentieth century. Chaplain Welch noted in his report for 1912 that "we have virtually a new institution" (E. Pen. 1913, 73).

In a real sense, Welch was ending more than a yearly report when he wrote the following reflection. He was announcing the termination of a century of direct religious guidance of the penal system: "the life and methods of today have practically but little similarity or relationship to those of a few years past" (E. Pen. 1913, 73).

The following July, Governor John K. Tener repealed the law of 1829 under which the separate system was organized. The Eastern Penitentiary was now a congregate facility and the penitentiary era was officially over.

American penology was thus on a course that was engineered by the religious community, but which had gradually lost sight of its origins. It now lacked a clear normative principle to guide its direction and help organize its data. The enthusiasm generated during the reformatory era would carry the penal philosophy for many decades, but, as with the penitentiary, it would eventually grind to a halt.

Chapter 6

AN INSTITUTION IN SEARCH OF
MEANING

In a study of administrative models in contemporary penal institutions, John DiIulio gives this description of a visit to the maximum security prison in Walpole, Massachusetts:

> Inmates roamed about virtually unimpeded, glaring, making threatening gestures, often shouting profanities at the officers. One cellblock was "trashed" by the inmates who lived there to underscore some grievance that nobody, including the inmates themselves, was willing or able to articulate. Officers wearing rubber boots and carrying shovels waded ankle-deep into the mess and were showered with insults and debris and human excrement. The inmates were rarely more charitable to each other than they were to the staff, and most assaults were inmate on inmate. Inmates spent their days in idleness punctuated by meals, violence, and weightlifting (DiIulio 1987, 2).

There is a necessary connection between this account, certainly as chaotic and violent as the early penal experiments before the birth of the penitentiary, and the scenario of the religious groups outside the prison that began this study. History suggests that the absence of a clearly defined moral organizational principle, one that articulates the justification and meaning of punishment, and to which each element of the penal environment is held accountable, is at the heart of the decisive problems in the American correctional experience.

Compare the modern depiction provided by DiIulio, with the accounts that hostile critics such as Louis Dwight and Charles Dickens provided of the Eastern Penitentiary, and one derives a far different impression. Dickens described the Pennsylvania method as "rigid, strict, and hopeless solitary confinement" whose effects upon its prisoners were "cruel and wrong" (1961, 120). Despite his revilement of the system his visit to the facility prompted these remarks:

> Every facility was afforded me that the utmost courtesy could suggest. Nothing was concealed or hidden from my view, and every piece of information that I sought was openly and frankly given. The perfect order of the building cannot be praised too highly, and of the excellent motives of all who are immediately concerned with the administration of the system there can be no kind of question . . . Standing at the central point, and looking down these dreary passages, the dull repose and quiet that prevails is awful. Occasionally there is a drowsy sound from some lone weaver's shuttle, or shoemaker's last, but it is stifled by the thick walls and heavy dungeon door, and only serves to make the general stillness more profound (1961, 121-22).

The point is not that what is required in the modern prison is "dull repose and quiet," although that may indeed be the case. It is that religious symbols, language, and ethics provided the American correctional system with an intelligible philosophy and direction throughout much of its history. The process of differentiation, and the conflation of liberal theology and progressive ideology, gradually terminated the conditions under which the religious community could supply such a role. The present status of corrections is aimless and vacuous due to its loss of a moral language, which alone can provide the meaning and motivation required for a system to function coherently.[1]

The progressive reforms embracing the environmental, hereditary, and psychological forces behind the criminal act have produced a wide array of experts, with elaborate sets of statistics concerning the social deviant. Penal professionals, and the public at large, are no longer in the dark as to the reasons for crime; nor is there lacking the breadth of programs, both within the institution and outside its walls, to meet the individual offender at each segment of age, criminal history, and emotional and physical dependency. What is lacking is an institutional logic that can bear the weight of incarcerating men and women against their will. There is abundant cynicism, a strong retributive component, and pragmatic responses brought on by the crisis of limits, specifically the periodic release of vast numbers of convicts by overcrowded facilities. None of these, however, is sufficient to meet the demands of a punishment process, based on time sentences, whose initial and ongoing motivation was the reform of its criminal subjects.[2]

In the opening chapter several theoretical understandings of social origin and cohesion were mentioned. Each claims that the organization and solidarity of a people can be traced to the cultural norms they espouse, and the non-cognitive, "religious" principle from which these norms emanate. The process of modernization, in which more complex interdependence and specification occurs, is a crisis point in societal development which "is always a moral and religious problem" (Bellah 1970, 64). This is so because increasing independence of societal actors and institutions "disturbs the preexisting structure of meaning and motivation in any society" (1970, 72).

This theory also holds true for institutions within a given system, as Weber among others pointed out. In contrast to Weber, however, what is needed is not necessarily a new eruption of charisma to offset the bureaucratic "iron cage," but the addition of voices attuned to the significance of symbols, and the moral language they evoke, to systemic integration. This is a reality which the descendants of inner-worldly Protestant asceticism failed to perceive.

In the penal context, when the momentum supplied by the reform spirit of Progressivism came to a halt with the prison uprisings at Attica and other institutions in the early 1970s, a defining principle was lacking from which the system could be reoriented. In an important study, Gresham Sykes relates correctly that the prison is a complex social system that produces its own norms, values, and methods of control, and that a simple, custodial or retributive philosophy is unable to govern it effectively. He states:

> [T]he lack of a sense of duty among those who are held captive, the obvious fallacies of coercion, the pathetic collection of rewards and punishments to induce compliance, the strong pressures toward the corruption of the guard in the form of friendship, reciprocity, and the transfer of duties into the hands of the trusted inmates—all are structural defects in the prison's system of power rather than individual inadequacies (Sykes 1958, 61).

With no professed foundational belief that can provide a direction, and from which a consistent set of norms and values can emanate, what remains are fragmented voices, most of which have abandoned the reformative vision that was the logic behind the cellular prison.

Recall the incongruity of the penitentiaries at Auburn and Sing Sing, constructed with a view to the moral reform of the inmate in his or her individual cell, when overcrowding forced double and triple accommodation.   The more profound incongruity is that those very facilities still exist today, with the same overcrowding, and without the belief in, or even the ability to articulate, a regenerative justification for incarceration. Both the architecture and logic of the prison "alternative" were based initially on the concept of the moral hospital, followed by the civic, psychological, and moral socialization of the reformatory. Without such a reformative vision, both the structure of traditional penal facilities and, indeed, the very concept of time sentences, face a crisis of meaning.

In the absence of a ruling moral logic, the penal system has become increasingly more cynical in its portrayal of human nature, its belief in the worth of its inhabitants, and its respect for the rights and privacy of the average citizen.   Surveillance of the discharged inmate has led to the sanction of a social environment in which every one has become a suspect, and in which controls and violations of liberty are woven into the fabric of social life:

> Delinquency, with the secret agents that it procures, but also with the generalized policing that it authorizes, constitutes a means of perpetual surveillance of the population: an apparatus that makes it possible to supervise, through the delinquents themselves, the whole social field (Foucault 1979, 281).

In a similar vein, Andrew von Hirsch states:

> The crime-control theorists began to feel that an effective system should give less emphasis to the criminal propensities of particular convicts and more to systemwide preventive effects. They thus drifted away from the positivists' individualized prediction theories and began to focus their interest on crime-control strategies that were addressed to potential offenders in general. Their attention turned, therefore, to general deterrence (1985, 7).

It would appear that the debate concerning the future course of corrections would be well-served by paying attention to the past, to the movements that created the structures with which current criminal justice professionals seem so ill at ease. If the history portrayed in this volume is correctly portrayed, then fundamental moral questions must be entertained, questions that have traditionally been the province of the religious community. This minimal requirement ought not be insensitive to some of the innovations this community brought to the development of the penal system in America. Often these programs were abandoned due to the pressure of external circumstances, not due to proven defects in the programs themselves. David Rothman asserts that New York and Pennsylvania "made an energetic and not unsuccessful attempt to put the programs into effect," and that "[t]he antebellum generation could rightly claim to have made a major innovation in criminal punishment" (1971, 94).

The central coordinates of the separate and silent systems, silence, work, and moral/religious training, were not found to be ineffective as formal guiding principles. It was the conditions surrounding their implementation, particularly in New York with its inordinate demand for financial stability, and its unfortunate misuse of corporal punishment, that eroded their value. Despite the fact that the statistical methods utilized to determine the effects of the penitentiary discipline on recidivism often missed reconvictions in other states, were certainly tinged with ideological bias, and cannot be necessarily equated with penal methods, it would be a mistake to ignore their findings out of hand. The chaplains who conducted them were not always blind supporters of the administration. History provides clear evidence that they were willing, to a significant degree, to critique institutional practices. Still, their data concerning recidivism was most favorable. Prior to the Civil War, the rates of reconviction were consistently less than 10%, with the data from the Eastern Penitentiary being the lowest.[3]

There are troubling and possibly insurmountable tensions in the decision to forcibly confine men and women. Two of the most constant are that public and governmental willingness to support reform programs is often linked to the financial cost of imprisonment, and that society's need to punish places limits on its ability to effect reformation. The history of the penitentiaries reveals, however, that it is possible to invest structures of control with meaning, as long as there is a stated moral organizational principle that is the channel through which an institution can be ordered and its inhabitants socialized. This task has been and always will be fundamentally religious in nature.

The data on the development of the American penal system has been presented not in hopes of painting an idyllic picture of the involvement of religion in the development of the penitentiary and the reformatory. It has been suggested, however, that the system has not generated a new theoretical and moral basis for its ongoing existence since the religious community withdrew from a vibrant, participative role. Historians and social scientists have too easily accommodated themselves to a positivist historical hermeneutic. In so doing, they have failed to comprehend the complex and dynamic nature of American religion, and its function in providing direction to the development of the prison and its related manifestations. This has led to more than an incomplete historical portrayal. It has contributed to the functional elimination of a critical element in organizing the system that administers to hundreds of thousands of confined men and women.

The historical period analyzed in this study was certainly different from our own, but it was a period when critical voices in the religious community debated each other and their social contemporaries in a public manner over the meaning and direction of punitive treatment. The leaders that emerged from this debate were not simply people of good will. They were educated, articulate, and involved in the life of the prison in a credible and respected way. Such voices may need to be heard once again if we are to find a way out of the current crisis in American penology.

Notes

Chapter 1

[1] Not all criminologists and social historians have dismissed the role of religion in American penal history. Scholars from various intellectual perspectives have maintained, by and large, that the religious community was an instrumental force in the social movements that led to the formation of the first penal institutions. They, however, have tended to argue that such movements were consciously or unconsciously motivated by prevailing class relations and the mode of capitalist production. The following pages will reveal the argument that religion has been the dominant motivational and ethical force in the development of American penal institutions, and, indeed, in the development of the scientific methodology for the study and treatment of criminal behavior.

[2] Perhaps the best source for documenting the covenental theology and the developments in Puritan theology preceding it is Perry Miller's, *The New England Mind: The Seventeenth Century* (Cambridge: The Belknap Press, 1939), chs. XIII-XV. See also Thomas Edward Zeman, "Order, Crime and Punishment: The American Criminological Tradition," diss, University of California, Santa Cruz, 1981, ch. 2.

[3] See Blake McKelvey, *The History of American Prisons* (Montclair, N.J.: Patterson Smith, 1977), 75: "This element [religion] was so prominent in the early days that its importance can scarcely be overestimated; its practical disappearance

in the course of the next fifty years was to be a significant factor in the story." The view that religious movements simply trailed in the wake of secular, political initiatives is expressed in David Rothman, *The Discovery of the Asylum* (Boston: Little, Brown & Company, 1971), 75-76: "[religious leaders] echoed prevailing social anxieties; they did not make a uniquely religious perspective relevant. Their vision of the well-ordered society did not indicate the influence of their special training. In this sense, they, unlike their predecessors, followed the pack rather than heading it." Similarly, Adam Jay Hirsch, arguing that pragmatic and not religious concerns motivated institutional initiatives in the Jacksonian era, calls the religious advocates "a handful of eccentrics" who attempted to "follow John Winthrop's lead and build a prison on a hill". See, The Rise of the Penitentiary(New Haven: Yale University Press , 1992), 68.

[4] The literature on social control as it relates to the penitentiary is extensive. The belief that penal development was directly related to the needs of capitalism and the prevailing relations of production is found in Georg Rusche and Otto Kirchheimer, *Punishment and Social Structure* (New York: Russell & Russell, 1968); Thomas Dumm, *Democracy and Punishment* (Madison: University of Wisconsin Press, 1987). Other accounts that give a high priority to capitalism and class conflict as controlling factors are: Michel Foucault, *Discipline and Punish* (New York: Vintage Books, 1979); Michael Hindus, *Prison and Plantation* (Chapel Hill: University of North Carolina Press, 1980); Michael Ignatieff, *A Just Measure of Pain* (New York: Pantheon, 1978). Although their approaches differ, both David Rothman, *The Discovery of the Asylum*, and Adam Hirsch, *The Rise of the Penitentiary* argue that the prison manifested the pragmatic need to control the social disharmony of the post-revolutionary era. Accounts that reveal penal and other lateral social developments as attempts to impose middle-class values on poor and working-class women are found in Nicole Hahn Rafter, *Partial Justice: women, prisons and social control* (New Brunswick: Transaction Publishers, 1990); David J. Pivar, *Purity Crusade* (Westport: Greenwood Press, 1973). For an overview of the subject see Stanley Cohen and Andrew Scull, eds., *Social Control and the State* (New York: St. Martin's Press, 1983).

[5] The overwhelming majority of writers on this subject are prone to agree with Hirsch, *The Rise of the Penitentiary*, 117, that the penitentiary declined because it was a "monument to failure." In his volume, *Prison and Plantation,*168-69, Michael Hindus suggests it was only when the religious movements for penal reform with their "impossibly inflexible ideology" started to "decline" that "prisoners began to enjoy some rights and privileges." A notable exception to this interpretation is provided by Carl E. Schneider whose review of Rothman's, *The Discovery of the Asylum,* emphasizes the foundational importance of the religious community in the penitentiary movement and of the rehabilitative ideal that it promoted. See "The Rise of Prisons And The Origins Of The Rehabilitative Ideal," *Michigan Law Review* 77 (1979): 707-746.

⁶ It is unlikely that the founders of the penitentiary in the United States knew of Mabillon's work but Roberts Vaux, a leading voice in the creation of the Pennsylvania system, had some knowledge of the "inquisitorial" prisons. It was in these institutions that many of the practices instituted by the Quakers were first introduced. See, Roberts Vaux, *Letter On the Penitentiary System of Pennsylvania* Philadelphia: Jesper Harding, 1827), 8.

₇ Christopher Lasch argues that many classical and neo-Marxists mirror the contempt of post-war liberalism for the uneducated masses. The latter are equated with the religious intolerance and small-mindedness of the age before scientific ideology proclaimed itself the executioner of such vestiges of our unenlightened past. What such intellectuals seek, according to Lasch, is a meritocratic rule of the experts. There are seeds of this tendency in both Lenin and Gramsci. Foucault's own theoretical approach leads to a similar conclusion. See Lasch, *The True and Only Heaven* (New York: W. W. Norton, 1991), 445-68; also Antonio Gramsci, "The Study Of Philosophy," in *Selections from the Prison Notebooks* (New York: International Publishers, 1971), 334-45.

Chapter 2

¹ Anxiety is by no means a novel development in Christian theology. The Reformation owed much of its theological and psychological underpinnings to the thought of Augustine. For an analysis of the impact of Augustine on Puritan theology see Perry Miller, *The New England Mind*, Chapter 1.

2 The controversial nature of Weber's thesis must be recognized. I use Weber with knowledge of the fact that neither Calvin nor the New England Puritans exalted the theological significance of wealth. Their's was an insistence on the value of work as a vocation in the service of the divine plan for humankind, as well as a refuge from the idleness that reflected "unregenerate" behavior. The New England preacher, Peter Buckley, stated: "Time was when we counted the proud blessed, and placed our felicity in other things, as in riches, preferments, favor and credit with men, etc. but now these are become vile and things of no value; faith makes us change our voice, and to speak with a new tongue." Nevertheless, there is not a strict aversion to material accumulation among the Puritans as long as one's primary focus is fidelity to God's commands. John Cotton, for example, stated: "we may indeed set our hearts on the blessings of this life, yet so, as therein we do God's will, build up his kingdom, honor the name of his grace, other wise, it will not be lawful for us to set our hearts upon them." See Phyllis M. Jones and Nicholas R. Jones, eds., *Salvation in New England, Selections from the Sermons of the First Preachers* (Austin: University of Texas Press, 1977), 32, 125-26. There is a significant departure from this ethical stance in the continued development of American Protestantism after the Great Awakening, when Calvinist and Puritan motifs were modified by the ethical rationalism of Arminianism and, eventually, by the rational subjectivism of Utilitarianism. The new shape of evangelical Protestantism, particularly in the

nineteenth century, was therefore accompanied by a more materialist component to the understanding of faith. Several accounts that underline the connection between capitalism and the development of evangelicalism are: Stephen Berk, *Calvinism versus Democracy* (New York: Archon Books, 1974), ch. 1; and Richard I. Bushman, :*From Puritan to Yankee: Character and the Social Order in Connecticut1690-1765* (Cambridge Harvard University Press, 1967).

3 See Richard Hooker, *The Laws of Ecclesiastical Polity* (Oxford: Clarendon Press, 1820); John Locke, *Two Treatises of Government*, especially Book II, Chs. VIII-XIII.

⁴ See Michel Foucault, *Discipline and Punish*, 104-114. See also Pieter Spierenburg, *The Spectacle of Punishment* (New York: Cambridge University Press, 1984). For an account that focuses on the metaphorical aspects of corporal punishment in line with the political and theological idea of the body politic, see Randall McGowen, "The Body and Punishment in Eighteenth-Century England," *The Journal of Modern History* 59 (1987), 651-79. A report that focuses on the religious aspects of the execution ritual, and how it was used as a platform to argue for moral cohesion as well as individual responsibility, is found in Louis Masur, *Rites of Execution* (New York: Oxford University Press, 1989), chapter two.

⁵ Cesare Beccaria (1738-1794) was born in Milan to a noble family. Although indisposed to concerted effort in any vocation, he was well trained academically and became associated with a group of intellectuals influenced by the Encyclopedists. Lombardy had only recently been freed of the domination of Spain and the penal methods of the Inquisition. Beccaria, aided by his associates, wrote *On Crimes and Punishments* in 1764. The work was an immediate international success and his ideas were to become standardized in the penal theory of the Enlightenment. He advocated a total revision of criminal law on the basis of general utility, denounced secret accusations and torture, questioned the necessity of capital punishment, and condemned existing penal jurisprudence. See Coleman Phillipson, *Three Criminal Law Reformers* (Montclair, NJ: Patterson Smith, 1975), 3-10.

⁶ Editions of Beccaria's work were published in Charlestown, MA in 1777 and Philadelphia in 1778, as well as serialized in several journals. See Louis Masur, *Rites of Execution*, 52.

7 *The Cambridge Platform,* enacted in 1648, gave a normative direction to Congregationalism based on biblical authority and Puritan tradition. It highlighted the three principles mentioned. See Alden T. Vaughan, ed., *The Puritan Tradition in America 1620-1730* (Columbia: University of South CarolinaPress,1972), 99-114.

[8] Several commentators on the period have suggested that the workhouses bore no resemblance to the later evangelically inspired institutions that emphasized the rehabilitation of the wrongdoer. They contend, incorrectly, I believe, that these houses of correction reflected the belief that the vagrant was a visible symbol of divine judgment on the sinner and held out no hope of reform. See Kai Erikson, *Wayward Puritans* (New York: Wiley, 1966), 196-98; Rothman, *The Discovery of the Asylum*, 53.

[9] Among the leading advocates in England for a religiously guided approach to corrections were John Howard, *The State of the Prisons* (London: W. Eyres, 1777). Jonas Hanway, *Solitude in Imprisonment* (London: J. Brew, 1776); Henry Fielding, *A Proposal for Making Effectual Provision for the Poor* (London: A. Millar, 1753). An overview of the impact of the above mentioned figures and their fellow reformers, albeit from the perspective of social control by the industrial elite, is provided by Michael Ignatieff, *A Just Measure of Pain*. For a more nuanced, "consensual" interpretation of these developments, see Margaret DeLacy, *Prison Reform in Lancashire, 1700-1850* (Stanford: Stanford University Press, 1986). For the impact of continental efforts on later criminological development, see Thorsten Sellin, *Pioneering in Penology* (Philadelphia: University of Pennsylvania Press, 1944).

[10] See Ernst Troeltsch, *The Social Teaching of the Christian Churches* (Chicago: University of Chicago Press, 1931), 684-87; Sydney Ahlstrom, *A Religious History of the American People* (New Haven: Yale University Press, 1972), 236-39.

[11] See Jacobus Arminius, *Writings* (Grand Rapids: Baker Book House, 1956). For a discussion of Arminian ideas see, Perry Miller, *The New England Mind: The Seventeenth Century*, 368ff; Stephen E. Berk, *Calvinism versus Democracy*, 11-12.

[12] See Sydney Ahlstrom, *A Religious History of the American People*, 7-8 ; Charles C. Cole, *The Social Ideas of The Northern Evangelicals* (New York: Octagon Books, 1977); Whitney Cross, *The Burned-over District* (New York: Octagon Books, 1981); Edwin Gaustad, *A Religious History of America* (New York: Harper & Row, 1966), 149-52; Timothy Smith, *Revivalism and Social Reform* (New York: Abingdon Press, 1957); Bernard Weisberger, *They Gathered at the River* (Chicago: Quadrangle, 1958).

[13] See Theodore Parker, "A Sermon on the Dangerous Classes in Society," in *Speeches, Addresses and Occasional Sermons*, (Boston: Horace B. Fuller, 1876) 296-332.

[14]   For further evidence on the wide involvement of the religious community in voluntary associations, see Cole, *The Social Ideas of the Northern Evangelicals*, 102; Mary P. Ryan, *Cradle of the Middle Class* (New York: Cambridge University Press,1981), 105; David J. Pivar, *Purity Crusade* (Westport: Greenwood Press, 1973), 159.

[15] See *Tenth Annual Report of the Inspectors of The Eastern State Penitentiary of Pennsylvania* (Philadelphia: Brown, Bicking & Guilbert, 1839), 17; *Thirty-First Annual Report* (Philadelphia: McLaughlin Brothers, 1860), 45; *Thirty-Seventh Annual Report* (Philadelphia: McLaughlin Brothers, 1866), 90. In this latter report, the physician, George C. Taylor, remarked that death among the inmates that year was "accelerated by that bane of prison life, self abuse."

[16] I am prepared to accept much of what Marty argues although he hints at a relationship between religion and politics that is quite different from the argument presented in this volume. The quote also overlooks the leadership of the evangelicals in the cause of anti-slavery. There is an impressive corpus of sermons, tracts, and articles promoting emancipation. See, for example, Reverend William Adams, *Christianity and Civil Government* (New York: Scribner, 1851); and Reverend James A. Thome, *Prayer for the Oppressed* (Boston: American Tract Society, 1859).

[17]   This is not to admit that the conservative economic agenda of evangelicals, coming as they did from a Calvinist social and economic paradigm, can be reduced to a synonym for capitalism and bourgeois values. I believe this opinion tendered by Edward L. Ayers, *Vengeance and Justice* (New York: Oxford University Press, 1984); Charles Dumm, *Democracy and Punishment*; Rusche and Kirchheimer, *Punishment and Social Structure*; and Hirsch, *The Rise of the Penitentiary*, among others, and with varying degrees of enthusiasm, misses the point that forms of economic exchange are themselves contingent on the moral parameters set by the religious community.

[18] Aside from the workhouse, there were several early and short-lived experiments in post-conviction detention, most notably that at Castle Island in Massachusetts. See Hirsch, *The Rise of the Penitentiary*, 11.

[19] Benjamin Rush was not a Quaker but a key figure in the American Enlightenment. The critical texts influencing this movement were provided by the moral sense theorists, especially Francis Hutcheson, and John Locke's *Essay Concerning Human Understanding*. In seeking to define human nature not in terms of innate ideas, but in emotion and sense impression the movement envisioned a penal setting where the control of sensory stimuli could refashion the person, leading to "habits of industry" and benevolence. Such ideas would have

been of interest to Quakers whose theology was centered on silence, internal conversion, and benevolent attitudes towards all. See D. D. Raphael, ed. *British Moralists, 1650-1800* (Oxford: Clarendon Press, 1969); Zeman, "Order, Crime, and Punishment," ch. 2.

[20] See Jeremy Bentham, "Panopticon or The Inspection House," in *The Works of Jeremy Bentham* (Edinburgh: W. Tait, 1843), 39-46.

[21] See also, Mary P. Ryan, *Cradle of the Middle Class*, 18-19.

[22] See Thomas Eddy, *An Account of the State Prison or Penitentiary House, in the City of New York* (New York: Issac Collins and Son, 1801), 6. Eddy mentions Howard, Beccaria, and Montesquieu, quotes Beccaria on the cover, and includes this quote from Montesquieu on the inface: "The Christian Religion, which ordains that men should love each other, would without doubt have every nation blest with the best civil and political laws; because these are, next to this religion, the greatest good that men can give or receive."

[23] In her study of domestic relations and class identity in Utica, New York during this period, Mary P. Ryan argues that social institutions were patterned on the New England family with its emphasis on economic productivity within a patriarchal system: "The internal relations and ideology of the family were colored by these economic imperatives and gave prominence to notions of hierarchy, authority, and patriarchy rather than either warm mutual ties or the free play of individual interests." See *Cradle of the Middle Class*, 50-51.

[24] The term "congregate" was used to describe any penal facility where the inmates either worked or were housed in common. Even when Auburn initiated separate accommodations for each resident, it maintained the practice of work in common and thus was considered a congregate penitentiary.

Chapter 3

[1] David Garland offers an interpretation of Durkheim's thought in his *Punishment and Modern Society* (Chicago: University of Chicago Press, 1990), chs. 2-3. The account is largely sympathetic, but argues that Durkheim has overstated the power of ritual and religious solidarity as foundations for punishment. Unfortunately, Garland centers his analysis on Durkheim's early writings when the author had not yet developed his mature theory on the role of religion in public life.

[2] Other authors have depicted this development in terms of a rising sentiment of empathy with other members of the society. The roots of this psychological characteristic are located in the increased privatization of the post-Enlightenment age, particularly among the middle and upper classes. See Pieter

Spierenburg, *The Spectacle of Suffering,* 183-199; Svend Ranulf, *Moral Indignation and Middle Class Psychology* (New York: Schocken Books, 1964).

[3] A polemical period document, attempting to defend the integrity of the Eastern State Penitentiary, emphasized its congruence with the professed merits of the Auburn system, among them the reformation of the inmate, habituation to virtue, solitude, religious instruction and trade development. See *A Vindication of the Separate System of Prison Discipline from the Misrepresentations of the North American Review* (Philadelphia: J. Dobson, 1839), 3-4.

[4] The Act of the General Assembly which established the Eastern State Penitentiary included among the duties of the inspectors: "They shall attend to the religious instruction of the prisoners and procure a suitable person for this object." See Richard Vaux, *Brief Sketch of the Origin and History of the State Penitentiary for the Eastern District of Pennsylvania, at Philadelphia* (Philadelphia: McLaughlin Brothers, 1872), 43.

[5] See John Sergeant, *Observations and Reflections on the design and Effects of Punishment* (Philadelphia, 1828), 4; Roberts Vaux, *Letter on the Penitentiary System of Pennsylvania,* 10.

[6] The resolution authorizing the appointment of the moral instructor was passed on 16 April, 1838. Prior to that volunteer clergy ' lfilled the duties accorded to chaplains. Richard Vaux writes: "There was   Moral Instructor appointed, but the Rev. Charles Demme', of the German   utheran Church, undertook to perform these duties, and was aided at variou: nes by the Rev. Samuel W. Crawford and the Rev. James Wilson, of the Refc   led Presbyterian, and Associate Reformed Churches." See Vaux, *Brief Sketch,* 77.

[7] One of the Quaker women remarked: "the female convicts could not be raised above their deplorable condition until they were placed under the superintendence of officers of their own sex." See *The Pennsylvania Journal of Prison Discipline and Philanthropy* 1 (1845), 114. For further insight into the work of Quaker women in prison reform, see Estelle Freedman, *Their Sister's Keepers* (Ann Arbor: University of Michigan Press, 1981), ch. 2.

[8] "The system of separate confinement afforded increased facilities to the members of the Association, in their labors for the religious instruction of the convicts, and they began to teach them regularly to spell and read." *The Pennsylvania Journal of Prison Discipline and Philanthropy* 1 (1845), 114.

⁹ Blanchard Fosgate, showing the wisdom of hindsight and the influence of developments critical of corporal punishment, reflected on the use of the shower bath during his tenure as physician at Auburn: "while the culprit may exhibit no signs of extraordinary suffering, portions of the interior organization, both in the function and structure, may have succumbed to its incomprehensible power. Phrenitis, amaurosis, epilepsy, insanity and death are among its darker phases, while those delicate shades of mental injury, seen only in occasional aberrations, must be of frequent occurrence." See *Crime and Punishment* (Auburn: W. J. Moses, 1866), 21.

¹⁰ Saint Benedict, for example, argued that the monk who committed repeated offenses was to be cut off from the common life of the monastery, working, praying, and eating alone "in penitential sorrow." Always the intention was the reinstatement of the erring brother who was to be visited by the abbot in his cell "lest he be swallowed up with overmuch sorrow." See Justin McCann, ed., *The Rule of Saint Benedict* (Westminster: Newman Press, 1952), ch. 27.

¹¹ The prison journal of one inmate provides some insight into the disciplinary advantages this structural addition might have provided: "the sneaks (night guards) come on. One follows another, gliding along, noiseless and specter-like, shod in thick felt-soled shoes. You hear nothing; they never utter a word; but there, at your door, suddenly stands a dusky figure, and the glim of the bull's eye (lantern) falls on you." See Julian Hawthorne, ed., *The Confessions of a Convict* (Philadelphia: R. C. Hartranft, 1893), 30-31.

12 A Senate Committee sent to investigate reported abuses at the New York penitentiaries described this common disciplinary tool: "The cat is the instrument used for the punishment of the convicts . . . the handle of which is a common cowhide whip, about eighteen inches long, wound with leather, and has six strands of twine, not exceeding one sixteenth of an inch in diameter, about twelve or fifteen inches long, and wound at the end with thread about one inch, to keep them from raveling" (N.Y. Sen. Doc. 37 1840, 18).

13 In this regard, as well as in many of the architectural features of Auburn, the shadow of Jeremy Bentham looms large. As noted in chapter two, the influence of English penal development was quite pronounced. Bentham intended to maximize the power of control over the inmate population by creating the phenomenon of the unobserved observer. The psychological effect, he argued, was to give not only prisoners, but also their keepers, the omnipresent reminder that their behavior was being monitored. The principal architect, Britten, would have been familiar with Bentham's ideas, as would John D. Cray, a retired British soldier, who had considerable input into the early developments of Auburn. See Bentham, *Panopticon or The Inspection House*, especially letter VI. See also Blanchard Fosgate, *Crime and Punishment*, 5-6.

[14] Not only were inmates required to attend Sabbath services, it was also a requirement for the guards: "except one in the north wing and one in the kitchen." See Gershom Powers, *A Brief Account of the Construction, Management, & Discipline of the New York State Prison at Auburn* (Auburn:U. F. Doubleday, 1826), 3.

[15] This statement must be understood within the limits placed on officials to mete out corporal punishment. State statutes required, for example, that two prison inspectors be present whenever a convict was to be disciplined by the whip. See Powers, *A Brief Account*, 1.

[16] Stephen Allen was one of the leading advocates of the silent system. He lobbied strongly for the new facility, as this letter from William Roscoe suggests: "At New York, it has been recommended, by you and your colleagues, that the present state prison in that city shall be abandoned and sold, and new prisons should be erected, where there are large marble quarries, with a facility of water conveyance, and that the convicts should be employed in quarrying, getting marble, and working it into proper shapes and sizes for building." See Roscoe, *A Brief Statement of the Causes Which Have Led to the Abandonment of the Celebrated System of Penitentiary Discipline in Some of the United States of America* (Liverpool, 1827), 19-20.

[17] The inspectors were displeased with the resignation: "This board will therefore only add, that in every respect he possessed their entire confidence and esteem, and that he left the situation very much to their regret" (Sen. Doc. 3 1831, 7).

[18] The transcript of the inquiry can be found in *Documents of the State of New York* (Albany, 1831), Doc. 60.

[19] The inspectors were victims of New York's volatile political structure. Each new administration in Albany would appoint a new body of overseers. This lack of legislative consistency was further compounded by a law providing that each year a new inspector would replace one currently in service.

[20] Chaplain Smith at Auburn shared these remarks with the Sabbath School Union of Cayuga County: "Who, that looks upon ignorance as the mother of crime, and regards intellectual light as essential to the virtue and happiness of a community, will not be glad that even one ray is thrown into this dark and frightful wilderness of mind? Who, especially, that acknowledge the efficacy of the 'sword of the spirit', will not rejoice in view of what the 'word of God', thus treasured in their memories, may be the means of accomplishing?" See *Report of Gershom Powers, Agent and Keeper of the State Prison at Auburn* (Albany:

Crosswell and Van Benthuysen, 1828), 60.

[21] John Hageman reported that "for sprinkling water on a convict," an inmate named O'Reily "was stripped entirely naked. . . whipped with a cat, the number of blows I cannot tell, say fifty or more . . . he was red all over his back and bloody" (Doc. 48, 48-49).

[22] In his commentary on the Massachusetts State Prison at Charlestown, Michael Hindus makes a similar claim: "As a substantial capital investment, the prison was visible proof of the seriousness with which the state took both crime and its elusive cure. And, by its quest for profit, the prison revealed the ultimate softness of that commitment while also reflecting in a ludicrously precise manner the entrepreneurial spirit of the age that produced the edifice." See *Prison and Plantation*, 162.

[23] In their landmark study of prisons in the United States and Canada, Enoch Wines and Theodore Dwight interviewed Benjamin Leggett, an official at Sing Sing during ten successive administrations dating to the first years of the facility. He was asked if reformation was the primary aim of penal philosophy, to which he responded, "I should think the view was to make the prison pay its way." See *Report on The Prisons And Reformatories of The United States And Canada* (Albany: Van Benthuysen & Sons, 1867), 288.

[24] Wines and Dwight quote chaplain Canfield at Clinton who offers a similar argument: "The teaching of morality and religion, to produce their best effect, need to be illustrated and enforced by the character and example of all who are allowed to associate with the convict officially or otherwise. The 'powers that be' may, if possible, employ an angel's tongue to enforce every command in the decalogue and all the teachings of the gospel, and yet if the same powers require the convict to systematically trample upon these commands, the practice will do much more to form his character than 'preaching'." See *Report on The Prisons*, 210.

[25] William James argues that the conversion experience, when sincere, rarely leads to "backsliding." See *The Varieties of Religious Experience* (New York: Collier Books, 1961), 209-210.

[26] Michael Hindus traces the employment of statistics to the Utilitarians in England who substituted "the hedonic calculus for scripture" and were led thereby to "a flexible response to social conditions." See *Prison and Plantation*, 230-31. The impact of the Utilitarians on American penology is unquestioned. This influence notwithstanding, Dwight and the chaplains were more the heirs of a religious tradition than a secular, philosophical one and the forerunners of the Social Gospel movement that sought to reconcile a historically grounded theological vision with the canons of scientific methodology.

[27] The Act of the General Assembly calling for the building of the Eastern Penitentiary allowed discharged inmates four dollars. See Richard Vaux, *Brief Sketch*, 49.

[28] This was not only the first prison library in New York but possibly the first in the United States. See Wines and Dwight, *Report on The Prisons*, 228.

[29] Georgiana Bruce Kirby gave this rather unceremonious depiction of Luckey and of the discord in the prison before Farnham's arrival: "The matron, a respectable, but incompetent person, had finally been attacked and the clothes torn from her body. A well-meaning, tight-skulled little chaplain had prayed frantically for the rebels—prayed to them also. They made a feint of yielding, then turned the prison into pandemonium again." See *Years of Experience* (New York: AMS, 1971), 190-91.

[30] By the end of the nineteenth century, thanks to the work of the Italian criminal anthropologist, Cesare Lombroso, the belief that the brains of criminals manifested "atavistic anomalies" was widespread among penal professionals and the public at large. Phrenology certainly had an impact on the development of this outlook. See Cesare Lombroso, *Crime: Its Causes and Remedies* (Boston: Little Brown and Company, 1911).

[31] Margaret Fuller, an acquaintance of Kirby's from the latter's previous experience at Brook Farm, was moved by the methodology employed by Farnham. She visited the prison and subsequently wrote to the women incarcerated there: "I wrote to some of the ladies of Boston on your account, and they will send you books which may, I hope, encourage the task for reading which it gives me pleasure to hear that so many of you show . . . I hope you will accept these books as a token that, although on returning to the world you may have much to encounter form the prejudices of the unthinking, yet there are many whowill be glad to encourage you to begin a new career, and redeem the past by living lives of wise and innocent acts, useful to your fellow creatures and fit for being gifted with immortal souls." See Kirby, *Years of Experience*, 212-213.

[32] Kirby later recalled the events leading up to this decision: "In the shop it was customary for one of the ladies to read aloud a part of the afternoon. The women would keep perfectly still and sew assiduously all the while, thankful for the privilege accorded them. Mrs. Farnham considered that the attempt to enforce continuous silence between human beings in close proximity to each other was worse than useless. She therefore gave permission to talk in a low tone to each other half an hour every afternoon, providing that they had conformed to the rule of silence during the remainder of the day." See *Years of Experience*, 199.

[33] One inspector is reputed to have told Edmonds: "I must say that I shouldn't like to marry Mrs. Farnham." To which the judge replied, "Thunder man! we did not hire her to marry you. We brought her here to manage this prison." See Kirby, *Years of Experience*, 218.

Chapter 4

[1] Warden Halloway at the Eastern Penitentiary stated in his report for 1866 that 70% of the male convicts received had been in the army or navy (Eastern Pen. Report 1867, 122).

[2] Ironically, the movement had the opposite effect on American religion and its public role. By seeking to elevate religious sentiments to the level of universal values, it served to secularize them. As the efficacy of parochial institutions was downplayed in favor of those accessible to all citizens, Beecher helped create the foundations for the modern liberal state. See David Pivar, *Purity Crusade*, 158.

[3] In another issue, Helen disobeyed her mother and took Minnie out on the swing. Minnie fell and smashed her head against a rock, nearly dying. The moral was: "Children, when tempted to be disobedient to your kind parents, or selfish and unkind to your brothers and sisters, think of what may happen in consequence, and how wicked it is to indulge in such feelings" (July 1866, 27).

[4] Warden Charles Sutton warned of the "dangerous classes" that exist as we drift "toward the Millennium" and called for support among those "who have the greatest faith in human nature and its ultimate perfection." See *The New York Tombs*, 17.

[5] Gideon Haynes, a renowned warden at Charlestown, sought to "reclaim" those confined under him and "fan into a blaze the smallest spark of manhood they may bring with them into the prison." See *Pictures From Prison Life* (Boston: Lee and Shepard, 1869), 246.

[6] Law takes on greater religious overtones to the degree that the religious sphere is relegated to the private realm. Pivar offers a similar argument in *Purity Crusade*, 164.

[7] Warden Cassidy remarked: "Heredity is one of the most prolific of all crime causes. The sins of the parents are visited on the child . . . It is a divine law, and it is human experience that such is the case." See *Warden Cassidy on Prisons and Convicts* (Philadelphia: Patterson & White, 1894), 29.

[8] In 1864, A. J. Ourt was appointed clerk of the Eastern Penitentiary. His yearly report was comprised of lengthy statistical tables analyzing the full range of personal and environmental factors seen as necessary to understanding the

origin of criminal behavior. In 1867, under Richard Vaux, the inspectors called for a state department whose exclusive duty would be the attainment and classifying of statistics which would "embrace all the social relations, and reach through all the stages of life from birth to death" (E. Pen. 38th Report 1867, 25).

[9] In their report for 1868, the inspectors of the Western Penitentiary claimed that the separate system was a necessary development over the early regime of strict solitary confinement. However, the lack of "mental resources" among the convict population demanded the implementation of a congregate format. See *42nd Report of the Inspectors of the Western Penitentiary*, 8.

[10] Were it not for the affection he harbored for the Eastern Penitentiary, and notwithstanding state budgetary considerations, it seems clear that Vaux and not Brockway would have inaugurated the reformatory. This early statement indicates how precisely he understood the future direction of American penology: "By this penitentiary discipline, each prisoner is treated individually; separated from convict contact and contamination; freed from the depressing and degrading consequences of association with other co-criminals; strengthened to effort for regaining lost moral and social health; brought within the direct personal influence of reformatory or curative treatment, and its most salutary modifying causes; subject to improvement from earnest effort of instruction in mind and handicrafts; placed in the most accessible relation to those creative forces, which in operation change the moral constitution. Thus each convict is surrounded by reformatory processes . . ." See *Penal: An Element in Social Science* (Philadelphia: King & Baird, 1862), 26.

[11] Vaux stated: "The elementary principles identified with social science are deduced by analogy from those of medical science, and the treatment of social maladies or crimes, is coincident with that of physical disease." See, *Penal: An Element in Social Science*, 21.

[12] Haynes was similarly vocal concerning these initiatives and implemented several of them during his tenure at Charlestown. He advocated the mark system (one good mark each month for good conduct and industry, for which one day for each year of the prisoner's sentence is deducted) and used the Bible in its defense: "Are not the Scriptures filled with promises of reward to those who repent and keep God's laws? It ill becomes us to criticize or raise our voices against principles enumerated from on high; it is too much like thanking God that we are not like other men." See *Pictures from Prison Life*, 244.

[13] Reverend Spring also wrote for the American Tract Society. In one of his publications he stated: "I should like to see an authentic and correct history of all the prisons in the land; and unless I am much deceived, such a statement would

not present an instance of an individual who had not broken over the restraints of the Sabbath before he was abandoned to crime, and who could not mark the profanation of that day as forming an advanced stage in his downward career." See *The Sabbath: A Blessing to Mankind* (New York: American Tract Society, n.d.), 5-6.

[14] A report by a Mrs. Child in a periodical dedicated to the abolition of capital punishment, said of Edmonds: "he has kept strong faith in human nature, and the omnipotence of Christian love." *The Hangman* 1(1 Jan. 1845), 1.

[15] For an account of the settlement of Australia and of the role of Maconochie in penal reform, see Robert Hughes, *The Fatal Shore* (New York: Knopf, 1987).

[16] Wines and his companion at the NYPA, Theodore Dwight (later appointed head of Columbia Law School, and the descendent of the president of Yale who so influenced Louis Dwight), founded the American Association for Promoting the Social Sciences in 1865 (NYPA 1866, 35).

[17] The ideas generated by the sojourn are described by McKelvey as having "an impact on penal developments in America and Europe second only to Howard's State of Prisons". See *American Prisons A History of Good Intentions*, 68.

[18] Although Elmira became synonymous with the reformatory movement, it was not the only institution of its kind when it finally opened. Indiana began its reformatory for Women in Indianapolis in 1873. See Nicole Hahn Rafter, *Partial Justice*, 29.

[19] For an overview of the institution see, David Dyer, *History of the Albany Penitentiary* (Albany: J. Mussell, 1867).

[20] In a letter to Wines and Dwight he revealed that, like Vaux, his evangelical roots were never far from the surface: "I trust, however, that as Christ's new dispensation of love submerged and practically annulled the old dispensation of law, so the new era of 'rewards', in the management of prisoners, will render the discussion of the subject of punishments comparatively unimportant." His administrative style at Elmira would reveal the irony contained in the letter. See Wines and Dwight, *Report on The Prisons*, 342.

[21] Brockway was in communication with Wines and the NYPA throughout his tenure at Detroit. He produced a paper in the 1868 report of the association calling for the abolition of the "preemptory character of the sentences imposed upon persons committed to these establishments." However, his essay, as well as his famous address at Cincinnati, came after earlier statements of Wines and

Dwight, such as this one: "Not a few of the best minds in Europe and America have, by their investigations and reflections, reached the conclusion that time sentences are wrong in principle; that they should be abandoned, and that reformation sentences should be substituted in their place." See Frederick Wines, *Punishment and Reformation*, 203-04.

[22] The governor of Massachusetts, Emory Washburn, in an editorial in the *Boston Daily Advertiser*, supported the concept of a reformatory for women. He wrote that "profit and loss" should not govern this decision but a "higher motive" that had planted the state's schools, "sustained her hospitals," "cares for the idiot and the insane" and "visits the sick prisoner in his cell with the consolations of religion." See *Reasons for a Separate Prison for Women* (Boston, 1874), 7.

[23] Since faith and metaphysics lacked empirically verifiable claims, moral propensities had to fall under some system of measurement, however suspect its method of calculation. The "moral condition" of incoming residents was statistically estimated according to "Susceptibility to Moral Impression" and "Moral sense . . . either Filial Affection, Sense of Shame, or Sense of Personal Loss." One entry for the last category ranked the inmates as follows: Positively none, 49.3%; Possibly some, 30.6%; Ordinarily sensitive, 15.2%; Specially sensitive, 4.9%. See Alexander Winter, *The New York State Reformatory In Elmira* (London: Swan Sonnenscein, 1891), 23.

[24] Rothman maintains that the "most problematic Progressive assumption" was "that the prison could perform both a custodial and a rehabilitative function, that there was no inherent conflict between guarding men securely and making them better." See *Conscience and Convenience* (Boston: Little, Brown & Company, 1980), 385-86.

Chapter 5

[1] In a similar example of the replacement of religion by ethics, a minister of the First Parish in Brookline spoke to inmates in this way: "Civilized life is, at bottom, not warfare, but mutual service. Every step of industrial progress that has been gained has been won by driving back the old predatory habits and instincts, setting men side by side to work peaceably, each for own advantage by serving the others' need." See Howard N. Brown, *A Prison-Sunday Sermon* (Boston: George H. Ellis, 1896), 8.

2 For a discussion of the press and its impact on attitudes towards crime and punishment, see Daniel A. Cohen, *Pillars of Salt, Monuments of Grace* (New York: Oxford University Press, 1993); Dan Schiller. *Objectivity and the News* (Philadelphia: University of Pennsylvania Press, 1981), 96 ff.; Masur, *Rites of Execution*, 114.

3 Haynes stated: "Without labor, reformation, or even ordinary discipline, in a prison is impracticable. If any general principle in prison discipline is certain, it is, that a society of prisoners in idleness will be a society of increasing depravity. See *Pictures from Prison Life*, 101-102.

4 Wines and Dwight had called Charlestown "the banner prison of the country." Yet there had always been a seam of violence woven into the fabric of the institution. After the "showering" of an inmate, Warden Charles Lincoln died (June 1843) after he "was stabbed in the neck with a shoe knife as he passed through the shop." Similarly, Warden Solon H. Tenney was murdered (December 1856) on his daily tour of the upholstery department. See Haynes, *Pictures from Prison Life*, 59, 71-72.

5 Wines and Dwight stated: "New York has six prisons, called penitentiaries, indeterminate between her state prisons and her county jails; but they are all local institutions, created by special statutes and managed by the authorities of the counties in which they are situated." See *Report on The Prisons*, 57. See also Dyer, *History of the Albany Penitentiary*.

6 McKelvey states: "[T]he principle that any man who helped build the political strength of a party was able to fill, and had a right to demand, any administrative post he chose, largely controlled the selection of wardens, and as long as this principle was maintained elaborate reformatory programs were doomed." See *American Prisons*, 176. Hindus makes a similar point, albeit cynically, with regard to the development of the reformatory: "Prison management was now in the hands of bureaucratic professionals, not evangelical reformers, and members of this new occupation would have been by temperament, as well as by training and inclination, incapable of proclaiming unattainable fantasies." See *Prison and Plantation*, 180-181.

Chapter 6

1 As a society in microcosm whose population reflects the pluralism of the larger society (racial issues not here considered), the idea of a civil religion is as critical to the common life of the American prison as it is to the nation. No society can function without a set of common rituals and symbols that provide moral meaning to its members. Lacking this, the critics of the penitentiary, many of whom are mentioned in this study, are correct in their observations as to its

futility. I am suggesting that the society *is* going to punish, some of those punished are going to be confined, and this punishment need not be a cynical charade of justice as long as its justification and intent are communicated and reinforced throughout the institution. Robert Bellah provides the classic essay on Civil Religion in *Beyond Belief* (New York: Harper & Row, 1970), 168-89. See also Robert Wuthnow, *The Restructuring of American Religion* (Princeton: Princeton University Press, 1988), chs. 10-11.

[2] Adam Hirsch offers this reflection on the paradoxical nature of the reformative ideal: "The irony is that even as advocates trumpeted the ideal of rehabilitation, the scheme they seized on to accomplish it merely reinforced the conception of a criminal underclass. It built a wall instead of a bridge between offenders and society. Paradoxically, this may well have been the penitentiary's foremost attraction. At a time when community involvement in punishment seemed unworkable, an institution that promised to rehabilitate offenders without need for such involvement held great appeal. But if rehabilitation is inherently a reciprocal process, if it requires not only contrition but forgiveness as well, then the very concept of carceral rehabilitation was flawed at the source." See *The Rise of the Penitentiary*, 116. Hirsch does not give proper recognition, I believe, to either millennial theology, which was far more inclusive in its reach than simply the "dangerous class," or to the social vision that sought to erect institutions based not simply on punishment but evangelical renewal. The religious figures featured in this study were by no means blind to the problems of the released offender, but such concerns did not mitigate the value, in their eyes, of a religiously motivated carceral regimen. In point of fact, Hirsch sheds light not on the failure of the penitentiary, but of the transformative or at least incapacitative ideal underlying the reformatory and the progressive ideology that was its inspiration.

[3] See W.D. Lewis, *From Newgate to Dannemora* (Ithaca: Cornell University Press, 1965), 113; NY Sen. Doc. 11 1839, 15; Doc. 13 1851, 223; Doc. 4 1858, 311; E. Pen. 1842, 4; 1852, 11; 1856, 16; 1869,13.

BIBLIOGRAPHY

PRIMARY SOURCES

GOVERNMENT AND ASSOCIATION DOCUMENTS

THE AMERICAN TRACT SOCIETY DOCUMENTS 1824-1925. NEW YORK: ARNO PRESS, 1972.

NEW YORK. SENATE. *DOCUMENTS OF THE SENATE OF THE STATE OF NEW YORK.* ALBANY: STATE PRINTER, 1831-1903.

NEW YORK. ASSEMBLY. *DOCUMENTS OF THE ASSEMBLY OF THE STATE OF NEW YORK.* ALBANY: STATE PRINTER, 1824, 1832-1833.

NEW YORK STATE COMMISSION OF PRISONS. *ANNUAL REPORT OF THE STATE COMMISSION OF PRISONS.* ALBANY: STATE PRINTER, 1898-1914.

THE NEW YORK PRISON ASSOCIATION. *ANNUAL REPORT OF THE PRISON ASSOCIATION OF NEW YORK.* NEW YORK: PUBLISHED BY THE ASSOCIATION, 1844-1849. ALBANY: STATE PRINTER, 1850-1874.

NEW YORK STATE SOCIETY FOR THE ABOLITION OF CAPITAL PUNISHMENT. *FOURTH ANNUAL ADDRESS.* NEW YORK, 1848.

166   Religion and the Development of the American Penal System

166   Religion and the Development of the American Penal System

166   Religion and the Development of the American Penal System

RULES AND REGULATIONS FOR THE GOVERNMENT OF THE MASSACHUSETTS STATE PRISON. BOSTON: J. BELCHER, 1811.

MASSACHUSETTS GENERAL COURT. INSPECTORS OF THE STATE PRISON. *REPORT OF THE INSPECTORS OF THE MASSACHUSETTS STATE PRISON AT CHARLESTOWN.* BOSTON: STATE PRINTER, 1831-1842.

DOCUMENTS PRINTED BY ORDER OF THE SENATE OF THE COMMONWEALTH OF MASSACHUSETTS, DURING THE SESSION OF THE GENERAL COURT. BOSTON: STATE PRINTER, 1853, 1871-1913.

DOCUMENTS PRINTED BY ORDER OF THE HOUSE OF REPRESENTATIVES OF THE COMMONWEALTH OF MASSACHUSETTS DURING THE SESSION OF THE GENERAL COURT. BOSTON: STATE PRINTER, 1871-1901.

THE PRISON COMMISSIONERS OF MASSACHUSETTS. *ANNUAL REPORT OF THE PRISON COMMISSIONERS OF MASSACHUSETTS.* BOSTON: STATE PRINTER, 1902-1914.

THE MASSACHUSETTS BOARD OF STATE CHARITIES. *ANNUAL REPORT OF THE BOARD OF STATE CHARITIES.* BOSTON: STATE PRINTER, 1865-1914.

THE BOSTON PRISON DISCIPLINE SOCIETY. *ANNUAL REPORT OF THE BOARD OF THE MANAGERS OF THE PRISON DISCIPLINE SOCIETY.* BOSTON: SOCIETY'S ROOMS, 1826-1851.

THE INSPECTORS OF THE EASTERN STATE PENITENTIARY OF PENNSYLVANIA. *ANNUAL REPORT OF THE INSPECTORS OF THE EASTERN STATE PENITENTIARY OF PENNSYLVANIA.* PHILADELPHIA, PA: STATE PRINTER, 1829-1913.

THE INSPECTORS OF THE WESTERN STATE PENITENTIARY OF PENNSYLVANIA. *ANNUAL REPORT OF THE INSPECTORS OF THE WESTERN STATE PENITENTIARY OF PENNSYLVANIA.* PITTSBURGH, PA.: STATE PRINTER, 1840-1845.

PECKMAN, GAIL MCKNIGHT ED. *THE STATUTES AT LARGE OF PENNSYLVANIA.* VOL I 1680-1700. NEW YORK: VANTAGE, 1976.

PENNSYLVANIA. GENERAL ASSEMBLY. *ACTS OF THE GENERAL ASSEMBLY RELATING TO THE EASTERN STATE PENITENTIARY.* PHILADELPHIA: J. W. ALLEN, 1831.

REPORT ON PUNISHMENTS AND PRISON DISCIPLINE BY THE COMMISSIONERS APPOINTED TO REVISE THE PENAL CODE OF PENNSYLVANIA. PHILADELPHIA: JOHN CLARKE, 1828.

REPORT OF THE JOINT COMMITTEE OF THE LEGISLATURE OF PENNSYLVANIA RELATIVE TO THE EASTERN STATE PENITENTIARY AT PHILADELPHIA. HARRISBURG: WELSH & PATTERSON, 1835.

REPORT OF THE SELECT COMMITTEE APPOINTED TO VISIT THE EASTERN PENITENTIARY AND THE PHILADELPHIA COUNTY PRISON. HARRISBURG: THOMPSON & CLARK, 1838.

REPORT OF THE SELECT COMMITTEE APPOINTED TO VISIT THE WESTERN PENITENTIARY OF PENNSYLVANIA. HARRISBURG: THOMPSON & CLARK, 1838.

THE PENNSYLVANIA JOURNAL OF PRISON DISCIPLINE AND PHILANTHROPY. PHILADELPHIA, 1845-1850. 1862-1864. 1895-1901.

MONOGRAPHS

A VINDICATION OF THE SEPARATE SYSTEM OF PRISON DISCIPLINE FROM THE MISREPRESENTATIONS OF THE NORTH AMERICAN REVIEW. PHILADELPHIA: J. DOBSON, 1839.

ADAMS, REV. WILLIAM, D. D. *CHRISTIANITY AND CIVIL GOVERNMENT.* NEW YORK: SCRIBNER, 1851.

BROCKWAY, ZEBULON. *FIFTY YEARS OF PRISON SERVICE.* MONTCLAIR, NEW JERSEY: PATTERSON SMITH, 1969. ORIGINALLY PUBLISHED IN 1912.

BURR, LEVI S. *A VOICE FROM SING SING.* ALBANY: 1833.

BROWN, HOWARD N. *A PRISON-SUNDAY SERMON* BOSTON: GEORGE H. ELLIS, 1896.

CALDWELL, CHARLES. *NEW VIEWS OF PENITENTIARY DISCIPLINE AND MORAL EDUCATION AND REFORM.* PHILADELPHIA: WILLIAM BROWN, 1829.

CASSIDY, MICHAEL JOHN. *WARDEN CASSIDY ON PRISONS AND CONVICTS.* PHILADELPHIA: PATTERSON & WHITE, 1894.

_____.WARDEN CASSIDY ON PRISONS AND CONVICTS. PHILADELPHIA: PATTERSON & SMITH, 1897.

CLEVELAND, CHARLES. *ADDRESS TO PRISONERS–FROM THEIR CHAPLAIN.* BOSTON, N.D.

DE BEAUMONT, G. AND A. DE TOCQUEVILLE. *ON THE PENITENTIARY SYSTEM IN THE UNITED STATES AND ITS APPLICATION IN FRANCE.* TRANSLATED BY FRANCIS LIEBER. PHILADELPHIA: CAREY, LEA AND BLANCHARD, 1833.

DIX, DORTHEA LYNDE. *REMARKS ON PRISONS & PRISON DISCIPLINE IN THE UNITED STATES.* MONTCLAIR, NEW JERSEY: PATTERSON SMITH, 1967. ORIGINALLY PUBLISHED IN 1845.

EDDY, THOMAS. *AN ACCOUNT OF THE STATE PRISON OR PENITENTIARY HOUSE, IN THE CITY OF NEW YORK.* NEW YORK: ISSAC COLLINS AND SON, 1801.

FOSGATE, BLANCHARD. *CRIME AND PUNISHMENT.* AUBURN: W. J. MOSES, 1866.

GRAY, FRANCIS C. *PRISON DISCIPLINE IN AMERICA.* LONDON: J. MURRAY, 1848.

HAWTHORNE, JULIAN ED. *THE CONFESSION OF A CONVICT.* PHILADELPHIA: R. C. HARTRANFT, 1893.

HAYNES, GIDEON. *PICTURES FROM PRISON LIFE.* BOSTON: LEE AND SHEPARD, 1869.

HOWE, S. G. *AN ESSAY ON SEPARATE AND CONGREGATE SYSTEMS OF PRISON DISCIPLINE.* BOSTON: WILLIAM D. TICKNOR AND COMPANY, 1846.

JENKS, WILLIAM. *A MEMOIR OF THE REV. LOUIS DWIGHT.* BOSTON: T. R. MARVIN, 1856.

KIRBY, GEORGIANA BRUCE. *YEARS OF EXPERIENCE.* NEW YORK: AMS, 1971. ORIGINALLY PUBLISHED 1887.

LIEBER, FRANCIS. *A POPULAR ESSAY ON SUBJECTS OF PENAL LAW.* PHILADELPHIA, 1838.

LIVINGSTON, EDWARD. *LETTER FROM EDWARD LIVINGSTON TO ROBERTS VAUX ON THE ADVANTAGES OF THE PENNSYLVANIA SYSTEM OF PRISON DISCIPLINE.* PHILADELPHIA: JESPER HARDING, 1828.

LUCKEY, JOHN. *LIFE IN SING SING STATE PRISON AS SEEN IN A TWELVE YEARS' CHAPLAINCY.* NEW YORK: N. TIBBALS & COMPANY, 1860.

MARTINEAU, HARRIET. *RETROSPECT OF WESTERN TRAVEL.* VOL. I. LONDON: SAUNDERS AND OTLEY, 1838.

POWERS, GERSHOM. *A BRIEF ACCOUNT OF THE CONSTRUCTION, MANAGEMENT, & DISCIPLINE OF THE NEW YORK STATE PRISON AT AUBURN.* AUBURN: U. F. DOUBLEDAY, 1826.

_____. REPORT OF GERSHOM POWERS, AGENT AND KEEPER OF THE STATE PRISON AT AUBURN. ALBANY: CROSSWELL AND VAN BENTHUYSEN, 1828.

ROSCOE, WILLIAM. *A BRIEF STATEMENT OF THE CAUSES WHICH HAVE LED TO THE ABANDONMENT OF PENITENTIARY DISCIPLINE IN SOME OF THE UNITED STATES OF AMERICA.* LIVERPOOL: HARRIS AND CO., 1827.

SERGEANT, JOHN. *OBSERVATIONS AND REFLECTIONS ON THE DESIGN AND EFFECTS OF PUNISHMENT.* PHILADELPHIA: JESPER HARDING, 1828.

SMITH, GEORGE W. *A DEFENSE OF THE SYSTEM OF SOLITARY CONFINEMENT OF PRISONERS ADOPTED BY THE STATE OF PENNSYLVANIA.* PHILADELPHIA: E. G. DORSEY, 1833.

SPRING, REV. GARDINER. *THE SABBATH: A BLESSING TO MANKIND.* NEW YORK: AMERICAN TRACT SOCIETY.

SUTTON, CHARLES. *THE NEW YORK TOMBS*. EDITED BY JAMES B. MIX AND SAMUEL A. MACKEEVER. NEW YORK: UNITED STATES PUBLISHING COMPANY, 1874.

THOME, JAMES A. *A PRAYER FOR THE OPPRESSED*. BOSTON: AMERICAN TRACT SOCIETY, 1859.

TIDYMAN, PHILIP, HENRY W. DE SAUSSURE AND SAMUEL R. WOOD. *LETTERS OF THE PENNSYLVANIA SYSTEM OF SOLITARY CONFINEMENT*. CHARLESTON, S. C., 1835.

VAUX, RICHARD. *BRIEF SKETCH OF THE ORIGIN AND HISTORY OF THE STATE PENITENTIARY FOR THE EASTERN DISTRICT OF PENNSYLVANIA*. PHILADELPHIA: MCLAUGHLIN BROTHERS, 1872.

_____. *THE CONVICT, HIS PUNISHMENT; WHAT IT SHOULD BE; AND HOW APPLIED*. PHILADELPHIA: ALLEN, LANE & SCOTT, 1884.

_____. *PENAL: AN ELEMENT IN SOCIAL SCIENCE*. PHILADELPHIA: KING & BAIRD, 1862.

VAUX, ROBERTS. *LETTER ON THE PENITENTIARY SYSTEM OF PENNSYLVANIA*. PHILADELPHIA: JESPER HARDING, 1827.

WASHBURN, HON. EMORY. *REASONS FOR A SEPARATE STATE PRISON FOR WOMEN*. BOSTON, 1874.

WINES, E. C. *THE STATE OF PRISONS AND OF CHILD SAVING INSTITUTIONS IN THE CIVILIZED WORLD*. CAMBRIDGE: CAMBRIDGE UNIVERSITY PRESS, 1880.

WINES, E. C. AND THEODORE DWIGHT. *REPORT ON THE PRISONS AND REFORMATORIES OF THE UNITED STATES AND CANADA*. ALBANY: VANBENTHUYSEN & SONS, 1867.

SECONDARY SOURCES

AHLSTROM, SYDNEY E. *A RELIGIOUS HISTORY OF THE AMERICAN PEOPLE.* NEW HAVEN: YALE UNIVERSITY PRESS, 1972.

ARMINIUS, JACOBUS. *WRITINGS.* TRANSLATED BY JAMES NICHOLS AND W. R. BAGNALL. GRAND RAPIDS, BAKER BOOK HOUSE, 1956.

AYERS, EDWARD L. *VENGEANCE AND JUSTICE: CRIME AND PUNISHMENT IN THE NINETEENTH CENTURY AMERICAN SOUTH.* NEW YORK: OXFORD UNIVERSITY PRESS, 1984.

BARNES, HARRY ELMER. *THE EVOLUTION OF PENOLOGY IN PENNSYLVANIA.* INDIANAPOLIS: THE BOBBS-MERRILL COMPANY, 1927.

BECCARIA, CESARE. *ON CRIMES AND PUNISHMENTS.* TRANSLATED BY HENRY PAOLUCCI. INDIANAPOLIS: BOBBS-MERRILL, 1963.

BEECHER, HENRY WARD. *THE SERMONS OF HENRY WARD BEECHER.* NEW YORK: J. B. FORD, 1869.

BEECHER, LYMAN. *THE AUTOBIOGRAPHY OF LYMAN BEECHER.* EDITED BY BARBARA M. CROSS. VOL. 2. CAMBRIDGE: THE BELKNAP PRESS OF HARVARD UNIVERSITY PRESS, 1961.

BEECHER, WM. C. AND REV. SAMUEL SCOVILLE. *A BIOGRAPHY OF REV. HENRY WARD BEECHER.* NEW YORK: CHARLES L. WEBSTER & COMPANY,1888.

BELLAH, ROBERT. *BEYOND BELIEF.* NEW YORK: HARPER & ROW, 1970.

BELLAH, ROBERT ET AL. *HABITS OF THE HEART.* NEW YORK: HARPER & ROW, 1985.

BENEDICT, SAINT. *THE RULE OF SAINT BENEDICT.* EDITED AND TRANSLATED BY JUSTIN MCCANN. WESTMINSTER: NEWMAN PRESS, 1952.

BENTHAM, JEREMY. "PANOPTICON: OR, THE INSPECTION HOUSE," IN *THE WORKS OF JEREMY BENTHAM.* EDINBURGH: W. TAIT, 1843.

BERK, STEPHEN E. *CALVINISM VERSUS DEMOCRACY.* NEW YORK: ARCHON BOOKS,1974.

BUSHMAN, RICHARD L, ED. *THE GREAT AWAKENING: DOCUMENTS OF THE REVIVAL OF RELIGION 1740-1745.* NEW YORK: ATHENEUM, 1970.

_____.*FROM PURITAN TO YANKEE: CHARACTER AND THE SOCIAL ORDER IN CONNECTICUT 1690-1765.* CAMBRIDGE: HARVARD UNIVERSITY PRESS, 1967.

CALVIN, JOHN. *ON GOD AND POLITICAL DUTY.* EDITED BY JOHN T. MCNEILL. INDIANAPOLIS: THE BOBBS-MERRILL COMPANY, 1950.

_____. *COMMENTARIES.* TRANSLATED AND EDITED BY JOSEPH HAROUTUNIAN. PHILADELPHIA: WESTMINSTER PRESS, 1958.

COHEN, DANIEL A. *PILLARS OF SALT, MONUMENTS OF GRACE: NEW ENGLAND CRIME LITERATURE AND THE ORIGINS OF AMERICAN POPULAR CULTURE, 1674-1860.* NEW YORK: OXFORD UNIVERSITY PRESS, 1993.

COHEN, STANLEY AND ANDREW SCULL, EDS. *SOCIAL CONTROL AND THE STATE.* NEW YORK: ST. MARTIN'S PRESS, 1983.

COLE, CHARLES C. JR. *THE SOCIAL IDEAS OF THE NORTHERN EVANGELICALS 1826-1860.* NEW YORK: OCTAGON BOOKS, 1977.

CROSS, WHITNEY R. *THE BURNED-OVER DISTRICT: THE SOCIAL AND INTELLECTUAL HISTORY OF ENTHUSIASTIC RELIGION IN WESTERN NEW YORK, 1800-1850.* NEW YORK: OCTAGON BOOKS, 1981.

DELACY, MARGARET. *PRISON REFORM IN LANCASHIRE, 1700-1850.* STANFORD: STANFORD UNIVERSITY PRESS, 1986.

DICKENS, CHARLES. *AMERICAN NOTES.* GREENICH, CO: FAWCETT PUBLICATIONS, INC., 1961. ORIGINALLY PUBLISHED IN 1843.

DIIULIO, JOHN J. *GOVERNING PRISONS.* NEW YORK: THE FREE PRESS, 1987.

DE TOCQUEVILLE, ALEXIS. *DEMOCRACY IN AMERICA.* EDITED BY PHILLIPS BRADLEY. NEW YORK: VINTAGE BOOKS, 1945.

DOUGLAS, ANN. *THE FEMINIZATION OF AMERICAN CULTURE.* NEW YORK: ALFRED A. KNOPF, 1977.

DUMM, THOMAS. *DEMOCRACY AND PUNISHMENT: DISCIPLINARY ORIGINS OF THE UNITED STATES.* MADISON: UNIVERSITY OF WISCONSIN PRESS, 1987.

DURKHEIM, EMILE. *THE DIVISION OF LABOR IN SOCIETY.* TRANSLATED BY W. D. HALLS. NEW YORK: THE FREE PRESS, 1984.

DYER, DAVID. *HISTORY OF THE ALBANY PENITENTIARY.* ALBANY: J. MUSSELL, 1867.

EDWARDS, JONATHAN. *THE NATURE OF TRUE VIRTUE.* ANN ARBOR: THE UNIVERSITY OF MICHIGAN PRESS, 1960.

ERIKSON, KAI. *WAYWARD PURITANS.* NEW YORK: WILEY, 1966.

FIELDING, HENRY. *A PROPOSAL FOR MAKING EFFECTUAL PROVISION FOR THE POOR.* LONDON: A. MILLAR, 1753.

FINDLAY, JAMES F. *DWIGHT L. MOODY AMERICAN EVANGELIST.* CHICAGO: UNIVERSITY OF CHICAGO PRESS, 1969.

FINNEY, CHARLES GRANDISON. *LECTURES ON REVIVALS OF RELIGION.* CAMBRIDGE, MA: THE BELKNAP PRESS OF HARVARD UNIVERSITY PRESS, 1960.

FOUCAULT, MICHEL. *DISCIPLINE & PUNISH.* TRANSLATED BY ALAN SHERIDAN. NEW YORK: VINTAGE BOOKS, 1979.

FREEDMAN, ESTELLE. *THEIR SISTERS' KEEPERS.* ANN ARBOR: UNIVERSITY OF MICHIGAN PRESS, 1981.

GARLAND, DAVID. *PUNISHMENT AND MODERN SOCIETY.* CHICAGO: UNIVERSITY OF CHICAGO PRESS, 1990.

GAUSTAD, EDWIN SCOTT. *A RELIGIOUS HISTORY OF AMERICA.* NEW YORK: HARPER & ROW, 1966.

GRAMSCI, ANTONIO. *SELECTIONS FROM THE PRISON NOTEBOOKS.* EDITED AND TRANSLATED BY QUINTIN HOARE AND GEOFFREY NOWELL SMITH. NEW YORK: INTERNATIONAL PUBLISHERS, 1971.

HANWAY, JONAS. *SOLITUDE IN IMPRISONMENT.* LONDON: J. BREW, 1776.

HINDUS, MICHAEL STEPHEN. *PRISON AND PLANTATION.* CHAPEL HILL: UNIVERSITY OF NORTH CAROLINA PRESS, 1980.

HIRSCH, ADAM JAY. *THE RISE OF THE PENITENTIARY.* NEW HAVEN: YALE UNIVERSITY PRESS, 1992.

HIRSCH, ANDREW VON. *PAST OR FUTURE CRIMES.* NEW BRUNSWICK, NEW JERSEY: RUTGERS UNIVERSITY PRESS, 1985.

HOOKER, RICHARD. *THE LAWS OF ECCLESIASTICAL PIETY.* OXFORD: CLARENDON PRESS, 1820.

HOWARD, JOHN. *THE STATE OF THE PRISONS.* LONDON: W. EYRES, 1777.

HUGHES, ROBERT. *THE FATAL SHORE.* NEW YORK: KNOPF, 1987.

IGNATIEFF, MICHAEL. *A JUST MEASURE OF PAIN.* NEW YORK: PANTHEON, 1978.

JACOBS, JAMES B. *STATEVILLE: THE PENITENTIARY IN MASS SOCIETY.* CHICAGO: THE UNIVERSITY OF CHICAGO PRESS, 1977.

JAMES, WILLIAM. *THE VARIETIES OF RELIGIOUS EXPERIENCE.* NEW YORK: COLLIER BOOKS, 1961.

JOHNSON, ALLEN AND DUMAS MALONE EDS. *DICTIONARY OF AMERICAN BIOGRAPHY.* NEW YORK: CHAS. SCRIBNER'S SONS, 1931. S.V. "RICHARD VAUX".

JOHNSTON, JAMES A. *PRISON LIFE IS DIFFERENT.* BOSTON: HOUGHTON MIFLIN COMPANY, 1937.

JONES, PHYLIS M. AND NICHOLAS R. JONES, EDS. *SALVATION IN NEW ENGLAND: SELECTIONS FROM THE SERMONS OF THE FIRST PREACHERS.* AUSTIN: UNIVERSITY OF TEXAS PRESS, 1977.

LASCH, CHRISTOPHER. *THE TRUE AND ONLY HEAVEN.* NEW YORK: W. W. NORTON, 1991.

LAWES, LEWIS. E. *TWENTY THOUSAND YEARS IN SING SING.* NEW YORK: RAY LONG & RICHARD SMITH, INC., 1932.

LEWIS, ORLANDO F. *THE DEVELOPMENT OF AMERICAN PRISONS AND PRISON CUSTOMS, 1776-1845.* MONTCLAIR, NEW JERSEY: PATTERSON SMITH, 1967. ORIGINALLY PUBLISHED IN 1922.

LEWIS, W. DAVID. *FROM NEWGATE TO DANNEMORA.* ITHACA: CORNELL UNIVERSITY PRESS, 1965.

LOCKE, JOHN. *TWO TREATISES OF GOVERNMENT.* NEW YORK: MENTOR, 1960.

LOMBROSO, CESARE. *CRIME, ITS CAUSES AND REMEDIES.* TRANSLATED BY HENRY P. HORTON. BOSTON: LITTLE, BROWN & COMPANY, 1911.

MALONE DUMAS, ED. *DICTIONARY OF AMERICAN BIOGRAPHY.* NEW YORK: CHARLES SCRIBNER'S SONS, 1936. S.V. "FRANKLIN SANBORN" AND "ENOCH WINES".

MARTY, MARTIN E. *PILGRIMS IN THEIR OWN LAND.* NEW YORK: PENGUIN BOOKS, 1984.

MASUR, LOUIS P. *RITES OF EXECUTION.* NEW YORK: OXFORD UNIVERSITY PRESS, 1989.

MCHUGH, GERALD AUSTIN. *CHRISTIAN FAITH AND CRIMINAL JUSTICE.* NEW YORK: PAULIST PRESS, 1978.

MCKELVEY, BLAKE. *AMERICAN PRISONS: A HISTORY OF GOOD INTENTIONS.* MONTCLAIR, N.J.: PATTERSON SMITH, 1977.

MILL, JOHN STUART. *UTILITARIANISM.* INDIANAPOLIS: BOBBS-MERRILL, 1957.

MILLER, PERRY. *THE NEW ENGLAND MIND: THE SEVENTEENTH CENTURY.* CAMBRIDGE, THE BELKNAP PRESS, 1939.

MILLER, PERRY, ED. *AMERICAN PURITANS: THEIR PROSE AND POETRY.* NEW YORK: ANCHOR BOOKS, 1956.

MONTESQUIEU, BARON DE. *THE SPIRIT OF THE LAWS.* EDINBURGH: DONALDSON AND REIB, 1762. ORIGINALLY PUBLISHED IN 1748.

NEWMAN, GRAEME. *THE PUNISHMENT RESPONSE.* PHILADELPHIA: J.B. LIPPINCOTT COMPANY, 1978.

NIEBUHR, H. RICHARD. *THE KINGDOM OF GOD IN AMERICA.* CHICAGO: WILLETT, CLARK & COMPANY, 1937.

PARKER, THEODORE. *SPEECHES, ADDRESSES AND OCCASIONAL SERMONS.* VOL. I. BOSTON: HORACE B. FULLER, 1867.

PARSONS, TALCOTT. *THE STRUCTURE OF SOCIAL ACTION.* VOL. I. NEW YORK: THE FREE PRESS, 1968.

PHILLIPSON, COLEMAN. *THREE CRIMINAL LAW REFORMERS.* MONTCLAIR, N.J.: PATTERSON SMITH, 1975. ORIGINALLY PUBLISHED IN 1923.

PIVAR, DAVID. *PURITY CRUSADE.* WESTPORT: GREENWOOD PRESS, 1973.

RAFTER, NICOLE HAHN. *PARTIAL JUSTICE: WOMEN, PRISONS AND SOCIAL CONTROL.* NEW BRUNSWICK: TRANSACTION PUBLISHERS, 1990.

RANULF, SVEND. *MORAL INDIGNATION AND MIDDLE CLASS PSYCHOLOGY.* NEW YORK: SCHOCKEN BOOKS, 1964.

RAPHAEL, D. D, ED. *BRITISH MORALISTS: 1650-1800.* OXFORD: CLARENDON PRESS, 1969.

ROTHMAN, DAVID. *THE DISCOVERY OF THE ASYLUM.* BOSTON: LITTLE, BROWN & COMPANY, 1971.

_____.*CONSCIENCE AND CONVENIENCE.* BOSTON: LITTLE BROWN & COMPANY, 1980.

RUSCHE, GEORG AND OTTO KIRCHHEIMER. *PUNISHMENT AND SOCIAL STRUCTURE.* NEW YORK: RUSSELL& RUSSELL, 1968.

RYAN, MARY P. *CRADLE OF THE MIDDLE CLASS.* NEW YORK: CAMBRIDGE UNIVERSITY PRESS, 1981.

SCHILLER, DAN. *OBJECTIVITY AND THE NEWS*. PHILADELPHIA: UNIVERSITY OF PENNSYLVANIA PRESS, 1981.

SELLIN, THORSTEN. *PIONEERING IN PENOLOGY*. PHILADELPHIA: UNIVERSITY OF PENNSYLVANIA PRESS, 1944.

SHILS, EDWARD. *THE CALLING OF SOCIOLOGY & OTHER ESSAYS ON THE PURSUIT OF LEARNING*. CHICAGO: THE UNIVERSITY OF CHICAGO PRESS, 1980.

SMITH, TIMOTHY L. *REVIVALISM AND SOCIAL REFORM*. NEW YORK: ABINGDON PRESS, 1957.

SPIERENBURG, PIETER. *THE SPECTACLE OF SUFFERING*. NEW YORK: CAMBRIDGE UNIVERSITY PRESS, 1984.

SYKES, GRESHAM M. *THE SOCIETY OF CAPTIVES*. PRINCETON: PRINCETON UNIVERSITY PRESS, 1958.

TEETERS, NEGLEY K. AND JOHN D. SHEARER. *THE PRISON AT PHILADELPHIA CHERRY HILL*. NEW YORK: COLUMBIA UNIVERSITY PRESS, 1957.

TROELTSCH, ERNST. *THE SOCIAL TEACHING OF THE CHRISTIAN CHURCHES*. TRANSLATED BY OLIVE WYON. CHICAGO: UNIVERSITY OF CHICAGO PRESS, 1931.

VAUGHAN, ALDEN T. ED. *THE PURITAN TRADITION IN AMERICA: 1620-1730*. COLUMBIA: UNIVERSITY OF SOUTH CAROLINA PRESS, 1972.

WALZER, MICHAEL. *THE REVOLUTION OF THE SAINTS*. CAMBRIDGE: HARVARD UNIVERSITY PRESS, 1965.

WEBER, MAX. *THE PROTESTANT ETHIC AND THE SPIRIT OF CAPITALISM*. TRANSLATED BY TALCOTT PARSONS. NEW YORK: CHARLES SCRIBNER'S SONS, 1958.

_____. "THE SOCIAL PSYCHOLOGY OF THE WORLD RELIGIONS," IN *FROM MAX WEBER: ESSAYS IN SOCIOLOGY*. TRANSLATED AND EDITED BY H. H. GERTH AND C. WRIGHT MILLS. NEW YORK: OXFORD UNIVERSITY PRESS, 1946.

_____. *ECONOMY AND SOCIETY.* EDITED BY GUENTHER ROTH AND CLAUS WITTICH. 2 VOLS. BERKELEY: UNIVERSITY OF CALIFORNIA PRESS, 1978.

WEISBERGER, BERNARD A. *THEY GATHERED AT THE RIVER.* CHICAGO: QUADRANGLE, 1958.

WINES, FREDERICK HOWARD. *PUNISHMENT AND REFORMATION.* REVISED AND ENLARGED BY WINTHROP D. LANE. NEW YORK: THOMAS Y. CROWELL, 1919.

WINTER, ALEXANDER. *THE NEW YORK STATE REFORMATORY IN ELMIRA.* LONDON: SWAN SONNENSCEIN, 1891.

WUTHNOW, ROBERT. *THE RESTRUCTURING OF AMERICAN RELIGION.* PRINCETON: PRINCETON UNIVERSITY PRESS, 1988.

ZEMAN, THOMAS EDWARD. "ORDER, CRIME, AND PUNISHMENT: THE AMERICAN CRIMINOLOGICAL TRADITION." UNPUBLISHED PH.D. DISS, UNIVERSITY OF CALIFORNIA, SANTA CRUZ, 1981.

PERIODICALS AND NEWSPAPERS

BACHE, FRANKLIN. "A LETTER FROM FRANKLIN BACHE, M.D. TO ROBERTS VAUX." *THE NATIONAL GAZETTE* (16 MARCH 1829) 1.

THE CHRISTIAN EXAMINER (BOSTON, MARCH 1851; JANUARY, FEBRUARY, MAY 1852; MARCH 1852; JANUARY, MARCH, MAY 1853).

COOPER, JOSEPH T. ED. *THE EVANGELICAL REPOSITORY* 1 (PHILADELPHIA, 1842).

DICKINSON, AUSTIN. "APPEAL TO AMERICAN YOUTH ON TEMPERANCE." *THE NATIONAL PREACHER* 4 (NEW YORK, JANUARY 1830) 313-320.

THE GOSPEL HERALD 1/47(NEW YORK, 1821) 191-92.

THE HANGMAN 1-2 (BOSTON, 1845).

MCGOWEN, RANDALL. "THE BODY AND PUNISHMENT IN EIGHTEENTH-CENTURY ENGLAND." *THE JOURNAL OF MODERN HISTORY* 59 (DEC. 1987) 651-679.

PREYER, KATHRYN. "PENAL MEASURES IN THE AMERICAN COLONIES: AN OVERVIEW." *AMERICAN JOURNAL OF LEGAL HISTORY* 26 (1982) 326-353.

THE PRESBYTERIAN QUARTERLY REVIEW (PHILADELPHIA, JUNE 1852; JUNE 1853; APRIL 1861).

THE PRESBYTERIAN MAGAZINE 1 (PHILADELPHIA, 1821).

THE PRESBYTERIAN SABBATH SCHOOL VISITOR 16 (PHILADELPHIA AND NEW YORK, 1866).

SELLIN, THORSTEN. "DOM JEAN MABILLON–A PRISON REFORMER OF THE SEVENTEENTH CENTURY." *JOURNAL OF THE AMERICAN INSTITUTE OF CRIMINAL LAW AND CRIMINOLOGY* 17 (FEBRUARY 1927) 581-602.

SCHNEIDER, CARL E. "THE RISE OF PRISONS AND THE ORIGINS OF THE REHABILITATIVE IDEAL." *MICHIGAN LAW REVIEW* 77 (JANUARY-MARCH 1979) 707-746.

VAUX, ROBERTS. "LETTER TO WILLIAM WHITE, THOMAS WISTAR AND ZACHARIAH POULSON OF THE PHILADELPHIA PRISON SOCIETY." *THE JOURNAL OF LAW* 1 (OCTOBER 1830) 120-21

INDEX

About the Author

Andrew Skotnicki is Associate Professor of Catholic Social Ethics at Saint Patrick's Seminary in Menlo Park, California

.